HIGH PRAISE FROM
PRISM PROGRAM PARTICIPANTS

The following are quotes taken from actual letters sent to the PRISM program. These letters were sent in over the past decade and are only a sampling of the comments made from tens of thousands of participants. The names in this section have been changed to protect the identity of those who sent in the letters.

"Even close friends didn't recognize me after being on PRISM. I lost 155 pounds and my friend lost 120 pounds but that was just the added bonus. The real victory was in being changed from the inside out. I am a different person today thanks to what God did for me through the PRISM Program."

PATTY DUDGEON, PRISM MEMBER AND LEADER

"Transformation for me has been all about the process of discovering who I am in Christ and walking by faith in the freedom of that knowledge and wisdom. The PRISM Program lessons walked me through the discoveries I needed to make for the renewal of my mind and attitudes toward food."

CHERYL, PRISM PARTICIPANT

"We have seen the fruit of the PRISM Program in the lives of...our members!"

PASTORS JACKSON AND MILLER, CROWLEY LAKE, CALIFORNIA

"Your program is sound and Christ-centered.... Thank you for your fine efforts in helping people in this very needy area of our lives."

PASTOR ELLIS, PRISM PARTICIPANT, WASHINGTON, INDIANA

"Much research went into our decision to offer a weight loss program as part of Women's Ministries at Hinson Memorial Baptist Church. Of all the programs we looked into, PRISM offered the most complete, well-balanced approach. Even so it was with fear and trembling that twenty-nine women gathered some fifteen weeks ago and began meeting. It has been exciting to see lives literally transformed. Many have experienced success for the first time. The weight loss has been wonderfully encouraging. But most thrilling has been the changed lives. It has been beautiful to watch the transformation that has occurred deep within."

WENDY, PRISM PARTICIPANT, PORTLAND, OREGON

"I must write to you to express my appreciation for the PRISM Program. It truly has saved my life! You understand what it is to be out of control with eating. I felt as though you were writing my life. I feel like the Lord used you to put my feelings down in words. Life the PRISM-way is good and it just keeps getting better!"

TERRI, PRISM PARTICIPANT

"What I've been given through the PRISM Program is priceless. This program has helped me enjoy the journey. It has taught me to live and love today!"

TRICIA, PRISM PARTICIPANT

"It's a blessing to be part of a program that enriches people's lives physically, emotionally, and spiritually. Are there no boundaries to the impact the PRISM Program can have on people's lives? Thank you!"

MERRILL AND JEAN, PRISM GROUP LEADERS, SALEM, OREGON

"Being on PRISM is like having God as your personal trainer. Your faith is strengthened and you know that you are not alone in your weight struggles."

ANNA-JEAN, PRISM PARTICIPANT, SANDY, OREGON

"This has been the only program that has been successful for all of us and we are so grateful. We feel great, look fantastic, and feel good about being the persons we were created to be. Praise the Lord! I get tears in my eyes whenever I think about the class members and the changes and success they are experiencing in their lives because of the PRISM Program. May the Lord give you the strength and wisdom to take this powerful ministry to all the world!"

CINDY, PRISM PROGRAM LEADER

THE
PRISM
WEIGHT LOSS
PROGRAM

KAREN KINGSBURY

with TONI VOGT

Multnomah Publishers® *Sisters, Oregon*

THE PRISM WEIGHT LOSS PROGRAM
published by Multnomah Publishers, Inc.
©1999 by TJL, Inc.

International Standard Book Number: 1-57673-578-8

Design by David Carlson Design

Multnomah is a trademark of Multnomah Publishers, Inc.,
and is registered in the U.S. Patent and Trademark Office.
The colophon is a trademark of Multnomah Publishers, Inc.

PRISM and the PRISM logo are trademarks of TJL, Inc.,
and are registered with the U.S. Patent and Trademark Office.

Printed in the United States of America

For information:
MULTNOMAH PUBLISHERS, INC.
POST OFFICE BOX 1720
SISTERS, OREGON 97759

99 00 01 02 03 04 05—10 9 8 7 6 5 4 3 2 1

Those we love and those we've never met,
who have suffered with overweight and food addiction,
perhaps for a lifetime, and are finally,
at this moment in time, ready to take
the first step toward lasting change.
This book, this program, this new life is for you.

And to God Almighty, the author of life,
who graciously gives us the desires of our hearts
and who is there to meet us at every turn
as we seek to become the people
he created us to be.

CONTENTS

Note to the Reader

◆──

PLEASE CONSULT YOUR DOCTOR BEFORE BEGINNING this or any other weight loss program. The PRISM program is not designed for children under age eighteen without parental approval. It is also not designed for pregnant women. Nursing women may participate with a doctor's approval and program modification.

If you are picking up this book for the first time, you want to know some details without a lot of reading. Perhaps you are deciding if you want to purchase this book. Maybe you want to know what else you'll need in order to reach your "right weight" and have a lasting transformation in your battle with overeating.

For you, we have included this note.

The book you are about to read includes the following:

- Everything you need to know to begin the PRISM Weight Loss Program
- The PRISM program guidelines, acceptable foods, and calorie guide
- Two weeks of workbook lessons

You won't have to make a phone call or join a group to get started. However, you are encouraged to locate your nearest PRISM support group as soon as possible since you will receive a complete set of workbooks when you register in a PRISM small group. Call PRISM for the location of the group nearest you. The PRISM program phone number is 1-800-755-1738.

If you are serious about losing weight and keeping it off for a lifetime, about analyzing what went wrong with your past efforts and correcting those attitudes so that you remain free from food addiction, then you will need to make the call.

The PRISM Weight Loss Program is a series of four six-week phases. Each phase requires an accompanying workbook (which will be issued upon registration in the PRISM program) and, ideally, group participation. Materials for phase five and beyond are available through your PRISM class membership. The people at PRISM will make sure you get set up with a local group.

In order to get started, you will also need a food scale and a comprehensive calorie-count book. These are available at book and department stores, or they may be purchased through the PRISM corporate offices by calling 1-800-755-1738. A Bible would also be helpful, since two suggested Scripture readings accompany each workbook lesson. While you do not need to be a Christian or even religious to be successful on the PRISM program, certainly we believe you will find strength, hope, and possibly an entire new outlook by heeding the suggested daily Scripture readings.

Finally, remember that this is not like any other program you've participated in before. Toni Vogt, president of the PRISM Weight Loss Program, likes to say this: "If at first you don't succeed, analyze what went wrong and try a new approach."

This is that new approach—the last time you'll ever find yourself struggling with food addiction and overweight.

Are you ready for the adventure of a lifetime? If so, read on. We'll see you at the end—if we still recognize you!

FOREWORD

"CONSULT YOUR PHYSICIAN before beginning any diet or exercise program."

As a doctor with a weight problem, this obligatory statement had always made me cringe. I agree that this is sound advice; but what if your doctor can't control his own eating habits?

Sure, I had been taught about weight control and exercise. The medical school I attended prided itself on its nutrition courses. And I had a good understanding of the biochemical processes that enable us to convert food into energy, muscle, or fat. In addition, my own lifelong struggle with my weight had made me an "expert" on what doesn't work. But despite this knowledge and experience with dieting, I was still unable to achieve and maintain a healthy body weight for myself.

So I would sit in my exam room while patient after patient would ask me—of all people—how they could lose weight. I would rattle off my usual "high carbohydrate, low-fat, more exercise" routine and hope they wouldn't ask me why I had a weight problem. The fact is, "high carbohydrate, low-fat, more exercise" had never worked for me, and it hasn't worked for our society. Despite all the fat-free snacks in our grocery stores and the billions of dollars spent on exercise equipment, Americans are fatter than ever. I was no exception. At five feet eleven inches and 255 pounds, I was one physician who definitely needed a consultant of my own.

Then a good friend of mine introduced me to the PRISM program. At first I was very skeptical about anything promising to help me lose weight and especially any program that claimed to help keep the weight off. But after a few weeks on the PRISM program, I knew I had found the answer to lifelong weight control. I have lost forty pounds and have twice as much energy as before. I look and feel great in every way that matters—physically, emotionally, and spiritually.

It's difficult to argue with these results.

Why was PRISM successful for me, and why will it work for you?

Simple. The PRISM program addresses sugar addiction and dependence on highly refined, nutritionally inadequate flour.

PRISM helped me realize how I had abused food all of my life. Through guidelines and KEY PRINCIPLES, it gave me the discipline I needed to overcome day-to-day temptations. But most of all, PRISM helped me tap into the most powerful force in the universe: Jesus Christ.

As a Christian, I had come to trust Jesus with my struggles and the uncertainties of life. I had even prayed for weight loss. But until I began the PRISM program, I had never realized what a dynamic role Jesus would play in my journey to my "right weight." The truth that Jesus cares about every aspect of my daily life, including my eating habits, had somehow escaped my recognition. I am certain that without Jesus' help, my battle with my weight would never have been won. Through Christ all things are possible, and the PRISM program has helped me realize that with Jesus' help, I can control my weight for a lifetime.

The PRISM plan uses discipline, fellowship, and sound physiologic principles to help you lose weight and maintain weight loss. It is completely sound from a nutritional standpoint and, unlike so many other weight loss plans, does not involve radical and harmful measures that encourage the body to regain weight that has been lost.

PRISM teaches you that all carbohydrates are not equal and that high insulin levels lead to overeating and weight gain. The daily readings and workbook lessons are insightful and filled with important tools to help you overcome food addiction and replace overeating with healthy life-sustaining practices. I look forward to my continued journey through the PRISM program and, with the Lord's help, to a long life with a renewed healthy relationship with food.

It's true. You should consult your physician before starting a weight loss program. But today if you come to my office and ask me how you can get beyond the miserable point of overweight and food addiction to the place of transformation, I am no longer embarrassed and tongue-tied. Instead, I will tell you plainly and with absolute confidence:

Find a PRISM group and get started. It is the only program that ever worked for me, and I know it will work for you also.

Those are doctor's orders.

—Bryce Cleary, M.D.

Preface

ANOTHER DIET!

How many does that make for you this year? Five? Ten? Perhaps it has been years since you have even tried to lose weight. Have you completely lost hope?

We understand being in that position. This program was created for people like you, people who have tried to lose weight but were never able to achieve real results or lasting success.

We, like you, are unique individuals with diverse backgrounds and attitudes about overeating and weight problems. However, we have found some common threads and principles of truth among people we have encountered through our own weight loss journeys. The simple principles upon which this program is based will facilitate your journey and give you the keys to open the doors to :

- Awareness
- Discipline
- Understanding
- Successful lifelong weight loss
- A continued lifestyle of freedom, health, and vitality

This program includes a method to help insure your success in overcoming the common problems of overeating and food addiction. That method is discussed in the section of this book that details the PRISM program.

As you find yourself willing and able to remain disciplined in the face of temptation, you will begin to believe with progressively greater conviction that you will be FREE FOR LIFE.

Near the back of this book, you will find two weeks of workbook lessons.

You will also find an Agreement of Resolution. Please read this book in its entirety before making a decision to join the PRISM Weight Loss

Program. Then please carefully consider the Agreement of Resolution, paying special attention to what it says before you sign it. By signing it, you give yourself or your leader written evidence of the seriousness of your decision to overcome undisciplined eating and do away with the problem of overweight and overeating. It will also help reinforce your own determination to reach your "right weight" and continue in a healthy, free lifestyle.

One of our deepest desires is that this program will give you principles for establishing eating behaviors that will stay with you for a lifetime.

Remember: A life free from the control of food is the only life to live!

But before we go on, we want to show you how sold we are on the PRISM Weight Loss Program by telling you our own stories and how PRISM has changed our lives.

THE

PRISM

WEIGHT LOSS

PROGRAM

OUR STORIES: HOW PRISM
HAS CHANGED OUR LIVES

Toni Vogt: The Beginning of PRISM

IT IS HARD TO PINPOINT EXACTLY when my weight problems really began. I realize now that, as a teenager, it was not necessary for me to lose weight because I was not "fat." Photographs of me at that time help me see that I did not need to lose weight. I looked just fine for my age and build. However, I began to think of myself as "fat."

Throughout my high school years I was very athletic and active. I was not heavy, but my frame and body type did not measure up to my taller, thinner friends. I constantly compared myself to people I could never resemble, even if lost ten pounds. I repeatedly tried to diet, but found myself unable to resist going with my friends to "Dairy Delite" after school or ball games. My self-worth diminished as negative tapes of self-rejection played over and over in my head: *Why can't I be taller, thinner, have flawless skin, be smarter, be blond with blue eyes...be like her?*

Throughout my journey, I identified myself as an "emotional" eater. I ate to fill the holes of loneliness, sadness, and a lack of self-worth. The lack of self-worth began early in my life. In fifth grade I began dealing with severe skin problems. I remember going on a diet for the first time in seventh or eighth grade. At that time—this was in the 1960s—"Twiggy," a supermodel from England, graced the cover of seemingly every teen magazine across the continent. She was beyond thin, but her look was considered very chic and vogue, and many of my friends and I strove (starved) to be more like her. I feel sad every time I think of that time in my life. I valued myself so little that I compared myself to unrealistic images of a thin body I could never attain. I was not as tall, small-framed, and slender as my friends, and I began to think of myself as fat and unlovable because of the way God had created my body.

I managed to keep my weight down fairly well until my first year of marriage, when the combination of several life changes spelled disaster for my weight. I took a desk job, stopped all athletic activity, began taking birth control pills, and tried to be Suzy Homemaker for my husband by cooking large meals that neither of us needed. In my first year of marriage I added about fifteen extra pounds. The war had begun!

Eventually I realized that I was eating large meals laden with an excess of refined carbohydrates. I loved that seratonin. I didn't snack much, nor did I ever reach the level of "hoarding" or "hiding" my eating. However, at mealtime, watch out! I had a very healthy appetite. I also ate during meal preparation and cleanup time.

Armed only with vanity and determination, I battled the bulge and the scale time and time again. Each time I would try the latest, newest craze in dieting. If I managed to take off enough weight to look good again, it was back to eating and normal life. I was either dieting or gaining weight. There was never a time that I could maintain my weight. I not so humorously proclaimed myself the "Queen of Yo" because my weight was like a yo-yo: up and down.

I had no idea how to get out of this pattern. With each new diet I tried, I found myself losing more heart, enthusiasm, and self-worth. I knew my diet history and that the latest new and improved diet was not going to bring me the lasting results I wanted. I became more and more desperate and tried just about anything that came along—always looking for that miracle plan that would help me get slender painlessly.

Pregnancy and breast-feeding became a license to eat. It was wonderful! They afforded me an excuse to eat whatever I wanted and loose clothing to hide the fat. My top weight was registered at the hospital shortly before I gave birth to my second child.

After the baby was born, I was back on the yo-yo. I lost hope of ever being slender again. I stopped caring about me and instead devoted myself completely to my children. They were a source of pride and joy—feelings I no longer had about myself. I was tired of trying and ready to give up the battle. I was ready to accept second best and learn to live with myself as I was—fat and depressed.

Eventually, my emotional and physical state hit bottom. The large quantity of food I consumed was only a temporary sedative for my emotional pain. Each time I gave in to food after promising myself I wouldn't, I reinforced my feelings of inadequacy and lack of self-control. I became totally absorbed with food, so self-centered in my own pity party that I began hurting the people closest to me.

Finally, I knew something had to change.

My first steps toward a commitment to change were very difficult, but I vowed that this time it would be a change for life. As in many other areas of my life, I have learned that honesty, self-control, and discipline are difficult at times—but they are also worthwhile and freeing. Every time I chose healthy foods in moderate portions rather than overeating, I felt better and better about myself.

A glimmer of hope ignited in me. I had found a way to conquer self-defeating behavior and regain self-control in my life.

After successfully reaching my "right weight" in 1988, I became a small group leader for a weight loss program. In late 1989, the program I was leading ceased to exist, and I was left without a program to share with others. The concept of the PRISM Weight Loss Program was born in the spring of 1990 from my desire to continue to share life-changing principles I had learned through years of personal trials and from the experiences of others like me.

My life has since been given back to me.

Discipline, knowledge, honesty, obedience, and self-worth—just to mention a few—are some of the things that rehabilitated me. The fact that I can look in a mirror today and see the beauty on the inside and outside of me is a miracle. I have accepted my "True Me," the way God created me. I now believe it is wonderful to be five feet four inches, medium-framed, with brown hair and hazel eyes. Why? Because I know it is right for me. I am grateful I do not have to compare myself with anyone else. All of us have our own beauty and unique qualities.

My story has a happy ending because I now have the knowledge and ability to lead a disciplined life. My prayer for each of you is that you, too, realize that you can take charge of your eating habits, weight loss, and life.

It is not too late to change. You must now take responsibility for yourself and your actions and persevere in your efforts.

Go ahead! Give the PRISM program your all! You truly can win the battle for a lifetime, and believe me, the rewards will exceed your dreams.

Now I want you to read the story of Karen Kingsbury, the author of this book; and herself a PRISM success story.

Karen Kingsbury: The Fat Lady at the Circus

When I was eight months old, the doctor told my mother I was too thin.

"Put Karo syrup in her bottle," he said. "That ought to fatten her up."

As far as I know that was the last time anyone worried about me being too thin.

When I was in kindergarten I began wearing Pretty Plus sizes. Even as a five-year-old I remember feeling different when my mother took me shopping and I had to try on special big clothes because of my size. I wanted desperately to be more like the other little girls in my class: smaller, prettier, and more popular. At the time I couldn't understand why they were different from me.

As I got older I began to understand.

My mother was a very good cook and enjoyed making rich dinners and even richer desserts. There were potatoes and gravy and buttered bread nearly every night and gooey sugar-laden desserts often. I remember how my mother made sandwiches. She buttered both slices of bread first, even if the next layer was peanut butter or mayonnaise. Every sandwich was buttered.

No need for a cookie jar in our family. We ate cookies the same hour they were baked. In fact, we never ate cold cookies in my home. All seven of us stood around the cookie sheet the moment it came out of the oven, and seconds later the batch was gone.

Batch after batch, year after year.

Ice cream was another favorite. My mother would dish out seven equal dishes, and an hour or so later my father would eat the remainder straight from the carton. I didn't know until I was an adult that ice cream could get freezer burn.

There was a lot of love in my family, and holidays were always a special time, ripe with tradition and merriment. We enjoyed laughter and afternoon pool parties, softball games and caroling, but every happy occasion seemed to center around food. We feasted from Thanksgiving right on into Easter with dozens of pies, Christmas cookies, candy-filled hearts, and mega-baskets of Easter chocolate.

Oh, there were times when my mother would draw in the reins of our family's growing food addiction—usually after my dad had visited the doctor and learned that his health was at risk from high blood pressure, diabetes, blood clots, etc.

But the diets were short-lived, in part because my parents loved to buy us "treats." We were always on the go, and every outing was associated with a show of love, a treat—some form of food. A drive to the lake meant frozen candy bars from the snack stand; the ride home took us through A&W for burgers and fries. At the movies we consumed boxes of Red Vine licorice, frozen bon-bons, oversized tubs of buttered popcorn, and sodas. All of that in two hours. It's no wonder that today I remember not the movies, but the food. We barely had time to watch the film as we feasted in the dark.

Even trips to the grocery store were an occasion to celebrate. My mother always allowed us kids to pick out a candy bar at the checkout, a "treat" for being good at the store. As we got older, average-size candy bars increased to half-pounders. Most people might break pieces off such a bar and take a week to eat it. Not us! We ate those as quickly as we once had eaten the smaller bars.

At that point, the sugar and food addiction was raging out of control, but none of us seemed to notice. Yes, we were all gaining weight. And when the seven of us went somewhere, we sometimes received strange glances from other people. But in those early days of pain, discouragement, and food addiction, at least I had company. In our own family circle, there was no judgment of overeating or overweight, and in spite of the increasing evidence of our problem, we continued to overeat.

Several times a year, we five kids participated in various fund-raisers for Scouts and school activities. We sold one-dollar candy bars, oversized boxes of M&Ms, Girl Scout cookies, and Christmas candy. And while we always won prizes for high sales, we were definitely our best customers.

I remember having boxes of chocolate in my room, under my bed. I was supposed to be selling them to neighbors and family members, but instead I ate one or two every day. I'd hide the chocolate stash and tell my family that I'd already turned them in or lie about how many I'd brought home to sell. Then I'd pay for the missing bars with baby-sitting money.

It wasn't that I felt uncomfortable overeating in front of my family. Rather, I didn't want them to know about my private supply because I didn't want to share. For reasons I did not understand, I couldn't get enough chocolate. I craved it constantly. The desire for the sweet stuff was a constant part of my waking thoughts, and only while I was actually eating it did I feel satisfied. I was eleven.

My ability to sneak food became an art form after I began baby-sitting. I would wait until the children were in bed and then rummage through their parents' refrigerator and cupboards. I was stunned to find whole boxes of cookies and snack bars, ice cream, and other sweets. At our house that kind of food would be gone within an hour of bringing it home, but some of the sweets in their cupboards actually bordered on stale.

It was during my baby-sitting days that I learned how to cover up my food binges. I would eat one-third of a package of Oreo cookies and then shake up the remaining cookies to make it impossible to tell how many were actually missing. I would eat two bowls of the family's ice cream, then dig a spoon deep into the container to fluff up what was left to hide the amount I'd eaten. I could easily consume an entire package of pudding, handfuls of cookies, a few granola bars, and the ice cream during one baby-sitting job. I became expert at covering my tracks and listening for the sounds of the couple's car in the driveway.

The feasting and binging continued unabated until I turned thirteen. By that time I was no longer wearing Pretty Plus clothes. I weighed 220 pounds, and the only clothes that fit me were in the Big Women section of clothing stores. There aren't many stylish junior high clothes in the Big Women section.

One day that year, I arrived late to class. I entered the classroom in my standard oversized sweatshirt and size twenty-two jeans. The teacher hadn't arrived yet, and in her absence, the kids snickered and pointed to the blackboard.

I looked and saw this: "Call Karen, Fat Lady at the Circus." Below it was, "Whale watchers, call Karen."

Blood rushed to my face and I trembled from the embarrassment. There was nowhere to run, nowhere to hide. At that moment the teacher showed up and quickly erased the board. Later that day, sitting by myself at my usual spot in the outdoor cafeteria, I ate my standard lunch of two brownies and two burritos. As I hurried through my lunch—hoping no one would notice the quantity of food I was eating—I gazed across the cafeteria at a group of popular girls who were laughing and squealing as several boys chased them around a table.

They were pretty, dressed well, and the boys liked them. All because they were thin.

I was homely, wore baggy clothing, and the boys mocked me. All because I was fat.

I stared down at my half-eaten second brownie, and suddenly I knew I was through. I hated what I'd become. I wanted desperately to fit into smaller clothes and to be accepted by my peers at junior high.

Filled with the hope of change, I raced home after school and searched my parents' bookcase. I found a book that promised a fifteen-pound weight loss the first week, snagged it, and read it in two days. The plan was neither balanced nor safe, but over the next three months I boycotted almost all the foods my mother prepared and starved my way down to a size fourteen. During that time I developed an irregular heartbeat, slammed my metabolism into low-gear, and had two episodes of fainting because of low blood sugar. But the grief I'd experienced because of my weight was so great I was willing to do anything to be thin. By the time my eighth grade year started, I had lost nearly eighty pounds and was a size ten.

No longer the Fat Girl at school, my true outgoing personality emerged; by the time I was in high school, I was dating the most popular boy on campus. He had come from a different junior high and hadn't known me when I was overweight. But after we had dated for a year, he began telling me something that stays with me to this day:

"Karen, you know, you'd be so pretty if you just lost five pounds."

Five pounds. That was all that separated me from being the most beautiful girl at Canoga Park High School. But there was a problem.

Although I'd lost weight, I hadn't learned how to break my addiction to the wrong foods. Once I went off the extreme diet, I immediately went back to the way my family was still eating: heavy dinners, large desserts, candy bars, and ice cream.

Soon I could tell I had put five pounds back on my hips, and I was frantic to stop gaining, especially since my boyfriend was so sure I could be wonderful if I just lost five pounds.

I remember one time when I was at his house for dinner. After the meal, when his mother brought out a carton of ice cream, my boyfriend looked at me and winked. "Don't give any to Karen, Mom...she's trying to lose five pounds."

I was mortified. My face got hot and I wanted to disappear. His mother chided him for being rude and asked me if I wanted some anyway. I politely declined, but inside I was sick. I didn't want to be abnormal, having to turn down desserts or having him turn them down for me simply because I had five pounds to lose.

That night I did something that became a dangerous habit and eventually a compulsion. I stopped at the ice cream store on the way home and bought a pint of my favorite flavor. There in the dark shadows of the front seat of my car, I consumed the entire container, bite by hurried bite. I was in such a rush to get the ice cream into my body that I don't remember tasting any of it. When I had finished, I tossed the container in a public dumpster and drove home, consumed by guilt and despair. After all, my boyfriend would never want me if I were *six* pounds overweight.

I went home and locked myself in the bathroom. Then, with the water running so no one would hear the noise, I stuck my finger down my throat. After gagging briefly, I lost the ice cream and the undigested parts of my dinner.

When I finished, I wiped my mouth, brushed my teeth and realized that I actually felt great—exhilarated and more than capable of facing the night. The depression was gone; in its place was a sense of wild self-control. I could cheat by tricking my body into not gaining weight while never denying myself the "treat" of having the sweets I so desperately craved.

The practice of binge eating and then vomiting so the food does not have time to digest is called *bulimia*. I did not know that then. For me it just seemed like a way to have the best of both worlds.

I continued in a fog of bulimia for the next three years. binging on donuts, ice cream, and lots of liquid, and then throwing it up so it wouldn't cause me to gain weight. After such an episode I would sometimes go three days without eating. Those days gave me even more exhilaration and a powerful feeling of self-control. Sometimes during my bouts of self-starvation, I would wish for the strength to become anorexic—to starve myself so long that I would no longer have an appetite. I thank God to this day that he did not allow me to succumb to anorexia, because it would have killed me. Instead, when my body screamed for nutrition, I would eventually give in. When I did, it was always in the form of another binge.

The cycle continued, even after I knew I was ruining my metabolism, my heart muscle, and perhaps even risking my life. As the years went on, my boyfriend remained unaware of my bulimia but continued saying "if you'd only lose five pounds...."

One night he admitted to me that even though he loved me, he could never marry me.

"Why?" I asked.

"Because, look at your family. They're all overweight and one day you will be, too. I couldn't handle that."

I dumped my boyfriend and stopped binging and purging. But still I could not refrain from my private gluttonous feasts.

Next I turned to exercise. Every day, hours a day. After a big binge, I would take as many as five exercise classes in a row in order to feel like I'd eliminated the bad foods from my system. It was while exercising that I met the man who eventually became my husband.

Over the course of our twelve-year marriage and relationship, I have grown increasingly aware that my body cannot handle the effects of refined sugar and white flour.

After giving birth to our second child, I took myself off sugar—even foods that contained a small amount of sugar—and in a few months I dropped sixty pounds and weighed less than I had on my wedding day. I realized that the common denominator was the sugar. It seemed that when I stayed away from the white stuff, I wasn't hungry. The binges disappeared. For the first time in my life I was free from my compulsion with food, and it was directly related to abstaining from sugar.

Even so, within a year I gradually allowed myself to begin eating sugar again and over the next five years put on thirty-five pounds. Oh, I still felt thin. I'd look in the mirror, hold in my stomach and smooth out the bulging areas. *Not bad,* I'd comment to myself. *Not really bad.*

But pictures told a different story. I was wearing my food addiction as obviously as if I'd had a sign around my neck.

I knew that part of the key was doing away with sugar, and for as many as three or four days in a row, I'd refrain from those products. Then I'd have a bad day or get invited to a party, and my commitment was out the window. For the first time in my life, my self-motivation to keep my weight down was not enough. The addiction was stronger than anything I'd known before; there seemed no choice but to give in to it and become, like my former boyfriend had once predicted, fat like the rest of my family.

Then a few years ago I heard about the PRISM Weight Loss Program.

A friend of mine told me her mother was in the program and loving it, losing weight and feeling free from a lifetime of food addiction. I asked about it and learned that it involved eliminating sugar and white flour through prayer and workbook lessons. By then I was a Christian, and I knew there had to be hope in such a program. I rushed to the bookstore to buy the PRISM book.

But there wasn't one.

As time passed, I eventually forgot about the PRISM program.

Then in July, 1998, I was at a booksellers convention. One evening, in my room on the ninth floor of a hotel in Dallas, Texas, I had a heart-to-heart talk with the Lord about eating.

It was not the first time since becoming a Christian in 1987 that I had related my food addiction to my spiritual life. I knew that in my relationship with Christ, there was power to break my addiction. But I found myself always in a cycle of binging, confessing, promising change, and then binging again.

That night in Dallas seemed different.

I had been signing books for store owners all day, smiling and playing the part of the happy author. But back in my hotel room I was miserable, unable to stop myself from overeating at every chance and frustrated with the way my pretty clothes no longer fit. I confessed it all to the Lord and asked for his help.

In the still small way the Lord often speaks to us, I distinctly heard two things from him that night. First, I realized I needed to be faithful to my decision to turn over my eating to him. Second, I knew that a book would come out of all of this, one that would touch the lives of thousands and thousands of people who had also suffered from a lifetime of food addiction.

I thought the idea of a book was strange at the time because, even if I did lose thirty-five pounds, there would be no earth-shattering example in that. Many food-addicted people today have one or two hundred pounds to lose. My message would miss them entirely.

But the Lord's prompting was clear and strong, and I prayed for him to show me how I could do both: be faithful in turning over my eating to him and write a book that would help those who had suffered like I had.

Weeks passed, and at first I was very conscious of my eating, trying to make healthy choices and avoid sugar. But the rationalization process began again, and I did what I had always done in the past. I gave in and started eating small quantities of sugar again. As always, first it was a little, then a little more. By August it seemed like my heartfelt time with the Lord had never even happened.

One day later that summer my husband and I were playing tennis when a friend of ours approached. I noticed immediately that she had shrunk. When I asked her what she was doing to lose weight, she smiled and said, "PRISM. It meets at your church."

PRISM. I remembered everything good about the program and asked the first question that popped into my head. "Is there a book on PRISM yet?"

"Just the workbooks." She smiled. "But they're great."

I could almost picture the Lord smiling somewhere. I had not been faithful in my eating habits, but he had been utterly faithful, even in bringing this woman by at that exact moment.

The next day the friend came over and brought material on the PRISM program. After reading through it, I felt sure this was the project God had placed on my heart weeks earlier in that Dallas hotel room.

I contacted PRISM president Toni Vogt. I suggested that we join forces and produce a PRISM book so other hurting, food-addicted people could have access to the hope it offers. She agreed, and the PRISM project was born.

There was one thing I knew I needed to do before I could write a book on PRISM. I needed to complete the program myself. Even though I agreed with its premises and was excited to share it with others, I was still terrified about whether or not I could follow the program guide-lines—especially what I call the "one-bite" rule.

Part of the PRISM program is an Agreement of Resolution, which the participant must sign, promising to inform their PRISM group leader or accountability partner if he or she takes one bite of a prohibited food.

I called Toni.

"I'm having a little trouble with the 'one-bite' rule. Are we sure we want to present it that way?"

I could almost hear Toni's smile at the other end. "Accountability sets us apart. It's why it works. Try it and we'll talk about it in six weeks."

Six weeks. An entire phase of the PRISM program during which I could not have one swipe or lick or crumb or taste of foods not allowed. Now I was really nervous.

The problem of overeating and overweight in my life, along with my abnormal attachment to food was stronger than ever. The night before I started PRISM I accepted an invitation to attend a barbecue at the home of some friends. There I consumed nearly a third of the Jello-pretzel-whipped cream salad.

"I won't be having this after tonight," I joked.

But inside I was terrified. What if I couldn't do it?

Then I remembered the Lord's message to me: "Be faithful." Sometimes that meant taking one step at a time and allowing him to lead me where I desperately needed to go. With a heavy, fearful heart I went to class and began the program.

The first three days were the hardest. It's like that for most PRISM members. The chemical addiction must be broken, and it takes an average of three days for the immediate effects of sugar to be eliminated from our bodies.

But after that there was no looking back. I lost twenty-three pounds in the first phase, and during that time my abnormal food cravings and desire to binge disappeared. There is no doubt in my mind that the daily workbook played a major role in keeping me on track and focused during that phase. Now I have completed the recommended four phases, even though I reached my "right weight" months ago. Total loss: forty-five pounds.

The benefits in my life have been amazing.

I am thin, attractive, healthy, and full of energy. But more than that, because of the tools and help I discovered in the PRISM workbooks, and because of God's faithfulness, I am finally free from food addiction. I am transformed—a new creation—living the life I was created to live in the body I was created to live it in.

A lifetime of obsession with food led me to PRISM.

Now it is your turn.

My prayers and those of many others are with you as you begin the journey of a lifetime, the journey to the TRUE YOU.

Godspeed, and don't forget to send us your stories once you, too, have been transformed. You can e-mail me at rtnbykk@aol.com.

EARLY IN 1997, NANCY ENDURED some of the darkest days in her life. She had been steadily gaining weight, and that year she peaked at 253 pounds and was growing out of her size twenty-four clothes. Her weight was affecting every area of her life: her relationships with her husband and children, her social times, her presence at the children's school, even her relationship with God.

"Many people did not know the severity of this problem in my life," Nancy says. "I woke up each day with a gripping fear, my heart beating wildly. I knew I needed a breakthrough."

Family gatherings had become drudgery for Nancy. She feared what others might think about her weight gain and had no motivation to join relatives in group activities such as softball, volleyball, or swimming. Instead she sat off to the side, often by herself, and watched everyone else live the life she longed to live.

"I felt like I was a prisoner in my own body," Nancy remembers. "I felt like my family just settled for me because they had no choice, as if they would replace me as soon as the right person came along."

Although her husband was utterly faithful to her during those dark months, Nancy began imagining that he stayed committed to her only because of their wedding vows. She imagined that if someone attractive came along at the right time, he would be gone.

Many days she was plagued by taunting voices reminding her that she was a fat slob, a no-good wretch. Other times the same voices would pacify her, assuring her that God loved her just the way she was and that fat people were beautiful, too. New clothes, the voices told her, will make you feel better. Buy new clothes and accept yourself the way you are.

When summer ended, Nancy found herself questioning God and what he wanted of her.

"I felt like he was directing me to the Scripture in Jeremiah that talked about having no other gods," she says. "But I thought it was referring to other people and their idols. It took a while before God showed me he was talking about me. I had made food my god."

In August, 1997, Nancy was introduced to the PRISM program.

"My friend told me it lasts six weeks at a time; you eat no white flour or white sugar; for six weeks you get no bread or potatoes; you limit yourself to twelve hundred calories a day...." Nancy recalls. "I told her to forget it. It wasn't for me. I couldn't do that. I told her to go ahead, but I'd do it my own way."

But that night God made it clear to Nancy that this was something he'd introduced to her for a reason. She realized that if only she could trust him, she might be able to find the strength to stay on the PRISM program.

Nancy and her husband prayed about the idea, and in September she started PRISM. Midway through her journey, she became a leader.

"This is a lifetime journey," she told the members in her class. "I'm in this with you. Remember, I didn't get where I am without making mistakes. But I kept picking myself back up and trusting in the Lord to take me further. I kept my eye on the vision of the TRUE ME and took it one baby step at a time."

By July, 1998, Nancy had reached her "right weight." She had lost 112 pounds, a total of 119 inches, and nine dress sizes. Her disposition was transformed in the process: instead of being depressed and grumbling much of the time, she is filled with peace, love, joy—the fruit of the Holy Spirit.

Today life is completely different in Nancy's home. She and her children communicate and share activities together. The bond between her and her husband has grown stronger. Because of the healthy foods in the house, her son has lost fifty pounds and her daughter two dress sizes. Her mother got on the PRISM program and lost nearly eighty pounds; her sister lost fifty.

Nancy says she learned that although God did love her before—regardless of her excess weight and lack of self-control—he was calling her to repentance. Food had become her god and she needed to change.

"I now enjoy a calm, peaceful life," Nancy says. "I'm not afraid to get up in the morning, and I feel fit spiritually and physically. I have the freedom that Christ intends for me to have. I have abundant life and I love it."

2

RECOGNIZING THE MONSTER

The Problem of Overeating and Overweight

THERE IS A MONSTER LURKING in our nation today, a monster who has taken up residence in every neighborhood, city, and state in the country. You won't see this monster in any horror movie or Halloween special on television. This monster isn't looked at as something to fear, but more often as an object of scorn, ridicule, and pity. At the same time, this monster is responsible for more death, illness, and emotional pain than just about any other factor in our lives.

It's the monster of overweight, and if you don't know it personally you know someone who does. Excess weight isn't an isolated problem in our culture today. Overweight is a condition common to men and women and boys and girls of all ages, races, and social groups. The most current studies show that 70 percent of Americans are overweight. Of them, more than a third are considered "obese," or at least 30 percent above their "right weight," the weight we believe God intended for us.

It's been said that some of the most dangerous weapons in our society today are the knife and fork. The facts back that up: There are a myriad of serious physical problems—some of them life threatening—associated with excess weight. Cardiovascular disease, hypertension, several types of cancer, diabetes, and problems in the joints and bones are just a few maladies that have been linked to excess weight. The latest statistics indicate that obesity is second only to smoking as a contributing factor in illness and premature death.

Medical costs associated with excessive weight are at an all-time high in relation to other illnesses. Consider the following:

- $11.3 billion is spent each year to treat, diagnose, and manage non-insulin-dependent diabetes mellitus and its related health problems. Eighty percent of those treated suffer from the condition because of overweight.

- Obesity accounts for $22.2 billion spent to diagnose and treat heart disease. Nearly 70 percent of the diagnosed cases of cardiovascular disease are related to excess weight.

- Obesity doubles one's chance of developing high blood pressure. The annual cost of obesity-related high blood pressure is approximately $1.5 billion.

- Almost half of breast cancer patients are obese. Overweight breast and colon cancer patients account for medical costs of $1.9 billion annually.

- Respiratory diseases have also been directly linked to obesity. These include chronic bronchitis, pneumonia, and sleep apnea.

- Heart failure can occur as a direct result of excess weight.

- Other health problems related to overweight include disorders of the thyroid, arthritis, spinal injury, joint or ligament injury, and psychiatric disorders—primarily depression.

- Perhaps most startling of all is the fact that Americans spend $33 billion annually on weight-reduction products and services, including diet foods, books, counseling, pills, shakes, and formulas.

In addition to the physical problems associated with overeating and overweight, there are the emotional ones, which can be devastating. Overweight people are far more prone to poor self-image and depression than those who are at their "right weight." Many live lives dominated by a pain that most of us can't imagine. Many of these people see themselves as trapped in a prison from which there is no hope of release.

If you are one of these people, take heart! There is hope for you. You don't have to allow the monster of overweight and overeating to dwell in your home. Your day of transformation is coming.

But before we talk further about how you can be free of the monster of overeating and overweight, we want to show you that you aren't alone. Others have been where you are. Other people have struggled with overweight and the pain, humiliation, and depression it has caused.

THE SORROW OF OVERWEIGHT

The following are testimonies from people who have gone through the PRISM program and found health, life, and freedom from overeating and overweight. These are people who have been transformed, just like you can be. Although each of these people has found freedom and transformation through the PRISM program, these are not their success stories.

These are their painful memories.

All names in this section have been changed to protect those who provided them.

Barbara:

Being overweight has always been a source of sadness and depression, but there are two things that will stick out forever as being devastating. Once when my friend and I attended a funeral in New York, I walked through the buffet line and filled my plate with food. At that point, I studied the seating arrangements and saw that everyone was sitting in canvas director-style folding chairs.

I hesitated a moment and studied the chairs from a distance. What if I didn't fit in them? What if they weren't strong enough to hold me? These concerns ran through my mind, but I quickly convinced myself they were unfounded. Surely they would be strong enough, I reasoned. After all, full-grown men were sitting in them.

Hoping for the best and having no other choice, I made my way to the table where my friend was already seated. I set down my plate, pulled out my chair, and sat down.

Immediately the canvas ripped away from the wood frame, and I landed squarely on the ground. My friend was at my side helping me to my feet, but the commotion caught the attention of the woman who was hosting the funeral dinner.

"Oh, hmmm... I guess we have a little problem here, don't we?" She seemed disdainful, annoyed by the broken chair and my presence at the funeral dinner. I wanted to disappear and go home.

"The chair must have been defective or something," my friend offered.

I appreciated her trying to rescue me from the embarrassment of the moment, but it was no use.

"No, these chairs were all just fine before the dinner," she insisted.

I was on my feet at that point, brushing grass clippings off my back side and wondering where I would sit for the remainder. I said the only thing I could think of to the frowning host: "I'd be happy to pay for it, if you just let me know what I owe you."

She waved her hand and spoke in a voice that was louder than necessary. "Oh no, that's all right. I can buy a new chair. Maybe something stronger next time."

My friend has probably forgotten that incident by now, but I haven't. I never will.

The other moment was even more devastating, although less embarrassing.

I had been suffering knee problems for several months—due in major part to my excess weight—when my doctor asked me to take my MRI test results to a knee specialist. Carrying the documents to the car, I was overcome by a desire to know what they said. What were all those strange notations doctors wrote, and what did they say about me?

I opened the envelope and began reading.

"Barbara is a morbidly obese person whose knees simply cannot bear up under the increasing pressure of her excess weight."

In that moment it felt like my entire world screeched to a halt.

I knew I was overweight, knew I had a problem. But "morbidly obese"! The words seemed like a death sentence, and that day I did the only thing I knew to do. I ate. Whatever I could get my hands on I ate, and I ate until I felt tranquilized from the blow that the doctor's remarks had delivered.

Cristy:

There were so many humiliating moments as an overweight person. When I was 120 pounds overweight, I was laughed at, mocked, stared at, and degraded in nearly every social setting imaginable. But the worst memories I have are of trying to discourage my husband from expressing physical love in our relationship.

I knew that even though I was extremely overweight, he still enjoyed sharing physical, sexual contact with me. But I dreaded those encounters because I hated my body. I couldn't imagine why he'd be interested in holding me or kissing me or touching me when all he felt was fat.

Over the years, I trained myself to use food as a way of preventing sexual contact. When I would see that he was getting ready for bed, I'd stand up, stretch, and make my way to the kitchen.

"I'm a little hungry—think I'll have something to eat," I'd say.

"Oh, okay." He'd look a little rejected, but then shrug and say, "Well, good night then."

Once he was in bed, I'd eat leftover dinner, bowls of cereal, whatever I could find. I ate until I could barely move, until I was sick to my stomach. Then I would trudge upstairs, brush my teeth, and fall into bed beside him. If he was still awake, if he had a modicum of interest in anything sexual, I would roll on my side—my back to him—and complain about the pain in my stomach.

Then, once I heard him safely snoring, the tears would come. I would silently cry myself to sleep, hating myself for binge-eating instead of making love with my husband, and promise myself that I'd never give in to the food cravings again. But the promises were hollow. There was no reason to believe I could ever follow through on any of them.

In that way, I avoided many physical encounters with my husband—all because I was too embarrassed of my body, too disgusted with myself to be intimate with him. There were other moments of heartbreak, of course, but those sad, painful nights will always stand out as the most difficult.

Jonathan:

I had been overweight all my life. I was also a very shy person. When I was an adult I had a very hard time talking to new people, especially women. It was impossible for me to look a woman in the eyes while talking to her, even if I managed to say something. Back in those days, I wore a size fifty-four pants and carried an extra 160 pounds on my frame.

One spring when I was that size, I went to an amusement park for a bachelor party. While there I suffered one of the most hurtful and humiliating moments of my life.

My friends and I stood in line to ride the Colossus, a roller coaster, until our turn came to climb aboard. I climbed in and my friends piled into the cars in front and back of me. I pushed the bar down, but it only clicked partially into place. I forced it with all my might, but when the ride workers came by to check my car, they said it had to go down further or I couldn't ride.

The commotion began to draw the attention of everyone in line, everyone on our train, and my friends, who sat nervously watching me suffer through this ordeal. When the ride workers finally decided there was no way the bar could possibly go down far enough, they told me I would have to get out. I was too overweight to ride. I walked out of there feeling a hundred pairs of eyes on me. Utterly humiliated, I vowed that I would come back and conquer the Colossus.

There were other embarrassments, including the fact that I could not fit into a booth at most restaurants. My stomach would hit the edge of the table, making it difficult to eat. The larger my stomach grew, the more eating became a chore. My plate seemed to keep getting farther and farther away so that I nearly always spilled food on myself trying to get it to my mouth.

When I look back on my days of being obese, these will always be sad, painful memories.

Rhonda:

I was 123 pounds overweight. I ate in hidden places: cars, closets, bathrooms—wherever I was sure no one could see me carrying out my addiction. Sometimes I felt like a criminal, but I ate anyway, stuffing wrappers in junk mail envelopes or wherever I thought my husband wouldn't look. I felt like I was in a car going downhill without brakes. I was depressed, devastated, and desperate. I didn't feel like life was worth living.

Bill:

I was letting God do what he wanted with every area of my life except food. That was my area, my privilege. I overate at every turn. Soon I was 100 pounds overweight and facing a lifetime of disease, limitations, and lack of motivation. I was at the end of my rope.

Cheryl:

I had forgotten who I was. I looked in the mirror and saw someone I didn't recognize, someone without self-control, someone devastated by the effects of a food addiction. I can remember lying on my bed crying, sobbing, wondering if there would ever be a plan I could stick to. All I wanted was my life back, the one I used to live before I got buried in overweight.

Take a moment to empathize with these people, who were brave and honest enough to share memories of their old selves. As we said, today these same people are all experiencing wonderful transformation because of the PRISM program.

If today you are where they once were, trapped by the problem of overweight, by even ten pounds of excess weight that you cannot seem to lose, take hope. There is a way out.

It's time to get excited!

Now we want to take some time to discuss why people get caught in the trap of overeating and overweight.

How Did We Get Here?

In the next chapter, we will discuss what we call "food addictions" and their role in weight gain. But for now, we want to talk about another common problem that leads to weight gain. It's a somewhat less obvious form of food abuse, but it's every bit as harmful to your efforts to maintain your "right weight."

A lot of people don't necessarily have a problem with food addictions. For them, eating is more of a pastime, something they do mindlessly even as they obsess about their weight. This leads to poor eating habits, which in turn leads to weight gain. On the surface, these people don't appear to have a problem with food, which can be frustrating for them because the weight gain continues.

Let's take a look at someone in this category. We'll call her Gina and put her in a familiar situation.

ONE SNEAKY MONSTER!

The morning dawned cool and wet. Washington state was often this way, and the fact that it was May made no difference. Gina sat up in bed and saw that her husband was already up. *Jogging,* she thought. *Good for him!* Gina was always proud that her husband took such pride in his physique and health. They were in their late thirties, and there was no time like the present to solidify exercise routines.

Gina thought for a moment about slipping into her sweats and hitting the treadmill she'd gotten for Christmas. It was the first time she'd actually enjoyed using a piece of exercise equipment. Many others were in the garage, waiting for an opportune neighborhood garage sale. But with the weather so wet and cold, she simply didn't feel like exercising.

She heard the kids watching television downstairs and thought about the day—housecleaning, bills to pay, grocery shopping. Then she had an idea. Getting up slowly, she stretched and headed for the bathroom. She glanced at the scale. *Should I?* She ran her hand over her stomach. She had been careful about what she'd eaten lately, skipped a few desserts, and cut back on the second helpings. Her stomach felt a bit flatter than yesterday. She pulled her nightgown over her head and stepped on the scale.

165.

That can't be right, Gina thought. She calculated when her period was due. Ten days. Maybe it was water retention. Maybe she'd stepped on the scale too hard and sent the needle to far to the right. Gingerly, she stepped on the scale again. The needle hovered between 165 and 166. Same as last week.

Gina's shoulders slumped and she walked away wondering what she'd done wrong. What could she possibly do to lose the weight? Forty pounds. Weight that had crept on after the children were born, and no matter what diet she tried, it never seemed to stay off.

For a moment, Gina stared at herself in the mirror. *I hate the way I look*, she thought. *Why can't I look like I did in high school?* For the tenth time that week she analyzed her eating habits. She didn't overeat; she didn't binge eat. She wasn't like those women who bought ten candy bars and stuffed them down when no one was looking. So what was the problem? Other women ate like she did and never struggled with their weight.

She thought about the scale again. If she could eat right for a week and still not lose a single pound, then what was the point? For today at least, Gina decided to put it out of her mind. She and the kids had been wanting to bake chocolate chip cookies, and why not? She wouldn't eat more than two or three, anyway.

That morning the children gathered in the kitchen. They spread the ingredients on the counter, softened the butter, and added sugar, flour, and the other ingredients. Bit by bit, Gina took swipes from the bowl. Not an excessive amount, but four, maybe five cookies before a single tray was baked. When the first batch came out of the oven, Gina and the children each had three cookies and a cool glass of milk.

Throughout the day, Gina tried to put the scale out of her mind. She wondered if maybe she was retaining water or if she'd eaten too much salt the day before. After lunch she drank two glasses of iced tea, and two hours later, when she went to the bathroom, she took off her clothes and stepped once more on the scale. 167. Gina sighed. The scale must have a defect. There was no way a person could gain that much weight in a few hours. It probably had a range of ten pounds one way or the other and today was just a bad day.

She pulled on her clothes and left the room. Again she thought about her eating habits and wondered why she struggled. What did she need to do? Eat carrots and cottage cheese all day? Maybe it wasn't worth it.

Dinnertime came, and Gina was ready to feel good about herself. If there was one thing her husband enjoyed, it was her cooking. The cookies lay on a nearby platter and Gina wasn't tempted to eat any while she prepared dinner. Enchilada casserole. It was a simple recipe, one the family loved. Bottom layer, crushed tortilla chips. Without giving it a thought, Gina munched on ten or twelve chips while she crumbled several handfuls and spread them over the pan. The next layer was chicken, mushroom soup, olives, and sour cream. Gina always seasoned the mixture by taste. A little salt, a little taste; a dash of garlic, another taste; dehydrated onions, a third taste. Gina thought it might need a bit more salt and added another half teaspoon. Another taste. By the time it was perfect, she'd had more than a full serving even though it wasn't something she noticed.

The next layer was grated cheese. Gina took out a block of Tillamook medium cheddar and began grating. A few jagged pieces fell into the bowl, and Gina ate them. It wasn't that she was hungry; it was just how she'd always cooked. When dinner was finally ready, Gina took a modest portion and skipped another serving of cookies afterward. That night she weighed herself one more time. 167. At least she hadn't gained more weight during dinner.

As she fell asleep, she wondered again why she couldn't lose weight. In the morning she went straight to the scale. 167. Nothing. Not a single pound. And she'd even passed up the cookies after dinner. What was the point? Nothing worked. Not ever.

Gina went through that day discouraged. What she didn't know was that the previous day her calorie total was approximately 3,000. Even if Gina were working out each morning, she would probably find that 2,000 calories was all she needed to maintain her "right weight." Instead, by the end of the year, continuing her same eating habits, Gina gained another seven pounds, and her self-esteem continued to plummet.

RECOGNIZING THE PROBLEM

Millions of overweight Americans get where they are the same way Gina did: overeating without being aware of it. They don't binge and don't eat too many rich desserts after dinner. These are people who truly believe they are eating right, but who are consuming more—oftentimes *many* more—calories than their bodies can use each day. The result? Excess stored body fat.

If you fit in this category, the PRISM program is for you. As you will see, the PRISM program works because it forces you to keep careful records of what you eat and when. This will help you put an end to the unhealthy practice of thoughtless eating.

But maybe you fit in another, more obvious, classification of overeaters. Maybe you are fully aware that you eat too much and that you eat the wrong foods. If so, read on. The next chapter is for you.

UNLIKE SO MANY OTHERS IN THE PRISM PROGRAM, Marcy never had a food addiction as a teenager or young adult. She enjoyed eating healthy foods because they gave her body energy and strength. In the process she avoided refined sugar and flour.

She took these eating habits into her first and second pregnancies and never gained a significant amount of weight. She also had no trouble losing the weight since she was still eating healthy foods and cooking that way for her family.

But when she became pregnant with her third child, she found herself with a two-year-old, a nine-month-old, and another on the way.

"Suddenly there simply wasn't time to eat the right foods," she says now. "We began eating fast and convenient foods when I got pregnant the third time."

Convenience foods led quickly to junk foods, including sugar-laden desserts and chocolate. By the time the third baby was born, Marcy was "very addicted to sugar and chocolate and sweets."

With three little ones underfoot and a husband who worked long hours, Marcy continued to rely on quick, convenience foods and to give in to her newly acquired junk food addiction. By the time her baby was a year old, Marcy weighed as much as she had the day before he was born.

"I realized I needed to get back to eating healthy and making better decisions about what I ate," she says. "I talked about making a change, but it just didn't happen. I was really hooked on the chocolate, especially. I wasn't disciplined enough on my own to break my addiction."

A few months later, she spotted a notice in her church bulletin about a PRISM Weight Loss Program group that was starting up.

"It was one of those things where I knew I needed to go, but my schedule was so crazy with the kids I couldn't do it. I sort of logged it away in my mind that it was there and in the spring a few months later, I was ready."

Marcy says that she was not afraid of the strict eating guidelines set by the PRISM program.

"By that point, I hated the way I looked, hated looking in the mirror. Nothing fit and I wouldn't buy new clothes. I wore a size fourteen or sixteen jeans, and I couldn't bring myself to buy that size. Instead I wore the pregnancy leggings that I'd been wearing all year. I was tired of the way I felt and looked and of all the wrong things I'd been eating."

Because her children took so much of her time, Marcy was not able to start a regular exercise program while she was on PRISM. However, she lost all the weight she needed to lose in just four phases.

"I was determined to make it through all four phases of the program, even if I reached my 'right weight' before then. I knew I had a problem, and I wanted to see the complete transformation take place inside and out."

Marcy says that when things got tough following PRISM—and there were those times—there was always someone in her group she could call for encouragement. In addition, she believes the strict program guidelines helped her stay on the program and find success.

Having been at her "right weight" for more than a year, Marcy thinks the PRISM program has many strengths that set it apart from other programs.

"First, it teaches you to eat the right way," she says. "You don't have to buy prepackaged food. You have to learn to eat right. This was realistic for me, even though it's not the quickest way."

Marcy also cites PRISM's discipline and daily lessons as helps that made her journey to breaking food addiction easier.

"It was exactly what I needed," she says. "Now I feel great inside and out, and because I relied on God for the changes, I'm even closer to Him. What more could you ask for?"

3

The Foods that Trap Us

A Look at Food Addiction

SOME YEARS AGO, A POPULAR DIET GURU told a national audience that there was no such thing as food addiction. His comments were repeated on news shows and in magazines across the world. They tickled the ears of thousands of overweight, food-addicted people. For a time they offered hope.

Good news! we all thought. This overeating thing wasn't really all that bad, after all. It was normal to consume entire packages of cookies or whole containers of ice cream. The diet expert was the icon of health, and he had spoken. If he said there was no such thing as food addiction, then there wasn't.

But as the echo of this man's words faded away, hundreds of thousands of people were still suffering from overweight, still helplessly growing larger and more unhealthy at the whim of their appetites.

It would stand to reason that if there were no such thing as food addiction, we would simply wake up one day and make a conscious decision to stop eating the wrong foods. We would gravitate naturally toward lean chicken and fibrous vegetables, and we would shed the weight.

But this is not happening. In fact, the percentage of overweight Americans today is up 20 percent from just ten years ago. There can be no other conclusion than the obvious one: Food addiction is indeed real and is running rampant in the lives of far too many people.

Often in this book you will read about "food addiction." In some ways, the term is an unusual one because by necessity we are all hooked on food. We need it to survive. But when we use the term, we are talking about an unhealthy urge to overeat, particularly the *wrong kinds of foods*.

Almost always, this type of unhealthy food addiction is to two highly refined carbohydrates: white sugar and white flour.

When we think about overeating, certain foods never come to mind. These include lean protein foods and fibrous fruits and vegetables. Have you ever found yourself thinking about food an hour after lunch and gravitated toward the bag of carrot sticks in the refrigerator? Would you overeat lean chicken breast or turkey slices dipped in mustard? Have you ever eaten one apple after another without being hungry and with no ability to stop yourself?

Probably not.

Instead, if you are like other food addicts, you crave buttered bread, muffins, cookies, cake, candy, and other starchy foods. All of these are high-carbohydrate foods. In later chapters, we will examine in depth carbohydrates and the relationship they have to food addiction, but right now let's take a look at a day in the life of a food addict.

FEEDING THE ADDICTION

It's Saturday morning. It is a beautiful day outside and there are forty-eight hours before another workweek begins, but Teri Taylor has her mind on one thing.

Pancakes.

Saturdays are pancake day at the Taylor household, and Teri's husband, John, is the chief flapjack maker. Regardless of the weather or what other activities are planned for the weekend, nothing is quite right until Teri digs into her first stack of pancakes on Saturday.

Teri is not obese; but she is thirty-five pounds overweight and plans to start a diet Monday morning. But today is Saturday, and she can smell the pancakes from the bedroom.

Completely focused, Teri quickly climbs out of bed—pancakes taste better hot—and makes her way to the kitchen. She eyes the serving plate—twelve pancakes. Eager to get her fork into her mouth, she bids her family a cheery good morning, ushers the children to the table, and serves them two pancakes each.

Then, with John still busy at the griddle, Teri takes the remaining eight flapjacks and slides them onto her plate. Checking to make sure her husband isn't watching, she takes several swipes of soft butter and swiftly hides them on the lower pancakes.

Taking what appears to be a dry stack of pancakes, she makes her way to the table. There she douses them in syrup and begins eating, moving as fast as she can so that her husband will not see how many she took or the syrup flooding her plate.

Eight pancakes later, Teri slows down and tries to make John think that she's enjoying a leisurely breakfast. Unaware of how many she has consumed, John asks if she'd like a few more before he sits down. She politely declines.

The truth is that if she could physically consume another pancake, she would. They still look good, and she knows they would still taste good. But at this point, she is sick to her stomach from overeating and couldn't possibly take another bite.

An hour later, the Taylor family heads for the tennis courts, where Teri loses to John in two straight sets. "Lack of energy," she complains, and adds that maybe she should have eaten a bigger breakfast. This comment, she believes, will give John the impression that she's been cutting back. Even if it is only an impression.

Back home, Teri showers and slips on extra-large shorts and an over-sized T-shirt. As she dresses, she pauses at the half mirror and holds in her stomach. *Looking thinner,* she tells herself. *Especially in this T-shirt.*

Suddenly she feels famished, and her body craves something sweet. *Nourishment,* she decides. She needs some nourishment. After all, she worked up an appetite playing tennis.

She rummages through the cupboards and finds a can of powdered vanilla protein shake mix.

This ought to be nourishing.

She pours a glass of milk, leaving plenty of room for the powder, and mixes in two scoops from the canister. Then she remembers how good the powder is when it balls up into little chunks that float on the top of the shake. She adds an extra scoop of powder for good measure and stirs it.

The rest of the family is upstairs, so she drinks the shake quickly and decides she needs a little something more to give her that boost she'll need to get her through the afternoon. She mixes another extra-powdery shake and sits down to sip it at the table.

While she is sitting and sipping, she remembers that she promised to make cookies for the children's ministry at church the next day. Baking cookies was Teri's way of volunteering and staying involved. She directs the children outside to play and suggests that John mow the front and back yards. That way she can take care of the baking, and they'll finish their chores at the same time.

Once the house is empty, she starts mixing.

Chocolate chip cookie dough is not good until the wet and dry ingredients are mixed, but the moment that happens, she begins sampling. By the time the chips are thoroughly mixed into the dough, she has eaten enough to make six cookies.

Humming happily to herself, anxious for the first bite of hot chocolate chip cookies, she slides the first batch into the oven. When it comes out ten minutes later, John enters the house, finished with the lawn.

"Mmmmm, smells good." He examines the tray of hot cookies.

"Too bad I have to take them to church." Teri playfully pushes John out of the kitchen. "Go take a shower."

He gives up on the cookies easily, flashes Teri a smile, and disappears upstairs. Alone again, Teri wolfs down four cookies so hot the chocolate chips burn her tongue. She sets the others on a cooling rack, arranging them so they don't look like a partial batch.

By the time John is finished with his shower, she has eaten four more and is hoping there will be enough left when she's done to provide the kids at church with two dozen.

The kids come in as she finishes with the cookies and ask for one. "Just one," she says." They're for church, remember?"

They agree and obediently take one each. "Can you come play with us, Mommy? Please?"

Not even if she were paid for it could Teri play outdoors with the kids. Not with warm cookies still calling her name and her stomach so full she can barely move across the kitchen. She tells them she has to clean the kitchen and then balance the checkbook. Maybe she can come out and play later.

By now, it's two o'clock in the afternoon, and John has decided to take an afternoon nap. Teri has prepared a snack for John and the kids, cleaned the kitchen, and found a way to eat four more cookies in the process.

On to the checkbook.

She begins reconciling her bank statement, but thirty minutes later she begins to feel something that seems like hunger. The remaining cookies are already wrapped and ready for church, so they're out of the question. She glances at the clock and sees how late it is. Hours after lunch. No wonder she's hungry.

After all, she never really ate lunch. Just snacks here and there.

Although she tells herself that she really doesn't need to eat anything, a thought has formed in her mind, and it relentlessly pursues her attention.

Granola bars!

There are two boxes of chocolate-covered granola bars in the cupboard. She decides it wouldn't hurt to have one, but once she's in the kitchen with the box in her hand, she grabs two bars and quickly heads back to the table to work on her checkbook.

She eats them slowly at first, then more quickly, enjoying the way the chocolate melts in her mouth, leaving the chewy granola behind as a bonus. Within fifteen minutes another thought has taken up residence.

There are more granola bars.

She thinks about the size of granola bars these days. *Why, they're smaller than ever before. In the old days they used to put two good-size bars in one package. Now the bars are no more than a few bites each.*

Moving quietly so she doesn't wake up John, she finds the granola bars and sees that there are only two left in the first box. Instantly she devises a plan. She will take the two remaining bars and assure anyone who misses them that she had purchased only one box in the first place.

She temporarily sets the bars under a dish towel—in case anyone should find her in the kitchen—and carefully folds the granola bar box into a tiny wad of cardboard.

The trash can is in the cupboard under the kitchen sink, but both doors squeak, so Teri turns on the water. In a move she perfected years ago, she reaches her hand deep into the trash can and buries the wad of cardboard near the bottom where no one will find it. She closes the squeaky cupboard door and shuts off the water.

Snagging the two granola bars from underneath the dish towel, she returns to the table to work on the checkbook. Ten minutes later the granola bars are gone, and another thought is consuming her mind.

Chocolate!

For some reason, she is craving chocolate. Not the kind of chocolate in chocolate chip cookies or chocolate-covered granola bars. Real chocolate. Pure chocolate.

She thinks about the calendar and realizes that it is ten days before her period. *Probably a hormonal thing,* she reasons. Happens nearly every month, and when it does she remembers an article she read once at the doctor's office. Best to give in to chocolate cravings, the author had advised. Otherwise a person might deny herself and overdo later.

Agreeing with that rationalization, Teri listens for her husband. Confident he is still asleep, she tiptoes into his office and finds the miniature candy bars he uses as a promotional item at work. There are hundreds of them with the company logo stamped on the outside.

At this point, Teri has consumed 3,600 calories, most of which she has eaten in the past two hours. But still, for reasons she cannot explain, she is hungry. As she begins filling her sweatshirt pocket with miniature candy bars, she briefly considers what kind of hunger this actually is. She realizes that even though she technically has not had lunch, she should not be hungry. But there is no denying the fact that she is craving chocolate so badly she can hardly breathe. With ten small candy bars hidden in her pockets, she returns to the checkbook.

About this time, John wakes up and makes his way into the dining room. She has not yet begun eating the candy bars and knows she must be careful not to stand up or move too quickly. They might rustle in her pockets and give her away.

Teri makes small talk with John for a moment and then begins to grow anxious. There is no real point to the conversation, and until he finds something else to do, the candy bars will have to wait. Finally she suggests he join the children outside. They need someone to play with and, well, she would do it, but she's trying to balance the checkbook. Someone's got to do it.

He agrees, bends to kiss her, and hesitates. A wave of fear rushes through her. Does he smell the cookies and granola bars on her breath? Does he know how much she's been eating?

"I love you," he says with a smile that reaches all the way to his eyes.

She feels her heart rate return to normal. He doesn't know. "I love you, too." She kisses him quickly and grins. "Now get. The kids are dying for someone to play with."

John heads outside. Once the door is closed, Teri stands up and spies on him through the front window. He tickles the children and begins spinning them around above the neatly mowed grass. When Teri sees that he's busy and that he won't soon be returning to the house, she makes her way quickly back to the table and begins eating chocolate bars.

Although she had planned to eat them slowly, allowing them to melt in her mouth so she could savor how the chocolate satisfied her craving, she has changed her mind. John could return at any moment, so she eats the bars quickly, rolling the wrappers into tiny nondescript balls that would not give her away even if they were discovered. Then she slips these balls back into her pocket.

As she nears the end of her stash, she hears her family returning and moves swiftly to the bathroom. By the time they enter the house, she's got the bathroom door closed and locked.

"Honey?" John sounds happy.

"In here...be out in a minute," she replies, her voice light. In a moment's time she empties her pockets, pulls off a piece of toilet paper, and places the tiny wrappers inside. Rolling all ten wrappers into a wad that resembles any other in the bathroom trash can, she flushes the empty toilet, runs the water at the sink for a moment, and joins her family.

She sees that their cheeks are red, their eyes shining from the playing and laughing and living they've been doing.

"Come on, honey, you should join us!" John approaches her and pulls her into a hug. "We're playing tag, and I'm outmanned."

The kids jump up and down. "Pleeease, Mom. Please!"

Teri smiles. "You know I'd love to, guys. I'm almost done. The minute I am, I'll be right out."

At that moment her son approaches and stares at something on her lip. "Mommy, is that chocolate on your face?"

Another wave of panic, but Teri deals with it smoothly, expertly. She wipes at the mark, and in a voice that betrays none of her anxiety she says, "Sweetie, Mommy gets chocolate all over her when she bakes. You know that."

The boy nods, and in a few seconds her family has accepted her refusal to play and gone back outdoors. This time, Teri has the distinct feeling she has more time than before. She snags another handful of candy bars and determines to eat these more slowly. After all, she barely tasted the last bunch.

Two hours later Teri manages to balance the checkbook just as her family finishes playing outside. They announce that they're hungry, and John suggests pizza. Another Saturday tradition.

Teri shrugs. Sure. The sooner the better. Especially since they hadn't really had lunch. She places the order, and an hour later she has consumed four pieces of pizza and half a serving bowl of potato chips.

Around ten o'clock she and John turn in for the night. She feels full, but not overly sick. Many years of overeating have left her almost immune to the effects it might otherwise have on her system. She tells John she's tired. Mental stress, she says, from all the work on the checkbook.

When she's sure he's asleep, she dons a bathrobe and heads downstairs.

Sunday morning. One A.M. This hour is hers, and hers alone. No one else is awake, and she can eat whatever she wants without worrying about being caught.

Except for the wrappers. There are always wrappers to hide.

She opens the freezer and sees half a box of ice cream bars.

Ice cream would be good, she reasons. *A milk product. Might even help me sleep better.*

Unwrapping a bar and rolling the paper into a sticky ball, Teri eats first one, then a second, and finally a third. At this point she realizes that there is only one bar left in the package. Someone might remember that there had been four bars and wonder what happened to the others.

With no remorse about planning to lie, she devises a plan she's sure will work. At breakfast she'll mention that the freezer must be having problems. The ice cream, she'll say, melted and made a real mess in the freezer. She cleaned it up, of course, but they'll certainly have to keep an eye on it so they don't lose any other products.

Satisfied with her story, she returns for the last bar. It wouldn't make sense that three would melt and one survive. She finishes it off, hides the wrappers near the bottom of the trash, and eats a turkey sandwich before returning to bed. *Turkey has protein,* she reasons, *something I really haven't had enough of lately.*

Besides, it isn't really mealtime, so what's eaten at night doesn't count.

Sunday is much the same for Teri, complete with more chocolate chip cookies and several trips through the church potluck line.

By Sunday night voices have come to taunt her.

Look at you! You're a fat pig!

All you've done is eat all weekend long.

You'll never lose weight.

You're worthless, hopeless. How could anyone ever love you?

Tomorrow, she responds silently, waging a war she has waged hundreds of times before. *I'm starting tomorrow, and after that I'll never eat like that again.*

You'll never last a day. A fat pig like you. And another thing—you're a terrible wife and an awful mother. You care more about food than you do about any of them. You can't do anything right....

The voices continue until she falls asleep.

Monday morning she wakes tired and weary, dreading the morning and the diet breakfast she knows she must eat. Not sure if she'll survive the day, she has low-fat, high-carbohydrate cereal with nonfat milk, half a grapefruit, and two glasses of water.

By the time she has the breakfast dishes done and the kids off to school, the voices are back, this time coaxing her to stop depriving herself.

You don't have that much to lose, you know.... It isn't fair.... You should get to eat what everyone else eats.... Come on, there's still a few granola bars left. You can always start the diet next week. After your period.

Gallantly, she wards off the temptation through a lunch of half a tuna sandwich.

By three o'clock her day has gotten increasingly hectic. The errands she'd planned to do have taken longer than she thought, and she's way

behind in her schedule. By the time she takes the children to choir practice, she's utterly frazzled and desperately wanting to tranquilize herself
with some kind of forbidden food. When she drops the children off, she's
met by an assortment of pastries and donuts and homemade cookies.

"Our treat to the mothers," one of the choir teachers says with a smile.
"For all you do for your children every day."

Teri rolls that thought around. She has done a lot for her children that day.
The teacher's right. It's about time someone decided to treat the mothers.
How often did that happen? She studies the pastries and chunky cookies.

"The plates are right over there." The choir teacher smiles and nods
toward a stack of small plates. It would be better to say no thanks, better
to stay with the diet and lose the extra weight. But the baked goods are
calling her name, and something deep inside Teri simply does not want
to be denied. Besides, it would almost be rude to turn down the offer.

Feeling her determination dissolve, she heads for the table and takes
a plate. Her children will eat no more than one pastry each, but she stacks
her plate high, taking two of everything offered. Speaking loudly enough
so anyone in range can hear her, she explains that she needs a few extra
for the children. They haven't had an afternoon snack yet, you know.

She makes her way to a circle of folding chairs set out for the occasion. While the other mothers are still in line, she eats as many pastries
and cookies from her plate as possible. This way no one will notice how
many she really took. If she's lucky, she'll finish before others have gotten
their plates. If she plans it out just right, she might even be able to get a
second plate without being noticed.

As she bites off whole sections of donuts and frosted cookies, she tells
herself this was a bad week to start her diet anyway. She has to bake
brownies for the school's PTSA on Wednesday, and there certainly would
be no point baking brownies if she couldn't eat any. Yes, it had been a bad
idea all along. No wonder she'd had such a rough morning. Especially
with her period right around the corner.

Next Monday, she tells herself. Next Monday she'll start the diet and
really make some changes in her life. Cut back on sugar, lose some
weight. Find the energy to play with the children and spend a little more
time with John.

Satisfied with this solution, she slips back to the table and graciously gives herself permission to take a few more pastries. She is actually excited about having another week to plan for her new diet. It feels good to know she has a plan and that starting next week, everything in her life will finally fall into place the way she has always wanted it to.

Starting Monday, she'd be a new person. And a few weeks after that she'd even be wearing a smaller size dress. She heads back to the dessert table. Yes, that was it. She'd start next week…next week…next week. Next week.

How about You?

If you have seen yourself in any or all of Teri's eating habits, if you can relate to the way she deals with food, even to the detriment of those she loves the most, then you must know one thing:

You are not alone.

And at this moment in your life, you have never been closer to finding the answers that will finally free you from addiction to high-carbohydrate food.

Take heart. Transformation is just around the corner.

But before you can begin, you need to examine your life and to be honest with yourself about how you got where you are.

PRISM Success Story: Larry Bellant

Weight loss: 75 pounds

AS A TEACHER IN THE PRISM PROGRAM, Larry Bellant is living a different life than he ever thought possible. Larry began gaining weight as a boy, when he used food as a sedative for comfort.

"My early life was a roller coaster of emotions," Larry says. "Sometimes the only way to make myself feel better was to eat."

His overeating resulted in an extra forty pounds that he carried through most of his school years, his work at a factory, and his married life. He maintained his overweight until 1991, when he injured his foot and was assigned a desk job.

"That's when my eating habits really caught up with me," Larry says. "I couldn't stop the weight from piling on."

Larry isn't sure what his peak weight was, but he knows it was in excess of 260 pounds. Too depressed to step on a scale, he tried an assortment of diets. Each time he would lose weight, but then quickly regain it. Then in 1997 he and his daughter, Sandy, discovered the PRISM program and brought it to Crossroads Community Church in Vancouver, Washington.

"The weight came off, but before that even happened I was thrilled with the program because of what it did for my relationship with my Lord," Larry says. "It taught me how to walk more closely with God, how to figure out why I ate what I ate, and how to train myself to respond in a healthier way to my emotions."

Larry has dropped his excess weight and kept it off for more than a year. In the process he has continued to lead the PRISM program at Crossroads and has helped hundreds of people find success. He looks forward to preparing for PRISM classes each week and is excited to learn something new about the process of transformation as he does so.

Now Larry says, "I think the most rewarding thing of all is watching other people find success and freedom from overweight and watching them grow closer to the Lord at the same time."

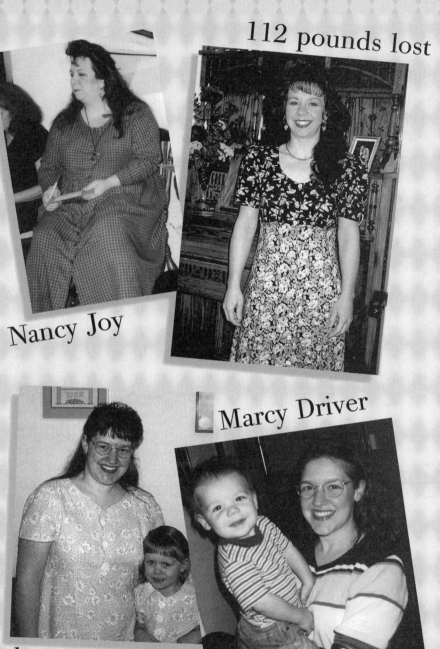

112 pounds lost

Nancy Joy

Marcy Driver

lost 37 pounds

4

A Time for Honesty

Admitting Your Problem

IN ECCLESIASTES 3:1–8, THE BIBLE TEACHES that there is a time for everything under the sun: a time to tear down and a time to build up, a time to cry and a time to laugh, a time to mourn and a time to dance. Now that you have become aware of the damage that overeating or food addiction has caused in your life and you are ready to do something about it, it's time for you to be honest with yourself.

If you are going to be successful in the PRISM Weight Loss Program, you have to be honest with yourself—maybe painfully so. You have to be willing to admit some things about yourself that may be unpleasant for you to think about. You must admit several things.

1. You have little or no self-control where food is concerned.

Many of us have tried to deceive ourselves about this truth. We have told ourselves we could lose the weight if we wanted to and that we certainly are not addicted to food. But time and again we have failed to walk away from the foods that harm us.

Think back to the last time you gave in to a food craving—not to actual physical hunger, but to a craving for a specific food. Let's say it was a piece of chocolate cake offered to you at a party when you were trying to follow a diet plan. You knew there would be cake, and you had told yourself ahead of time that you would not under any circumstances have any. You planned to just sip your water or stir your hot tea and politely say no when the cake was offered.

Now, though, the cake is being passed to the other partygoers and already you have declined twice. Still the cake plates flow through the room, and on the third offer you hear yourself accept. Warning bells, however loud or soft, sound, but you pay no heed. *This piece,* you reason, *is not so big. Just an end piece. Mostly frosting. How many calories could be in a piece of cake that's mostly frosting?*

You eat it and find yourself feeling passed over and left out. Your piece was much smaller than the others. Glancing around, you see that others are enjoying their large pieces, and you tell yourself it isn't fair that you should be deprived of a normal-size piece of cake—especially when parties like this happen so infrequently. You quickly finish the piece of cake, and when you think no one is looking, you drop the dirty paper plate and plastic fork in the trash. Through a series of strategic but brief conversations you wind up near the cake table and casually take a plate with a large piece—a rose on the frosting even. *That's more like it!* you tell yourself. *A regular piece like everyone else.* And while still engaged in conversation, in a manner so smooth you are sure no one has noticed, you eat your second piece of cake.

Although the conversation is interesting, and the one talking is telling you personal details that should demand your strict attention, you find yourself glancing once more at the cake table. Two choices remain: You will either consume a third piece, still trying to appear to be slowly nibbling your way through your first piece, or you will leave the party dissatisfied and intent on satisfying the craving some other way. Perhaps you will stop at the store and buy a cake for the family's dessert that night. Or maybe a quick stop at the bakery for a few cupcakes to eat on the way home.

You either obey the cravings, allowing the problem of overweight to continue ruling your life, or you remain frustrated, anxious, short-tempered, and distracted until you find some other way to satisfy them—perhaps a secret binge later that night or the following day.

If this picture is familiar to you—and for most of us it is a weekly if not daily occurrence in some form or another—then you need to recognize your lack of control and admit your weakness. You need to admit that you have little or no self-control where food is concerned.

The truth is that you are addicted to overeating and it is gradually killing you. In many ways, it is little more than a slow form of suicide. In addition, you feel the guilt, self-hatred, self-repulsion, and shame associated with every binge.

One PRISM program member likened this type of overeating to placing yourself on train tracks as a locomotive bears down on you. Every time you give in to the problem, you tie another rope around your body, binding yourself tighter to the tracks. Only by admitting the truth about your lack of self-control will you begin to untie the ropes.

This is a painful admission to make to yourself, but there are others. Read on!

2. Deception has become a part of your lifestyle where your eating habits are concerned.

For the person whose life is dominated by overeating and overweight, deception comes in many forms. In fact, your life as a food addict can be one of utter deceit to yourself and those around you.

Food addicts lie to themselves about the way they look and about what and how much they eat. If you have been involved in this type of deceit, you will be shocked when you realize how much you actually have been eating. (This is why it is so important to keep track of your food intake while trying to break your problem with overweight through the PRISM program.)

If you struggle with overweight and overeating, you have probably deceived yourself in many other ways. First, you have convinced yourself that you aren't really all that overweight. If you are twenty pounds overweight, you may have convinced yourself that if you dress a certain way no one will really notice and that you can continue overeating. A closet full of long, dark jackets and black slacks will cover just about any problem, you tell yourself.

You look in the mirror each day and assure yourself that you certainly could be worse off. Then you work to think of someone who is fatter than you. This is the way many of us have rationalized our weight for years and years.

"I may be twenty pounds overweight," you tell yourself. "But Suzie across the street is two years younger and thirty pounds overweight. Therefore, I'm not really that bad—not as bad as I could be."

If you are fifty pounds overweight, you think of someone in your circle of friends and acquaintances who is seventy-five pounds overweight. When you enter a room, you are able to spot immediately the person who is heavier than you. *Whew!* you tell yourself. *No one will notice my overweight with that person in the room. That person is much bigger than I am, so I'm not really all that fat after all.*

These lies never stop.

But we don't lie to ourselves alone. We also lie to those we love.

We deceive most those who share our home. We would like them to think that we have a slow metabolism, that we have done everything we can, and that there must be something wrong with the way our bodies burn food. Certainly our overweight cannot be caused by undisciplined eating! At least that's what we want them to think.

And we are willing to go to great lengths to keep them believing our lies.

The deceit we practice on those we love takes many forms, but initially it manifests itself in hidden wrappers, stolen moments, and secret places where we consume food. Perhaps we have a ritual of taking the children to school, stopping at the market, and buying a "goodie" for ourselves. Whatever that food item is, we consume it privately—usually in the confines of our car.

If you doubt this, look around sometime at the people stopped alongside you at a busy intersection and see how many are eating. We are a nation of food addicts, and it's often in the private world of our own vehicle that we have our destructive feasts. Of course, wrappers and crumbs must be disposed of in a public dumpster so no one in our family will find them or suspect the truth.

Whatever our individual rituals are, they exist, and we nurture them carefully so no one will find out. We even worry about being caught by someone who knows our family members. *What if they tell on us, or mention in passing that they saw us at the donut store?* This fear drives us to cover our tracks carefully.

When we binge at home, we must deceive our families by stashing food in secret places. We hide chocolate bars or cream-filled cookies in places where no one would look, and when we eat them, we carefully hide the wrappers so we can continue to deceive.

When we feel sick from overeating, we must lie and say we just don't feel well. If we are anxious and uptight because of our self-hatred and repulsion, we must blame it on the type of day we had. If we neglect our home and work because of the time and energy we spend on feeding our addiction, we must lie and say that we have not been ourselves lately and that we mean to get more organized.

All of this is deceit, and it is an integral part of the problem of overweight. It is time to admit that in your misery and eating binges you have become deceitful.

3. How you see yourself is distorted by deception.

Deceiving yourself about your overweight will eventually distort the way you see yourself. When that happens, you no longer need to lie to yourself about your overweight because you actually do not see it as such. You have been so successful in deceiving yourself that now you honestly see yourself as not having a problem. You consider your weight normal, when in fact you may be carrying a dangerous amount of excess weight.

Distortion about the state of our personal health and weight and attachment to food are firmly in place when we begin to believe the lies we tell ourselves. When this happens—whether you have twenty or two hundred pounds to lose—you actually begin to feel thin and see yourself as slender based on your constant comparisons with someone larger than you.

In the worst cases, this distortion will cause a food addict to scan the headlines of gossip magazines while waiting in supermarket checkout lines. "Rescue Workers Airlift Eight-Hundred-Pound Man from Family Kitchen" is the type of article that will give a five-hundred-pound food addict hope and encouragement. It will even make that person feel thin.

4. You desire to be slender but are unwilling or unable to give up overeating.

If there is no such thing as food addiction, then you would be able to give up overeating or poor eating anytime you choose. You could consciously choose to stop, and immediately overeating would no longer be a problem. Since this is not the case, you have either been unwilling or unable to give up binge-eating and/or excessive eating.

5. *Have underestimated the impact of overeating on your total life.*

If you fully understood the depth of your overweight and the problems that are associated with it, you would be horrified every time you reached for a fifth cookie or finished off a carton of ice cream.

The reality is that you have compromised your health, your home, your peace of mind, and the lives of those you love by continuing your food addiction. You are not a happy, self-assured person free to love and care for those around you. Instead you are trapped in the prison of overweight, caught up in a myriad of negative emotions and self-hatred. This, in turn, spills over into the way you treat your loved ones. You are angry, unloving, and impatient with coworkers, children, and spouses because you are disappointed in yourself.

Another important area we greatly affect is our health. A lifetime of overeating has made us a virtual time bomb: at any moment we could suffer a heart attack, stroke, or serious illness related to our weight. If you thought you might be taking ten minutes off your life every time you reached for a french fry or bite-size piece of chocolate, you might think twice.

But you don't think about it, and the nightmare continues.

Overweight also affects our careers. We are passed over for promotion and overlooked when recognition is being passed out. Most of us have lost far more workdays because of illness or injury related to our overweight than we care to admit.

Finally, we suffer spiritually when we overeat and binge. Our focus is on food and all that surrounds it. We think of food when we are sad, reward ourselves with food when we are happy, and tranquilize ourselves with food when we are anxious. We have taken the spot in our hearts and lives that rightfully belongs to God and given it over to food. In many cases food has become nothing less than our idol.

When our lives reach this point of destruction, common sense seems to suggest that we take notice and work to eliminate the problem. We don't because, in overvaluing food, we have devalued its cumulative effect on our lives. It is time to recognize the fact.

6. What you think of as nurturing your body through food is really self-abuse.

Overindulging in highly refined, sugary carbohydrate foods pacifies, tranquilizes, and satisfies us for a brief time. But as with every addiction, we must constantly consume more, and in the process we are literally killing ourselves with a fork and spoon. The medical statistics on obesity are clear. It is the second-leading cause of premature death among adults in many nations today. Willingly participating in an activity that will shorten your life cannot be considered caring for yourself. It is not nurturing or self-gratifying or good or any of the other words we use to describe our private feasts. It is dangerous, deadly, self-abuse.

7. You don't understand how God views the problem of overeating and how he desires to help you overcome it.

Many people chafe at the idea that overeating could be a spiritual problem, even a sin. But the first of the Ten Commandments is clear: We are to have no other gods before him. When we make food an idol, using it to meet needs that God alone wants to meet, we are in sinful territory. Also, when we eat out of a fleshly desire to overfill ourselves, we become gluttons and again venture into sin.

Scripture is God's Word, and it teaches that overeating can be a grave problem in our spiritual lives. At the same time, we serve a God who desires to help us out of the snare of our overeating and overweight. He stands ready to help us so that we might find the strength we need to destroy our problem with weight and overeating or poor eating. His Word and his Holy Spirit will be crucial helps on the journey to the TRUE YOU.

Our goal is to help you have freedom from overweight and overeating. In the next chapter we will begin to take a look at how we will do that.

PRISM Success Story: Karen

Age: 40

Weight loss: 40 pounds

WEIGHT WAS NEVER A PROBLEM FOR KAREN until after she had her second child. During that pregnancy, she had become a Christian and given her life to the Lord. In the process, she recognized that she had weight to lose and figured the best way to lose it would be with God's help.

At that time—the early 1980s—the church Karen attended offered a Christian weight loss group that basically followed a balanced diet and offered small group time for prayer.

"The problem was we were exclusive. If you didn't have a very deep faith, the program wasn't for you."

While involved with that group, Karen told herself that if she practiced a certain thing long enough it would become a natural part of her life. This meant that if she stayed devoted to eating healthy foods in average quantities for a long enough time, eventually she would eat that way without having to think about her choices.

"I believed it while I was on the program, but it wasn't true."

Although she lost weight and stayed involved with the group for several years, Karen eventually left and gradually began eating sugar and other foods that had led to her original weight gain.

"It was a very emotional time in my life," she says. "I didn't have anything left to give to my weight loss group, so I pulled out of it and turned to food to smooth out the rough spots in my road. I did it without even realizing that was what I was doing."

She reached her all-time highest weight about eight years later and not long afterward heard about PRISM from an announcement at church. At the first PRISM meeting, she heard talk of transformation, renewed thinking, and destroying the food addictions she'd developed over the years.

"I was very leery of that," she says. "I didn't want to have a lot of hope that this program could actually change me. That was something I used to believe, but it never worked before. Why would I be able to change now?"

Although she didn't believe she could change on the inside, Karen knew it was time to make a change on the outside. She reluctantly decided to commit herself to the PRISM program because it was the best way she could imagine to lose the extra weight she was carrying.

"I had a very bad attitude at first, and as a result I ended up dropping out in the middle of the first phase."

Back at home, still stuck in her bad food habits and unhealthy eating patterns, Karen knew there was no hope unless she changed her attitude and tried PRISM once more. This time she noticed that her workbook answers were different from before.

"It occurred to me that maybe, just maybe, I was actually starting to change the way I viewed food," she says. "It was almost too good to be true."

She made a much more decided commitment to the program and in the process realized one change after another in both her spiritual journey and her relationship with food.

"Suddenly it wasn't so important how quickly my attitudes were changing," she says. "Just to know that I'm in God's will, participating in the only program I know of that daily addresses my inner self and the reasons I eat."

One difficult part of the program was the day she was asked to put away her bathroom scale.

"I must have been using the scale for all the wrong reasons, but it wasn't until I had to put it away that I realized how much I'd been depending on it. Of course, it never helped me anyway. It either made me feel good or bad, and I developed a dependence that was unhealthy. Eventually, it felt good to put it away."

Karen was able to reach her "right weight" without using the scale. As a result, today she maintains her weight by using mirrors to tell her if she's where she should be. Now, because she has committed herself to eating right and nourishing herself the way God intended, she does not feel she will ever need to use a scale again.

In addition, Karen says that through the workbook lessons she has drawn strength and made progress on her path to total transformation. The Agreement of Resolution has also helped her in this area.

"I did my lessons and read my agreement every day. Some days it may not reflect how you actually feel, but it puts you in touch with your focus and intentions and helps you to move ahead. It defines you all over again every day."

Because the PRISM program doesn't presume anything spiritual, it is more useable for "the average overweight bear," Karen says. "This program is for anyone, believer or unbeliever. And either way it will change your life."

HELP IN DESTROYING
THE MONSTER

Why the PRISM Program Works

FOR THOSE OF US WHO HAVE STRUGGLED WITH THE MONSTER of overweight, it is difficult to imagine a day when we will be free from its talons. Most of us recognize the effects of food addiction and overeating on our lives. We have watched the pounds pile on and have been forced into larger sizes and even stores for larger people. Inevitably there have been times when we have been dissatisfied, even disgusted, with our outward appearance and have made a decision to change.

The next step was a diet.

Diets are designed to change our food intake for a specific amount of time, and as a result they cause us to lose weight. But because they deal only with food intake and the outward appearance, they are unable to transform us permanently.

So many of us have been there.

Start a diet, lose twenty pounds; fall off the diet, gain twenty-five pounds; start a diet, lose thirty pounds; fall off the diet, gain thirty-five. This is the dieting yo-yo syndrome discussed earlier, and much has been written about its damaging effects on our bodies. Our metabolisms are greatly affected by fluctuating weight and calorie intake. When we fall off the diets, our bodies store greater amounts of fat in anticipation of the next period of starvation.

On again, off again, and so it goes—our weight steadily climbing, our health steadily declining with each passing year. This is what it is to fight a losing battle with the monster, overweight.

If you find yourself losing this battle, there is hope. There is a way to slay the monster, move ahead, have the trim, healthy body you are intended to have, be at your "right weight," and be the TRUE YOU.

I'm not talking about another in a seemingly endless line of diets or exercise devices that flood the weight loss market today. I'm talking about the PRISM Weight Loss Program, a program that involves changes not only in your diet, but in how you approach issues related to food and your self-image. This is not a short-term fix or a quick weight loss program; rather, it's the beginning of a lasting change in your life.

The PRISM program has three facets: food guidelines, helpful workbooks, and support provided by small groups. Here is a brief look at each of them.

1. The PRISM Program Food Guidelines

The PRISM food guidelines are specifically designed to break your food addiction by holding you accountable for both the quantities and types of food you eat. Phase one is the most stringent, but it also provides the most cleansing for your battered metabolism and body. The food guidelines are detailed in chapter 7.

Included in the food guidelines is a PRISM Agreement of Resolution which helps establish participant accountability.

Before starting PRISM you must sign an Agreement of Resolution like the one given here.

The Agreement of Resolution

I, _____, resolve my desire to change my eating behaviors and learn methods for continuing this control for my lifetime. I resolve that I will follow the food guide (including calorie levels), the guidelines, and KEY PRINCIPLES of this program exactly, without any deviation from its standards. I agree that there are no foods more important to me than becoming slender and reaching my "right weight." Even one bite of extra or prohibited food cannot compare with the freedom I will know when I take steps to become the person I was created to be.

I understand that in the event I decide to revoke this resolution through violation of the program guidelines and KEY PRINCIPLES, I will inform my PRISM group leader or my accountability partner of my decision.

I willingly submit myself to receive the support, strength, and guidance I will require from my leader, fellow class members, and God to complete this program.

Signed: Class Member _____

Implicit in the Agreement of Resolution is a very strong rule, one you must acknowledge and consider carefully before you make a commitment to participate in the PRISM program. This rule states that if you choose to take one bite of foods prohibited by the food guidelines, you will inform your PRISM group leader or accountability partner.

I call this "success in accountability," and at first I rebelled against it. Every other aspect of the PRISM program seemed wonderful to me. Although I was anxious about whether or not I could stay within the program guidelines, I couldn't wait to get on board and watch the transformation begin. But the accountability implicit in the Agreement of Resolution really threw me for a loop.

When I first understood the severity of the one-bite rule, I called PRISM president Toni Vogt and begged her to change it.

"I like everything else about the program so much," I told her. "But the Agreement of Resolution is really tough."

Toni was sympathetic because she'd heard this concern expressed so many times before. She said it was a form of tough love for a problem that has resulted from a lack of discipline.

"Nearly everyone is afraid of the Agreement of Resolution at first. But after making it through the first few weeks, those same people usually embrace it. Try it for six weeks and then we'll talk," she said.

And she was right.

Toni told me that when she teaches classes, she sometimes makes the point that if her husband or child were diagnosed with life-threatening diabetes, she would not consider having sugar in her house. Likewise, she tells her students that if someone in their family had a problem with alcohol or drugs, they would not consider having those items in their homes. Most families pull together and eat or drink differently in support of the one with the problem.

I agree with Toni. For too long the problem of overweight and food addiction has been whitewashed as "not that serious." It is time to face the facts and make changes that will last a lifetime.

I know now why I was troubled by the Agreement of Resolution. It terrified me. I simply didn't think I could do it. Certainly the food addict within me didn't want to be pushed into a corner with no way out, no way to cheat.

Three weeks into the program I knew one thing for sure. The one-bite rule was the reason I was still on it and the reason I felt great and had more energy than I'd had as a teenager. It kept me on the program when I was still far from a complete transformation and hadn't lost enough weight to keep myself motivated. I couldn't stand the thought of calling my small group leader or accountability partner to tell her I'd chosen to have a brownie.

Since I knew I didn't want to make that phone call, I had no choice. I had made my commitment, and I was going to keep it. Therefore, there was no need to salivate over the brownies, because I wasn't going to eat them.

2. PRISM WORKBOOKS

Workbooks are available for each of the first four PRISM phases. Supplemental material for those who have finished phase four is available through PRISM. This material includes journals, books, and other resources. By the time participants are in phase five and beyond, they have often identified a specific area that needs to be addressed—such as *we need to help identify this for ppl beyond phase 5*

a lack of exercise, lack of self-esteem, sexual abuse. Some class members decide to tackle a particular problem on their own rather than repeat a PRISM curricula for one or more phases. They may do this within their PRISM membership.

Workbooks are issued in a PRISM support group when you register in the program. Each workbook includes an Agreement of Resolution, which you must read and sign before you start each phase. It also includes daily lessons complete with inspirational Scripture to help you through difficult aspects of the program. In the following chapter, we give you a breakdown of many themes discussed in the phase one and phase two workbooks. Also, the workbooks include enough food journal sheets to get you through that phase.

The following is a sample of a food journal sheet (see page 82 for a full-sized one):

Note that the food journal sheets make it simple to keep track of the daily aspects of PRISM:

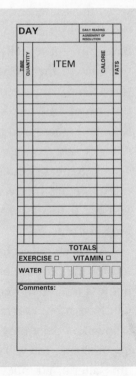

- Reading your Agreement of Resolution

- Doing your workbook lesson

- Writing down your food intake for the day

- Acknowledging that you drank enough water and took your vitamins

- Getting your exercise

In a sense, the PRISM program is akin to voluntary rehabilitation for a condition that may have haunted you and stolen from you all of your life. The workbook is designed to be a constant companion, a tool that will be close at hand while you are on the program and help you find motivation each day as you continue your journey toward transformation.

This daily workbook lesson sets PRISM apart from other programs because it does not force you to rely on weekly encouragement for success. You will be encouraged daily and given help to deal with the daily struggles of transforming your eating behaviors.

Workbooks are issued upon registration in a PRISM small group. To find out where your nearest PRISM group is located, contact the PRISM office at 1-800-755-1738.

There is a different PRISM workbook for each of the four primary six-week phases. Phase five and beyond include additional material provided to all PRISM small group members. The lessons do not take long—perhaps ten or fifteen minutes each day.

DOING AWAY WITH THE SCALE

Very early in the PRISM program, participants are asked to stop weighing themselves. There is a reason for this. Many of us are so emotionally tied to the scale that we weigh ourselves every day and base our entire self-worth on the number that flashes in the tiny window. In the PRISM program you are working toward transformation from the inside out. You will lose weight and you will lose inches. But proof of your success is not found in those numbers alone. Success is measured by your change in attitude toward food and your ability to stay away from foods you have been addicted to in the past. These changes cannot be measured merely by stepping on a scale. Too often, we are motivated or discouraged by the number on the scale and for that reason you must simply do away with it while on the PRISM program.

At the end of each phase you will have an opportunity to weigh yourself for the purpose of charting your weight loss and to be sure you do not lose too much weight. But this weigh-in is optional if you are certain you have more weight to lose. No longer will you be losing weight and following a daily program for the reward of a lower number the following morning. You will be making changes that will stay with you for a lifetime, altering attitudes for a lifetime. The number on the scale has nothing to do with that transformation.

3. The PRISM Program Small Groups

Currently thousands of people are finding freedom from overweight within the safety net of a PRISM small group. These groups meet once a week in offices, churches, and homes across the country and even in some foreign countries. You may call PRISM at 1-800-755-1738 to discover the meeting place nearest to you. Or you may decide to start a PRISM group at your workplace, church, or home.

There are four ways you may become part of a PRISM small group meeting. They are the following:

ESTABLISHED GROUP MEETINGS.

You may call the PRISM offices and provide your zip code. A PRISM representative will look up the official group meeting closest to you and provide you with the name of the group leader and a local telephone number to call to determine meeting times and places. Established group meetings follow a standard agenda. The group may open in prayer, allow time for shared victories, watch a PRISM video with encouraging and informational material, and then split into smaller groups for discussion.

If there are no established group meetings near you, there are other options to meet your needs.

ESTABLISH YOUR OWN PRISM CHURCH SUPPORT GROUP.

In order to start a support group for your church family, you must have your pastor, minister, or priest's approval and six people including yourself ready to begin the PRISM program. These groups will be open to anyone who chooses to come and may be advertised through your church newsletter, bulletin, inter-office memos, or bulletin boards. Advertising materials and leadership guides are provided by PRISM at no charge. Contact PRISM to obtain a free, no-obligation introductory packet and video if you are interested in starting a support group at your church.

ESTABLISH YOUR OWN PRISM SUPPORT GROUP AT YOUR PLACE OF WORK OR AT HOME.

As few as two or more people may form a support group to get together and encourage each other on a weekly basis. Perhaps you are interested in meeting during a lunch hour once a week with a group of people from work. Maybe you want to form a group in your neighborhood or join with friends and family members and meet in someone's home each week. This type of meeting is more intimate and allows for more time spent in discussion and individual needs. Again, contact PRISM to request free, no-obligation introductory materials if you are interested in starting a work or home support group.

PRISM CORRESPONDENCE COURSE.

If you are unable to find or attend a regularly scheduled meeting due to time constraints, or if you would prefer to follow the program privately, you may decide to work toward transformation through the PRISM correspondence program. PRISM will send all pertinent materials to you as if you were in a group. Correspondence members will go through the program one on one with their own personal PRISM consultant via the telephone each week. During that time the consultant will listen to and discuss your personal struggles and successes and offer encouragement for the coming week. Please contact PRISM to request free, no-obligation correspondence program information materials.

Now that you understand the key facets of the PRISM program in general, we can take a more in-depth look at some of the topics discussed in the workbooks.

PATTY HAD BATTLED EXCESS WEIGHT ALL HER LIFE. Although she was only five feet tall, she hadn't weighed less than 200 pounds since her mid-twenties. Three decades of overweight brought about a dozen diet attempts, none of which helped her lose more than a handful of pounds and none of which had any lasting results.

In addition to the standard diets, liquid diets, and other diet plans, Patty tried strange concoctions. She once received serum injections from a doctor as part of a weight loss strategy. Later she learned that the serum contained monkey urine and urine from pregnant women.

"Isn't that gross?" she asks now.

She tried self-hypnosis, Weight Watchers, and any other diet that came along, but nothing worked. Patty hit an all-time low in 1993 when she was diagnosed with chronic fatigue syndrome and could no longer work. She had seriously high blood pressure and doctors told her she was likely to suffer a stroke or a heart attack because of her poor health and excess weight.

She refused to discuss these issues with the doctor or the Lord, although she had been a Christian for more than a decade. "I figured this is the way God made me, so I would just have to live with it."

In reality, Patty admits now, she was destroying the only body God had given her.

"For the next four years I could do little more than sleep and eat. I ached all over and I was miserable with life," Patty says. "I had tried everything in my own power and nothing was working."

In 1997 she reached the end of herself and her own efforts. About that time she heard about the PRISM program.

"A friend of mine had lost 120 pounds on PRISM," Patty says. "The whole source of the program was developing a commitment to God. I decided to give it a try and I never looked back."

Patty began PRISM in February 1997 and asked God to heal her of her overeating and food addiction. Sixteen months later she had lost 155 pounds and had to relearn a host of activities. For several months after losing her weight she would often fall when sitting down on the toilet or in a chair.

"I used to have a whole other person there to catch me when I sat down," she says. "Now I have to back my legs up to a chair to know where I am when I sit."

She wears smaller shoes, smaller glasses, and smaller dentures as a result of her weight loss. Once when she and her husband were at the store, they ran into a longtime friend they hadn't seen for a year. The woman stared at them and then started to turn away.

"I called to her and asked her if she recognized who I was," Patty recalls. "I told her I was Patty, and she just shook her head. When she realized it really was me, she ran to me, hugged me and started crying. She thought my husband had gotten a new wife. She couldn't believe it was really me."

Other changes she appreciates include the fact that her grandchildren can hug her and circle their arms easily around her petite frame. In addition, she is in charge of a group of sixteen women who are also on the PRISM program.

"The success rate with this program is better than anything else I've seen," Patty says. "I had weighed over 200 pounds for more than thirty-two years, and on every diet there is. I even considered having my stomach stapled, but my insurance wouldn't cover it."

Today when Patty runs into old acquaintances, they often tell her they recognize something about her eyes and her voice. But when she tells them who she is they generally gasp.

"No one can believe it's me," Patty says. "That's how different I look."

But like others who have found success on PRISM, it isn't just her looks Patty is excited about.

"This is a program that is about so much more than the food," she says. "We believe that with God all things are possible, and we have been finding that this is exactly what happens. God has given me the strength and willpower to complete this diet program."

Patty says her faith is stronger and her personality is different than before. "I'm the same person, but I feel so much better and am more bubbly. I am so much better in every way than I was before I started PRISM. I will be forever grateful for what God has done for me through the PRISM program."

One other benefit: Patty is back to work now. Her job? A food demonstrator at Costco.

"People come up and say, 'Oh, no thanks. I can't have white sugar or white flour.' So I ask them if they're on PRISM," Patty says. "You know what? A lot of people out there say yes. They're finding the same success I did through the Lord and the PRISM program."

DAY

TIME QUANTITY	ITEM	DAILY READING AGREEMENT OF RESOLUTION	CALORIE	FATS

TOTALS

EXERCISE ☐   VITAMIN ☐

WATER ☐☐☐☐☐☐☐☐

Comments:

DAY

TIME QUANTITY	ITEM	DAILY READING AGREEMENT OF RESOLUTION	CALORIE	FATS

TOTALS

EXERCISE ☐   VITAMIN ☐

WATER ☐☐☐☐☐☐☐☐

Comments:

DAY

TIME QUANTITY	ITEM	DAILY READING AGREEMENT OF RESOLUTION	CALORIE	FATS

TOTALS

EXERCISE ☐   VITAMIN ☐

WATER ☐☐☐☐☐☐☐☐

PRISM® and PRISM® instructors do not give advice regarding the nutritional adequacy of your diet. Any questions about your dietary or nutritional needs should be directed to a medical professional.

T.J.L. INC 1992
ALL RIGHTS RESERVED

NAME:

CLASS TIME:

PHASE:

WEEK #: _____   CALORIE LEVEL: _____

PRISM

FOOD JOURNAL

Consultant Comments

A New Perspective

Changing How We View Food

ONE OF THE TOP OBJECTIVES OF THE PRISM PROGRAM—other than weight loss—is to change your behavior when it comes to food by changing how you view food. We want to give you a new perspective on what you eat, when you eat it, and why you eat it.

In our culture, if there is one place the problem of overweight thrives, it's in our emotions. Over the years we have learned to eat when we are happy as a means of celebration and when we are sad as a means of comfort. We use food as a way to add excitement to our lives and commemorate the good things that come our way. We use it as a tranquilizer to mask our feelings of depression, anxiety, and boredom.

It is important to understand each of these areas and how they have contributed to our problems with overweight. For that reason, the PRISM workbooks deal extensively with each of these issues.

We believe that in order for transformation to occur, it must take place throughout the entire person—body, mind, and spirit. This being the case, weeks of workbook time are devoted to the emotional aspect of overweight and food addiction.

Most of us already know the emotional triggers that cause us to overeat. Still, we will touch on a few of them in this chapter. Remember, there is no easy solution to the emotional problems associated with overweight. The only way to be transformed into a person who is no longer subject to them is by analyzing and examining them in depth.

CELEBRATING BY OVEREATING

Celebrations are often the scapegoat for the overeater. We avoid starting diets when any sort of celebration is looming, and once we have committed to an eating program, happy occasions give us permission to throw our commitment out the window. Since getting involved with PRISM, I've talked with several people who were desperately interested in the program. But because of an upcoming celebration they were reluctant to start.

Holidays or celebrations that might sideline us from breaking our food addictions in any given year include: New Year's Day, Super Bowl Sunday, Valentine's Day, President's Day Weekend, Passover, Easter, spring break, Mother's Day, Memorial Day, Father's Day, Fourth of July, summer vacation, Labor Day, Halloween, Thanksgiving, and Christmas.

Somewhere in there add your birthday and anniversary and the birthdays of your immediate family members. Also add special occasions, including the visits of out-of-town guests, weddings, graduations, promotions, report cards, etc. When you plot these events on a calendar, you will notice there will never be a six-week block without a celebration. Never time for even the first of the four PRISM phases.

If you are going to be successful in breaking your problem with overweight, you will need to relearn how to eat during holidays and celebrations. This means that, instead of associating the hallmarks of our lives with food (Grandma's New Year's pudding, Mom's Fourth-of-July brownies, Aunt Susie's Labor Day cookies, etc.), we must make new associations and look forward to other aspects of the celebration.

NEW WAYS TO HANDLE THE SITUATION

1. Look forward to feeling good in the midst of friends and family members, confident in the knowledge that you are taking good care of yourself that day, physically and emotionally.

2. Remember how obsessed you were with food at previous celebrations and how you always ended up feeling guilty and miserable.

3. Plan out your conversations the way you once planned your food *Hmmm* intake. Look forward to talking to specific people about specific things.

4. Look forward to the energy you will have: energy to be lead batter at the family softball game, energy to play tag with the children, or energy to provide the hostess with a little help cleaning up after the party.

5. Think out your right food choices ahead of time or bring something that will work into your calorie allotment for the day.

6. Save up and buy a new outfit for the occasion. The longer you've been on the program, the closer to your right size you will be!

7. Be in charge of creating activities that go along with the celebration and have nothing to do with food.

8. Offer to help plan the menu. This will ensure that healthy food will be served as an alternative, allowing you to make good choices during the celebration. You may also be surprised at how many guests appreciate and choose the healthier food.

THE TEMPTATION OF TRIALS

Another area where we nurse our friendship with food is during trying times. Trials will come for all of us. Deaths, injuries, illness, financial woes. It is often during these times that we allow ourselves wild binges with high carbohydrate, sugar-laden foods. There actually is a physiological reason for this. An overload of sugar in our systems causes the chemical seratonin to be released into our bloodstreams, which in turn gives us a twenty-minute feeling of well-being. Sometimes it is this chemical reaction and temporary feeling that subconsciously send us to the kitchen when we are facing life's greatest trials.

However, when this feeling wears off, our blood sugar plummets, which in turn sets off a feeling of darkness and depression. Combine that feeling with whatever real emotions are happening because of the trial and we feel left with only one option: eating more.

The sad truth is that eating may temporarily pacify you, but the problem that sent you to the refrigerator is still there. You have not solved it. Instead, you have created additional problems. These problems lead to a furious cycle characterized by:

- Increased food addiction

- Weight gain

- Depression

- Reduced immune system

During times of stress, our immune systems are already compromised. Binge-eating causes additional physical stress on our bodies, and high-sugar foods have been proven to reduce our ability to ward off illness. The result is that on top of dealing with a trial, you will likely be dealing with an illness, anything from a common cold to a raging sickness.

All because you sought the wrong outlet as a way to numb yourself, instead of handling a crisis.

NEW WAYS TO HANDLE THE SITUATION

1. When you receive news of a specific crisis or difficulty, take a moment to pray. Ask God to help you through the situation and then stay connected with him throughout the ordeal. This will establish your basis of strength and support, something food can only pretend to do.

2. Pay special attention to your food choices and avoid high carbohydrate foods. Always avoid all foods containing refined sugar and white flour.

3. Make certain to get extra protein. Foods high in protein will keep your energy levels high, your brain functioning clearly, and your blood sugar even. This will give you the staying power necessary to meet the physical demands of a crisis—including late nights, little sleep, and emotionally draining days.

4. Drink extra water. This, too, will keep your body operating at its optimal level and will help keep your immune system strong.

5. Remember to exercise. Movement is a natural stress reliever. Although there are many times when our routines are interrupted by a crisis, try to find time to take a walk with friends or family members, ride a bike, or get some sort of aerobic exercise. Again, your immune system will be stronger for your effort and you will be much more capable of handling the given situation. (We'll cover exercise in more detail later.)

6. Take your vitamins. Vitamin C, antioxidant multiple vitamins, and garlic capsules are likely to boost your immune system and help counter the physical effects of stress. (We'll cover vitamins in more detail later.)

7. Don't stuff your emotions. Express your feelings when they arise, even if it's only to your spouse or a close friend. Those of us who are addicted to wrong foods often don't deal with our emotions. Instead, we find ourselves staging a major binge as a way of finding the comfort we are not receiving. Only when we share our emotions and truly address our problems and needs can we receive real comfort and support from loved ones around us.

FOOD: RX FOR FRUSTRATION

It's 4:30 in the afternoon. You're unloading the dishwasher when the rice begins boiling over on the stove. Reaching to turn down the flame, you notice that the sink is backing up as the dishwasher runs. Potato peelings from yesterday's dinner float lazily atop the backup of dirty water now filling the sink. Searching for a place to set the cooked rice, you settle for a stack of newspapers that has been cluttering the kitchen counter for three days. At that moment the baby grabs for the rice container, knocks it over, and spills tiny grains of rice across the entire kitchen floor.

"Mom, where's Antarctica?" your third-grader asks.

"Antarctica? Who wants to know?" You reach for the broom just as the baby grabs a dinner plate from the open dishwasher and drops it on the floor, shattering it into twenty-seven slivered pieces.

"All done," you tell the baby. "No, no, no."

You pick him up, take him to his playpen, and set him inside. Immediately he begins whimpering, which leads to a full-blown scream—the kind that sends feelings of electrocution through your body strong enough to perm your hair from fifteen feet away.

Forgetting about the rice to focus on the shards of china, you bend over and begin sweeping.

"Mom, the dog threw up all over Dad's new shoes." It's your son with the announcement, and by the smile on his face it seems he is almost happy about the fact.

Sighing, you look up from the floor and above the sounds of the baby's cries, you calmly say, "Please clean it up as best as you can. Daddy will be home in an hour."

"Where's Antarctica, Mom? Teacher says I need to know by tomorrow."

"South. It's south."

You manage to get up most of the glass before your son reappears. "I used that old sweater, Mom. Is that okay?"

This news causes you to straighten more quickly than you have since your junior high phys-ed class. "What sweater?"

"The gray one on that rack out there."

"My pearl gray sweater? The one I was air drying on the rack? You used it to wipe up the dog's...."

"Mom, is Australia one of the states in the U.S. that doesn't border another state?"

"I couldn't get all the throw-up out so I put the shoes in the tub to soak."

"Or is Italy one of those states, Mom...."

Just then the telephone rings.

You look toward the phone—across the cluttered kitchen counter and open dishwasher and rice-covered floor—and you see an entire basket of Christmas cookies. Suddenly there is only one way the night will ever seem right.

Certainly you can relate to this scenario. Frenzied, harried moments in the course of the day that cry out for peace, quiet, and tranquillity. At times like these we reach for something to pacify us, and far too often the pacifier is an unhealthy type or quantity of food.

People who deeply desire to feel in control of their lives are especially prone to overeating during times of frustration. Circumstances may be spinning out of control, chaos may reign, but if we can get to our stash of comfort foods, we can dim the effect this craziness has on our sense of well-being. By taking the focus off the frustration and placing it onto the food, we can somehow trick ourselves into believing that all is right with the world.

Of course if you gobble six cookies, the reality is that there are still dishes to put away, rice to sweep up, papers to stack, and vomit to clean out of Dad's soggy shoes (not to mention your sweater). Only now you'll have to deal with those things while harboring a heavy guilt for doing the very thing you know is destroying you.

NEW WAYS TO HANDLE THE SITUATION

1. Be aware and plan ahead. Frustrating situations tend to come at the same time each day. Late afternoons, for instance, or school-day mornings. Know your schedule and be aware that such a moment may be approaching.

2. Stay one step ahead. If clutter bothers you, keep things tidy so that when an overwhelming number of demands land squarely on your shoulders, you will not have the added frustration of clutter. This is true of whatever bothers you—dirty bathrooms, dishes, etc.

3. Ride it out. When the frenzied moments come, remember that they will also end. Remind yourself that this, too, shall pass. And try to focus on meeting the needs one at a time. Eventually, dinner will be served, kids will go to bed, and life will again be quiet. There is no point in punishing yourself with destructive eating and its aftereffects. These will last much longer than the frustrating moment.

4. Pray. Keeping your perspective during times of frustration is especially important. You can do this by establishing a prayer connection. Tell God that you are frustrated and ask for his help. He may not sweep up the rice for you or locate Antarctica on a world map, but he will help you keep

your focus. Also, remember that we would do better when tempted to focus more on the escape than on the temptation (1 Corinthians 10:13).

5. Have a backup plan. Many times frustration comes as a result of being overwhelmed in a specific moment. When these moments arise, have a different plan of action. In the past you have turned to food to tranquilize you and help you through them. Now you will need to find something else to do on such occasions. Here are some suggestions:

- Take a nap.

- Sip a tall glass of water—perhaps adding a lemon slice—and find a quiet place to sit.

- Find a quiet place—even a closet—and pray for strength and peace to get through the situation.

- Memorize a Scripture verse.

- Take a walk or get thirty minutes of aerobic exercise.

- Make a phone call to someone with whom you can share the situation.

- Do housework or something else constructive. Sometimes the sense of accomplishment helps ease feelings of frustration.

- Work on a hobby.

- Sing. Smile. Laugh. Breathe deeply. Remember, the moment of frustration will pass.

THE DIET ROLLER COASTER

The problem of overeating will stay with us as we ride the roller coaster of up-and-down dieting. Our desire for excess or wrong food lessens as we lose weight and force ourselves to eat healthy foods. But eating correctly can translate into a feeling of self-denial, even punishment. Once we have allowed ourselves to "fall off the wagon," once we have given up on our diet, the problem will come back bigger, fiercer, and more demanding than ever.

Most of us have ridden the roller coaster ourselves. Gain thirty pounds, lose twenty; gain thirty, lose twenty. In a matter of years, we can wind up with fifty extra pounds despite the fact that we spend half our time dieting. Here's an example of how this pattern can make our food addiction worse over the years.

Cindy first chose to lose weight when she was twenty and wanted desperately to fit into a smaller size for her sister's wedding. Knowing no other way, she went on a crash diet and did, indeed, lose twenty pounds in only five weeks. So intense was her struggle during that time that she could hardly wait for the wedding reception. At that point, she told herself, she could eat whatever she wanted. After all, the pictures would be taken, the dress would be zipped, and there would be no reason to continue to deny herself the food she'd been craving for more than a month.

At the reception, Cindy was first in line for cake. She ate three pieces and dozens of melt-away mints from the centerpiece bowl. Before the evening was over she had also helped herself to several slices of cheesecake from the buffet line. She intended to eat in moderation once the wedding was past. But there were parties and movies and get-togethers with friends. Despite her good intentions, she continued to overeat, occasionally participating in a full-fledged binge and feeling guilty much of the time.

One year and thirty-five pounds later, Cindy wound up in a bookstore looking for the latest diet book. This time she chose a plan that helped her count her food as exchanges. The program offered many packaged foods available at local supermarkets and even a variety of diet desserts that could be eaten if worked into the exchange program. She lost thirty pounds; but in the next five years she gained a husband, a child, and forty pounds.

She didn't come to the PRISM program until she'd ridden the roller coaster another three times, losing weight and gaining it all back plus a few additional pounds. Each time she began gaining weight it was because of repeated binge-eating—sometimes triggered by a special event, other times as a way of rewarding herself for reaching a weight loss goal.

Most likely, you have seen yourself in some of Cindy's actions and in the way your weight has gradually crept up over the years. The effect this kind of dieting has on the metabolism is devastating. It forces our bodies to alternate between a state of starvation and a state of excessive carbohydrate supply or excessive insulin. Anticipating a state of starvation, our metabolism slows down to store fat during the eating stage and slows down to conserve fat when our body is dieting. The end result is fast weight gain and a metabolism that can no longer efficiently burn fat.

If you, like so many others, have done this to your body, it is not too late to get off the roller coaster and begin the process of transformation.

NEW WAYS TO HANDLE THE SITUATION

1. Decide to start the PRISM program, then do it! Decide also that you will never weigh more than you do at this moment. Your success on the PRISM program will be a lifelong change and not merely another trip down the roller coaster. You will not be starting merely another diet in a string of many, rather you will be taking the first step on the road to lasting transformation. At the end of that road you will find freedom from the problem of overweight and overeating and a new attitude toward food. With exercise and healthy eating, your metabolism will pick up speed until it is working as it was intended to.

2. Rid yourself of the idea that food is a reward. When we reach our "right weight," we must not see food as the reward—the pot of gold at the end of a dreary, dull rainbow. Nothing could be farther from the truth. Food is for nourishment only. Nourishing your body may be enjoyable, but it is not healthy to view food as a comfort, a friend, a support system, or a source of entertainment. We eat to live, not the other way around.

The PRISM program will help you change your mind about the purpose of food and free you to view it as God intended. You will enjoy the foods he created but refuse to make food an idol in your life. (See Exodus 20:3.) Once you allow your mind to be changed, you will no longer reach your goal weight only to binge as a reward. You will have taken yourself off the roller coaster.

3. Begin an exercise program. The damage you have done to your metabolism by riding the diet roller coaster is reversible, but only with consistent exercise. If you are one who has experienced numerous weight losses and gains, your body's engine burns fuel at a sluggish pace. Regular exercise will help speed up your body's motor and get your body burning efficiently once more. There will be more on exercise and its benefits, along with a simple program to follow, in a later chapter.

It's Your Choice

You've had a chance to examine a few of the ways in which a person's relationship with food can become skewed. Our guess is that you may have one or more of these problems. If that is the case, take heart. Millions of people have experienced the same trouble areas with food and are faced even now with a choice.

The choice is this: Continue in the grip of the problem, or break free and allow God to transform you through the PRISM program. There are so many people standing by to help you make the right choice and follow through with your decision.

Now that you have a better understanding of reasons for food addiction and the problem of overweight, it's time to talk about the solution: the PRISM Weight Loss Program.

AS FAR BACK AS CANDY COULD REMEMBER, she had been twenty to thirty pounds overweight. Every few years she would reach a point of intolerance with herself and go on a diet.

"I'd lose the weight and gain it back almost immediately," Candy remembers.

By the time she'd had her second child, Candy realized that she had done something many mothers do—center celebrations and evening dinner hours around heavy, carbohydrate-laden foods. When daily problems arose as they do for all of us, Candy found herself using food as a solution. The most difficult aspect of this habit was her occupation. Candy was a nurse, and although she was unaware of food addictions, she knew she was not eating in a healthy fashion.

For Candy, sweets and white-flour products made up a majority of her calorie intake each day. After numerous diets had failed, she was looking for a way to kick these foods and lose weight when she ran into someone who was on the PRISM program. As she looked into PRISM, she realized that many of her coworkers were on the program. Many of them had lost weight and were feeling more energy than they'd had in years.

"Everything about it sounded wonderful, but the religious part of the program was very frightening to me," Candy says now. "I don't really consider myself a Christian, and I didn't know if I'd feel comfortable about the faith element in PRISM."

Still, Candy decided to give PRISM a chance. The results have been amazing. Not only has Candy lost twenty-four pounds and four dress sizes, she's also developed a liking for Scriptures.

"I enjoy reading the daily Scriptures and doing my lesson. I've talked to God several times recently, and I've never done that before," Candy says. "I enjoy the strictness of PRISM—the regimen of it."

Candy says that she is careful not to miss a lesson and that she goes through her workbook each morning. The bathroom scale is collecting dust in the garage, and people around Candy notice a dramatic change.

"It's amazing how the fat falls off when you stop eating sugar and white flour," she says. "And I enjoy the lessons so much that when I'm through with the workbooks, I'm going to take that morning time to read the Bible."

Nancy Boydston

after losing 80 pounds

Patty Dudgeon

155 pounds later

The Heart and Soul of PRISM

What We Stand For

AS SHOULD ANY PROGRAM BASED IN THE CHRISTIAN FAITH, PRISM has a mission statement, which states the purpose of everything we do and all we want the program to do for you.

The PRISM Mission Statement

The mission of the program is to communicate principles for change in eating behaviors of the overweight, overeating, food-addicted individual. These principles are based on truth, hope, and encouragement, and they promote understanding, strength, and discipline. We rely on biblical principles for direction in all aspects of administration, business, teaching, and program content.

This mission statement can be broken into four parts:

1. The purpose of PRISM is to communicate principles for lifelong change in eating behaviors of overweight individuals.

We believe that overeating and overweight point to a much deeper and more complex problem. Individuals who are aware of their need to lose weight lack the tools and direction to deal successfully with the total problem. It is our desire to give them the keys to a new lifestyle with clarity, simplicity, and compassion. (See Proverbs 8:5–9; 12:17; 16:6; John 8:32; 2 Corinthians 4:2; Ephesians 4:15.)

2. These principles are based on truth, hope, and encouragement.

We believe that, as we teach solid techniques for gaining self-control and insight into the causes of overeating and being overweight, we must convey a totally honest message. Our message will also provide hope and the positive encouragement necessary for success. These qualities will insure the transformation necessary for lasting benefit. (See Psalm 42:11; Proverbs 13:12; Romans 5:3–5.)

3. These principles promote understanding, strength, and discipline.

Our goal is the transformation of the whole person—body, mind, and spirit. As we assist them in evaluation and education, participants will gain new insights, revived stamina, and discipline, which will last a lifetime. We understand that the time it takes to acquire these characteristics will vary for each person. We will seek to be flexible and adaptable to fit individual needs. (See Proverbs 3:5–6; James 1:12.)

4. Biblical principles will direct administration, business, teaching, and program content.

In our desire to see the total person changed for a lifetime, we must have a basis of truth for all our efforts. We believe the Bible is the perfect Word of God, who is the author of life. It is an infallible source of knowledge and information. Therefore, we resolve to base all creative thought, direction, and problem solving on his Word. (See Proverbs 19:21; 2 Timothy 3:16–17.)

THE KEY PRINCIPLE TO REMEMBER

The following statement is your first KEY PRINCIPLE. It carries with it the expectation that you will follow this teaching and all other KEY PRINCIPLES with no variation.

DEVIATION FROM OR VARIATION OF ANY GUIDELINES WHILE PARTICIPATING IN THE PRISM WEIGHT LOSS PROGRAM IS STRICTLY PROHIBITED. NO VIOLATIONS OF THE GUIDELINES ARE ALLOWED.

Please understand that this KEY PRINCIPLE does not infer rejection or a lack of compassion for your struggle. It is our intention to help you understand the importance of discipline and adherence to all program guidelines.

Think of your problem with overweight as a prison, where a problem has tormented you for months, years, or even a lifetime. The PRISM program will destroy the problem, but it will require your commitment to adhere to the program guidelines. Think of it as self-imposed rehabilitation, a plan that will, perhaps, save your life.

Having been through the program ourselves, we understand that sticking to the PRISM guidelines takes no small commitment on your part. We want to do everything we can to help you stick to the guidelines, and we believe the most effective tool we have for doing that is the PRISM workbooks.

WHY THE WORKBOOKS WORK

Workbook lessons are the heart and soul of the PRISM program and the reason why it is so different from any other. Each day you will start your morning with a workbook lesson, which includes some review, some new material, and usually a personal evaluation. Optional Scripture readings accompany each lesson.

The daily workbook lessons include guides that will lead you to a place of transformation and help you do away with your food addiction and struggles with weight. The PRISM Weight Loss Program deals with a variety of issues that will help loosen the grip of overweight and set you free. The following are themes covered by the PRISM workbooks for phases one and two:

PERSONAL EVALUATION

The PRISM program begins with a deep look at your relationship with food. You chart your current weight and measurements and answer questions about your thoughts on starting PRISM and your eating habits. Many of us have never given thought to the reasons we eat what we do or to the emotions behind our choices. This personal evaluation will offer a time for self-reflection and get you ready to begin the PRISM program. It will be repeated at various times throughout the program to enable you to watch your inner transformation as it takes place.

A NEW BEGINNING

The starting place for people who begin the PRISM Program is accepting the truth that this is a new beginning. This is not merely another diet plan, another way to take off twenty pounds only to see that much and more return in a few months. This is the beginning of the rest of your life, the start of a transformation that will leave you changed inside and outside. The workbook section on new beginnings helps you understand this and why it is important to leave the past behind.

SELF-IMAGE

Generally, people who suffer from food addiction and overweight have a distorted view of themselves. A few of us see ourselves as heavier than we truly are and as having more of a problem than we really do. But the majority of us see ourselves as "not that bad off" or thinner than we really are. We wear dark or loose clothing in order to hide our overweight and we compare ourselves to others in order to justify our size. In this way we are able to continue in a form of denial, feeding our addiction and ignoring our problem. Often we even delay regular medical checkups in an attempt to hide the truth. *I'll go after I lose a few pounds,* we tell ourselves. *The doctor will only tell me I need to lose weight—something I already know—so I'll skip my appointment this year.* Meanwhile, we continue to grow larger and more unhealthy while our food choices flare out of control.

This section of the workbook will help you better understand your true self-image. You will learn about the "skinny pig" syndrome, which can lead you to go on food binges with someone larger than you. You may also find that you allow yourself to eat large quantities of wrong foods because you are comparing yourself to someone across the room or across the state who is larger than you. So long as you can justify your addiction and overweight, you can keep from making a change. You must deal with this problem with your self-image in order to understand why you are in need of a transformation.

OUT OF THE "EATING CLOSET" AND INTO THE LIGHT

Everyone who has ever battled excess weight and perhaps a food addiction knows the places where he or she has staged dozens, sometimes hundreds, of food binges. For some people this may be their car, for others it's in their homes—in a bathroom perhaps, or in a certain area of a walk-in closet, or even in front of a kitchen cupboard. Wherever it is, this place offers the food addict a place to do business. Food is often stored there, and there the most serious binge-eating takes place. These places need to be identified and acknowledged. That done, we can move out of the eating closet into the light.

ACTIVITIES THAT TRANSFORM

It is important to examine closely the activities that lead to overeating or binge-eating. In this workbook section, you will have an opportunity to examine them and consciously replace them with activities that will lead to transformation.

FOUNDATIONS FOR THE TRUE YOU

This section of the workbook allows time to reflect on previous lessons. It includes another personal assessment of where you are in the transformation process and how the foundation has been laid for success.

IDENTIFYING THE LEVEL OF YOUR ADDICTION

Again, personal evaluation is used to determine how deeply rooted your problem with overweight is. This section is designed to create greater awareness in PRISM participants so that they can have a better understanding of how badly the transformation process is needed and how long it will take.

CODEPENDENCY: REACTING VS. RESPONDING

Many of us feel we have an overweight problem because of someone else. Perhaps we believe it is our parents' fault for feeding us fattening foods and getting us hooked on chocolate and sugar at an early age. Perhaps we think it is the fault of a nagging spouse who seems to drive us to distraction and ultimately to overeating. Whatever the excuse, it is time to be done with it. This section of the workbook deals with letting go of the excuses and responding to those issues in ways that do not involve food.

Overeating is a reaction we have learned over the years. It is a way of dealing with the issue at hand quickly and as painlessly as possible—or so it seems. While on the PRISM program you will learn that while you need to respond to family and lifelong issues, you do not have to react by overeating. Learning appropriate behaviors and responses is a key aspect of your transformation and success on PRISM.

IDENTIFYING AND BREAKING THE SNARES

There have always been, and probably always will be, obstacles on the road to bettering ourselves. The way to overcome them is not to eliminate them, but to identify them. Once they are recognized for what they are, they become nothing more than bumps in the road to change. Once you have recognized them and planned how to respond, things that might have tripped you up in the past will barely slow you down in the future.

SUCCESS VS. SABOTAGE

Fear of success will sometimes cause even the most determined of us to sabotage our own efforts. By the time you reach this point in the workbook, you will have undoubtedly experienced much success. Still, the old habit of sabotaging yourself lurks in the shadows, waiting to welcome the problem of overweight back into your life. This section teaches you to recognize and eliminate self-sabotaging behavior.

THE GRIEVING PROCESS

Often people who are in the process of giving up a lifetime food addiction or letting go of poor eating behaviors experience grief. They grieve because they will never again find themselves on a food binge, out of control, and eating their way toward a sick stomach and further weight gain. Overeating and food binges have become familiar, and letting go of them causes grief for many people. This section will help you identify the grief and deal with it without making choices that will defeat your weight loss efforts.

TRIUMPH OVER TEMPTATION

These workbook sections will help you identify temptation and be prepared for the moments when it hits the hardest. By developing a plan of attack before the temptation hits, you will experience triumph over temptation.

REMEMBER TO PRAY

These letters stand for PRISM, Recognize, Acknowledge, and You. Each has a role in stopping temptation and each is examined fully in the PRISM workbooks.

THE APPETITE UNDERSTOOD AND TAMED

Sometimes we are unclear about how our bodies work and how appetite plays a role in our eating. Generally, it takes our bodies four hours to experience true hunger after eating a meal. The lessons in this section of the workbook help you identify the difference between true hunger and emotional hunger. Food addiction, specifically sugar addiction, can cause our bodies to experience what feels like true hunger even when we do not physically need to eat. Understanding the difference is a big part of your success in the PRISM program.

THE PIG SYNDROME

PIG stands for the Problem of Immediate Gratification. Many times it is this syndrome, which is explained in the workbooks, that leads us to binge and sometimes sabotages our weight loss efforts. By anticipating this syndrome, it is possible to avoid it and eliminate it on the road to transformation.

FILLING THE HOLES CREATED BY CHANGE

Letting go of damaging eating habits will leave you with holes in your life. This section of the workbook helps you learn new ways to fill them. You will have the opportunity to examine your habits and identify those that must no longer be a part of your life. You will learn how to choose new habits and ways to fill these holes. In this way you will become a completely whole, transformed person free from the habits of food addiction and misuse.

TAKING YOUR THOUGHTS CAPTIVE

As with any temptation, success or failure begins with the battle of the mind. Self-talk—positive or negative—can make the difference when temptation comes. It is very important that you learn to identify your thoughts and self-talk so that you come to recognize the ways in which you actually invite temptation. You will learn how to hear the negative ideas you place in your mind. This will be a crucial step in the process of transformation.

CHANGING YOUR VIEW OF THE OUTSIDE—FROM WITHIN

Once you have learned to identify the negative thoughts that fill your mind, you must learn to replace them with positive thoughts. In chapter 10 we will look at this issue more closely. But you should know that throughout the first four phases of PRISM and beyond, you will be encouraged to develop and practice positive self-talk. You will tell yourself that you are successful and that you are in the process of transformation. You will also tell yourself that you are capable of completing this process.

THE EMOTIONAL EATING CYCLE—ANXIETY, DEPRESSION, FEAR, ANGER, APATHY

When you reach phase two of the PRISM program you will have the opportunity to take a deeper look at the emotions that led to your problems with overweight and food addiction. You will focus on anxiety, depression, fear, anger, and apathy and make a personal evaluation with regard to each of these emotional pitfalls.

AVOIDING THE FLIP OUT SYNDROME

These letters stand for Frustration Level Involving Perfection. This section of the workbook addresses the excessive need some people have to be in control of their situation. For these people, anything less than perfect control is often akin to failure. The drive for control can lead to frustration because our emotions are not always easy to control. When weight loss does not happen fast enough for you, you may be close to reaching the "FLIP out" point. Being aware of this frustration level helps you avoid its pitfalls, including binge-eating or dropping out of the PRISM program.

ACCEPTING THE TRANSFORMATION

Another key aspect of transformation is accepting the change you are observing. As the weight falls off and you begin to see the TRUE YOU in the mirror, you must accept this change. This involves letting go of large clothing, preparing for compliments, and going out in public aware of your new image. The workbook lessons on this topic help you understand and appreciate your transformation and the effect it has on your appearance.

TRANSFORMING, NOT CONFORMING

At various points along your journey to transformation, you will have to make the choice to continue onward despite the opinions of others. People will say many negative things to you as you journey toward change. They will ask if you're tired of dieting; they will comment that you've lost enough weight already; they will tempt you with foods; and they will even make you feel guilty for not eating them. This section focuses on keeping the right attitude toward transformation and helps you avoid giving up just short of your goal.

RIGHT ATTITUDE, ENERGETIC ACTION

As you examine once more your attitude toward change and right eating habits, you will take one step closer to your destination of transformation. Along with right thinking comes energetic action and a renewed focus on exercise. As you lose weight and rid your body of excessive refined carbohydrates, particularly sugar, you will experience an amazing increase in energy. It is important that you find something positive to do with it. At this point, you will want to focus an increasing amount of time on regular exercise. This will continue to restore your damaged metabolism and will help change your body into the fit image you know to be the TRUE YOU.

SET FREE TO REMAIN FREE

Many people believe they must celebrate a successful weight loss with an eating binge. This negative thought belongs to the old, overweight, food-addicted self, and you must remove it from your thinking. The workbook will help you understand that you have been set free from overweight to remain free. Again, this is not a program we intend for you to repeat year after year. It is a rehabilitation process that will leave you changed from the inside out. It is the only program available that seeks to destroy the problem of overweight. Once you are at the glorious stage of transformation, you must develop tools and the mind-set to remain there. This section will help you acquire these tools.

ONE DAY AT A TIME

There will always be times, even on a program like PRISM with daily lessons and encouragement, when the process seems long and arduous. At this stage of your transformation, many of you—especially those of you with a hundred or more pounds to lose—will have achieved only a portion of the weight loss you hope to see. Because of that, there will be times when you might feel discouraged or even depressed about your ability to continue the PRISM program. Again, in an attempt to avoid common pitfalls before you stumble into them, the PRISM workbooks will help you understand that even in the midst of wonderful change, you must go through the process one day at a time. Personal evaluation questions help you see how well you work on a one-day-at-a-time basis and will help you gain strength in this area.

TRANSFORMATION—A FAMILY AFFAIR

Inevitably, the changes you are going through will affect your entire family. You will probably find that everyone at home is eating healthier foods and staying away from sugar-laden, highly refined carbohydrate junk. You will be encouraged to involve your family as much as possible so they can appreciate your transformation and learn from your new healthy eating habits.

There are more overweight children in our society today than ever before. While it is important not to stress weight too often with children—especially girls, who are more prone to eating disorders—it is important to model healthy eating. Talk about your success in your PRISM weight loss journey, share the victories, and be sure to verbalize how energetic and happy you feel now that you are eating better.

The workbooks will give you more ideas about ways to involve your family in your transformation process.

These are a few of the specific themes dealt with in the first two phases of the PRISM program. Personal evaluation questions are provided in nearly every lesson. Phases three, four, and beyond will continue to help you work through the process of breaking food addiction and growing toward transformation. The daily lesson material in the PRISM workbooks makes up the heart and soul of the PRISM program. It is another aspect of what sets PRISM apart from other plans.

The PRISM workbook lessons will encourage you to be as honest as you have ever been about your problem with overweight. On PRISM you will not fantasize about diet cakes or packaged diet foods. Rather, you will come clean about your emotional food addiction so that lasting change can begin.

In the next chapter we will take a look at the PRISM food guide.

ALL HER LIFE, JULIE THOUGHT OF HERSELF as the thin one in her family. Nearly everyone else—her mother, father, sisters, uncles—was very overweight. But while the others packed on the pounds, Julie convinced herself she was different.

As she grew older, Julie needed more effort to maintain her thin body. When she turned thirteen she began putting on weight, but by imposing strict guidelines and forcing herself to eat small amounts, she stayed thin through high school and the early years of her marriage.

"My husband has always been this wonderful man— athletic, full of energy," Julie says. "I always felt good about being the same way as him."

Together they were fit and thin and energetic, and Julie assumed she would be that way forever. But the first time she got pregnant everything changed.

By then, she and her husband had moved to California for his work, but the move had taken her away from everyone she knew.

"Suddenly I was in a town where I knew no one, I was pregnant, and it was one hundred degrees outside," she remembers now. "There was nothing to do, so I ate. I ate everything I'd never given myself permission to eat. It was almost like I had a free ticket of some kind. I figured I could eat whatever I wanted because I was supposed to gain weight."

Julie gained seventy pounds with that first pregnancy, eating donuts, candy, cookies, chips. But when the baby was born, the weight didn't melt off as she had planned.

"I became really obsessed," she says. "I had developed this food addiction, this way of eating junk food constantly and now I wanted to stop."

The problem was, she couldn't.

The more she ate, the more she weighed. With her weight gain came a feeling Julie had never experienced in her thin days of popularity in junior high and high school: self-repulsion.

"I hated myself and I took it out on everyone around me," she says. "Including my husband."

Every time he offered to help Julie lose weight, tension developed between them. Julie understands now why her weight problem bothered her husband. It caused her to become snappy, depressed, and lethargic. Gone were the days of playing together and being active. But when he mentioned her weight, she became very angry, and the pattern nearly destroyed their marriage.

Because he was already sensitive to her weight problem, Julie's husband began taking more careful note as to what she was eating and how much.

"I couldn't stand being scrutinized," she says. "It was like he was watching my every move wondering what I was eating."

So Julie did something she'd seen her other family members do. She began to hide her food. She would stash candy bars around the house and eat entire meals on the way home from the store, tossing the bag in a dumpster before pulling into the driveway.

"I must have a slow thyroid," she would tell her husband. "I hardly eat anything, and I can't lose any weight."

It was a lie, she admits now, and as such it only added to her misery and desperate situation. There were times when she would purchase a large quantity of candy and eat it in the car, popping one piece after another into her mouth. She remembers that she didn't even enjoy the taste of it, but still continued eating.

Julie remembers that when she was growing up her mother once told her she couldn't have a candy bar because they couldn't afford to buy one.

"I told my mom I couldn't wait till I was a grown-up. I'd stop and buy a candy bar anytime I wanted to."

In those days after having her first baby, Julie devoted herself to making good on that promise.

Over the next year she joined several different weight loss and exercise programs. She lost part of her excess weight, but gained it all back during her second pregnancy.

"At that point my husband and I almost got divorced because I hated myself so much," she says. "I was angry and depressed, and I took all my aggressions out on my husband and kids. I was miserable."

Since she couldn't stop eating, she figured she would never be thin again. It was at that point she realized she had finally joined the "fat club" and become like everyone else in her family. She was just like them now.

In some ways, her overweight actually brought her closer to her sisters. It was as if they suddenly had everything in common. She remembers sitting at a table in a cafeteria one day with her mother and sisters when her brother came up.

"Well, if it isn't the Roseanne Barr family," he said with a smile.

The comment was a humiliating blow to Julie. Until that moment, she hadn't realized how big she'd gotten, how far from the thin, athletic young girl she had once been. She realized that she looked in the mirror only to put on makeup. She knew well what her eyes and lips looked like, but not her entire body.

"If I took a look at the whole image, I'd start crying," she says. "And that day at the cafeteria it all became clear how far I'd gone with my food addiction."

Not long after that her husband sat her down. "Honey, you're fat and you're getting fatter all the time," he said earnestly. "I want to help. Tell me what I can do to help you."

Although his comments humiliated her again, she accepted his gift of another exercise video and tried her best to pretend she was interested. She also convinced her husband to stop mentioning her excess weight, which he did except when there was tension in the marriage.

"When we fought, he would always comment about my weight, which meant that even though he didn't say anything the other times, it was always on his mind," she says. "I was lying to him about my eating and exercise; he was lying to me about the way he felt about me. It seemed like our whole marriage was a lie at that point."

In the pit of despair and depression about her overeating and obesity, when it seemed things couldn't get worse, Julie began eating more. Every television commercial involving food triggered an instant response in her.

"Whatever it was, I had to have it right then. Immediately," she says. "I'd even make up reasons for having to go out just so I could get that cheeseburger or piece of cake. Whatever it was, I had to have it."

About that time, Julie got pregnant with their third child, and this time she gained only sixteen pounds. She felt as if she'd eaten so much for so long that she simply couldn't eat any more. After she had the baby, she tried a liquid meal replacement diet plan, but that soon fizzled. By then she was carrying an additional one hundred pounds on her petite frame, and she was desperate for help.

She remembers once being at a Christmas party with her husband and hovering near the dessert table. She started sampling from several of the dishes and couldn't seem to stop.

"My husband kept asking me to go talk with various people," she says. "I knew what he was doing. He was trying to get me away from that table, but I wouldn't leave. I wanted those sweets and I was going to eat them. It was sick. By that point I had a problem that was completely out of control."

Later that month, she ran into a friend who had lost weight on the PRISM Weight Loss Program.

"I've never felt better," the friend told Julie. And somewhere in the core of her depression and devastated self-image, Julie felt a ray of hope. She contacted another friend, and the two agreed to attend a PRISM meeting the following week.

At the last minute, her friend backed out.

"I decided that if she wasn't going to go, I wouldn't go either. I would stay overweight and continue eating whatever I wanted, whenever I wanted it, and I would just stay fat. It was easier, I figured."

But when her husband came home from work that afternoon, he seemed very excited and anxious to know what time she was going to leave for the PRISM meeting.

"I was so mad at him for being concerned about whether I was going or not, that I just said 'Fine!' I'd go, and then maybe he'd leave me alone about it."

Angry, afraid, and doubting herself with every step, Julie went to the meeting. She sat in the back, and listening to the group leader speak, she did something she never planned to do. She cried.

"I couldn't stop crying," she says. "Everything they said was me, and suddenly I knew that this was a program that wouldn't just change what I was putting in my mouth, but why I was putting it there."

Even though she doubted her ability to follow through with the program's strict guidelines, Julie agreed to turn the entire issue over to God.

"I couldn't do it anymore. Julie couldn't do it. I had to give it to Him. He took it over for me after that."

Because of the program guidelines, Julie knew she couldn't touch anything with sugar in it. She treated the foods she had been addicted to as poison, believing that to eat even a lick or a small taste of such food would cause her to be struck by lightning.

"It was the first time I'd been honest in such a long while," she says. "I was like a drug addict. I didn't let other people know what I was eating. I'd eat a small amount at the table with the family, but no one knew how much I'd eaten before and how much I'd eat after.

"That first week on PRISM, I guess that was the most amazing thing. I was finally being honest."

By following the PRISM guidelines and being faithful to do her daily workbook lessons, Julie lost the hundred pounds that plagued her. Today she feels like she's been given a new lease on life.

"My whole life has changed," she says. "Yes, I'm different on the outside. People are noticing me, and my husband has fallen in love with me all over again. But the biggest changes are on the inside, in the way I view food."

Thanksgiving, for instance, is no longer a time to get excited about overeating rich, sugar-filled foods. Rather, it is a time to be with loved ones and give thanks to the Lord for all he's done for her.

"I'm not focused on the food at all. I don't have to be stuck at that table anymore. I'm a butterfly now, flitting about the party having fun and loving life."

Another benefit, Julie says, is that her entire family is eating healthier food. This started when her children and husband watched her make separate meals for herself.

"It didn't take long before they were saying that's what they wanted. The healthy food, not the junk. Now we all eat better."

Julie has kept her weight off for several months by maintaining a transformed view of food and its role in her life. Because she is happier with herself, she has found a wealth of other benefits, including patience and joy in dealing with her children.

"I've found a whole new life. Everything's new," she says.

Perhaps most exciting of all, is that Julie does not view the weight she has lost on the PRISM program as temporary.

"I really feel like I'll never be fat again. I know I won't. God has given me a way out through the PRISM program. I feel like my eyes were clouded over before and now they're clear. I don't have to be a slave to food—that typical have-it-your-way kind of person who has to run out and feed myself tons of junk food. I don't need it. I'm perfectly happy eating foods that sustain me and make me healthier."

8

What We Eat and Why

The PRISM Program Food Guidelines

THE PRISM PROGRAM IS MORE THAN A LIST OF FOODS you can and cannot eat. It can change your life in many ways, including how you view food and how you view yourself as a person. But, as with any weight loss program, PRISM is only as good as your willingness to follow the guidelines we've laid out both in this book and in the PRISM workbooks.

In this chapter we will tell you the foods you can and cannot eat when you are in the different phases of the PRISM program, the amounts of those foods you can eat, and the all-important caloric guidelines.

Why the Phases?

Each phase of the Prism program is six weeks long. There are several reasons for this format, and they all have to do with helping you track your progress and make lasting changes in how you view the role of food in your life.

At the end of each phase you must reevaluate whether you are at your "right weight" and whether you are consuming the correct amount of calories. If you are not at your "right weight" at that point, you will have the choice of whether or not to commit to the next phase of the program.

People who are not at their "right weight" after four phases, or approximately six months, may start over with the first phase as often as necessary. Some people who have lost as much as two hundred pounds on PRISM have taken two years to do so and have gone through phase one four separate times before going on to phase two, three, and four. Others will go through the four phases then continue on with the supplemental material provided by PRISM. There is more about this in chapter 13.

Do not be concerned with how long it will take to reach your "right weight." The key to your success and transformation is changing your mind and the way you think about and use food. In some cases this will happen much more quickly than the loss of your excess weight. In other cases, the weight will come off before you have time to completely transform how you feel and think about food.

For that reason, we advise you to complete the four phases of PRISM, even if you have reached your "right weight." If you no longer need to lose weight, you may add calories, but you should still complete all four phases of the PRISM program so that the workbook lessons can provide you a complete course in transformation and breaking food addiction.

By going through the four phases of PRISM, overweight individuals can change their attitudes about food and eating. Encouraging the eating of healthy foods in the right amounts allows the process of renewal to take place. The PRISM Weight Loss Program lets these changes take place gradually, which produces lasting results.

THE FOUR FOOD PHASES OF PRISM

There are different sets of food guidelines for each phase of the PRISM program. If you are just beginning, you will be in phase one. Each phase after the first one allows more variety in the foods permitted.

Common to all four phases is our emphasis on the importance of an adequate intake of water and the use of vitamin and mineral supplements. An adequate intake of water is important for your body to function properly and is vital when you are trying to lose weight. In all stages of the PRISM program you must drink eight to ten large glasses of water, mineral water, or herbal tea per day to help your body eliminate fat and toxins.

We also strongly advise that every day you are on the PRISM program you take a quality multivitamin plus iron and a sustained release B-complex vitamin.

The following discussion explains the differences in the food guidelines for the four phases of the program.

PHASE ONE FOOD GUIDE

1. Women may have no less than 1,000 calories and no more than 1,200 calories per day. No more than 700 calories should be eaten before the evening or main meal. Exceptions: There are exceptions for people with specific needs or health concerns. Also, if you are a woman who weighs more than 250 pounds, you may eat 1,300 to 1,500 calories per day. You may also have up to two servings of cereal as listed on package and count it as one bread/cereal exchange.

2. Men may have no less than 1,300 calories and no more than 1,500 calories per day. No more than 800 calories should be eaten before the evening or main meal. Exceptions: If you are someone who does physical labor, you may have up to 1,600 to 1,700 calories per day. You may also have up to two servings of cereal and count it as one bread/cereal exchange.

3. You must write down any and all foods you eat and their caloric value on a food journal sheet every day. This completed food journal sheet will be turned in to your leader at your local PRISM group each week.

4. You must weigh, measure, and accurately count calorie values of any and all foods you select.

5. Liquid beverage meal replacements are NOT ALLOWED.

6. Any food bars, breakfast bars, granola bars, etc., are NOT ALLOWED.

7. ALL dessert products are NOT ALLOWED, with the exception of sugar-free diet gelatin.

8. Sugars, brown and white, are NOT ALLOWED. Foods with sugar added are also not allowed. Some salad dressings or condiments with sugar as the fifth or later listed ingredient are allowed.

9. Other than those with sugar as a primary ingredient, condiments, diet sodas, coffee, tea, sugarless gum, artificial sweeteners are allowed. You must count their caloric value.

10. Gravies are NOT ALLOWED.

11. Popcorn, popcorn rice cakes, and white flour snack foods are NOT ALLOWED.

12. Vitamin supplements should be taken daily in the form of a multi-vitamin plus iron and a B-complex timed release.

13. You may have up to 1/4 cup of oat bran or wheat bran per day. You must count the calories.

14. Deep-fried or breaded foods are NOT ALLOWED.

15. Communion is sacred and part of worship. Bread for this purpose is allowed in all phases of this program.

16. If you are unsure about any food or any recipe you may want to try, please check it first with your leader or by calling PRISM.

17. If you have to ask yourself whether it's okay to eat it—don't!

PHASE TWO FOOD GUIDE

In the second phase of the PRISM Program you will be reintroduced to bread—but only 100 percent whole grain or whole wheat sandwich bread. You will also be able to add corn or whole wheat tortillas—baked or steamed, but never fried. Potatoes are also reintroduced to the diet, but only baked or boiled and only three times a week. A five-ounce frozen dessert or pudding dessert may be added three times a week, but it must not be sweetened with white or brown sugar. Fructose or other natural sweeteners are allowed in this dessert product.

PHASE THREE FOOD GUIDE

The third phase of PRISM allows the addition of whole wheat or whole grain English muffins and pita pockets. Up to one cup of 100 percent whole wheat, grain or vegetable pasta is also allowed per day. All other guidelines remain the same.

PHASE FOUR FOOD GUIDE

In the fourth phase of PRISM you are allowed to add 100 percent whole grain or whole wheat hamburger and hot dog buns and bagels, but only on a limited basis.

MAINTENANCE

You've made it—you've reached your goal weight and are looking at the TRUE YOU every time you glance in the mirror. You look better, feel better, and are healthier than you've been in years. It's the culmination of a transformation that began when you first picked up this book—or stepped into a PRISM class for the first time. Either way, now that you've made it, you need to maintain it.

Because the PRISM program is not a diet, not something you enter into and then exit from, maintenance is really very simple. Once you have reached your right weight, add one hundred calories a day to your daily intake for one week. At the end of the week, weigh yourself. If you have still lost weight, add two hundred calories per day for the second week. Continue adding a hundred calories per day, per week until you reach a plateau that is right for maintaining your "right weight."

At this point you may be staring wide-eyed at the page wondering if you haven't missed something. You may have been expecting to be reintroduced to the world of sugary snacks and floury pastries. But in the transformation that comes as a result of the PRISM program, there is no need, no desire, and no room for these foods. However, some people choose to include these products again while maintaining the proper calorie levels to keep their weight steady. For those of you who plan to eat white sugar and flour in the future, keep reading.

Sugar and Flour—Again?

Through the PRISM program you will learn the damaging effects white sugar and white flour have on the body. However, it is possible that sometime while maintaining your "right weight," you will eat these items again. When you do, remember your weaknesses. You did not follow the path of transformation and lifelong change only to fall again under the yoke of slavery to these foods. If you eat them, do so in small quantities and only on rare occasions. And notice how you feel. You will find that you are energetic, relaxed, positive and full of hope while eating the God-given foods allowed on the PRISM program. But when you reintroduce white sugar and white flour to your diet, you may spend the ensuing hours feeling bloated, cramped, heavy, and depressed.

In the long run, many PRISM participants decide it is not worth the pain to eat those foods. Transformation is best maintained while staying away from the very items that put you in bondage in the first place.

What if I Get Out of Control Again?

If you do choose to reintroduce small quantities of sugar and flour, realize there is a chance that they will sabotage your efforts and put you once again at the mercy of unhealthy foods, overeating, and eventually overweight. A word to the wise: Give yourself a five-pound cushion or have a pair of pants that will set off warning bells when the zipper starts to groan with use.

When this happens, return to phase one of PRISM. Jump back on the train and remember what got you to your destination in the first place. Then when you again arrive at your "right weight," think twice about including white sugar and white flour in your daily diet. Healthy alternatives are widely available.

Maintaining a Healthy Outlook

As you maintain, enjoying life at your "right weight," reread your PRISM workbooks or this book now and then. The transformation will be long-lasting, but there is nothing like a refresher course to keep your eyes on the prize, especially when the world around you is so busy eating the wrong things.

Remember the new habits you've developed and the ways in which you've managed to stay within the PRISM guidelines while at parties, barbecues, and backyard socials. Practice these habits so that, with each passing week, month, and year, your transformed lifestyle becomes second nature.

As you follow these guidelines, maintaining your "right weight" in the PRISM program is not only possible, but probable. A majority of PRISM participants—particularly people whose faith is strong and active—have kept their weight off and maintained their "right weight" for more than three years. You have every reason to believe that you, like them, will find lifelong success in the same way.

GUIDELINES FOR CALORIC INTAKE

In addition to the food guidelines for each of the four PRISM phases, the program includes caloric guidelines that are essential for your success on the PRISM program. These guidelines are based partly on the body's basic metabolism, or the amount of energy it takes to maintain life. Most women must consume at least 1,000 calories and most men must have 1,300 each day in order to keep their systems operating at the healthiest level. If we allow our caloric intake to drop below these minimum levels—as many fast weight loss programs recommend—our bodies may begin to metabolize muscle and other healthy tissue in an effort to prevent starvation.

On the other hand, maximum calorie levels are also a part of the PRISM program. Maximum calorie levels allow our bodies to begin burning excess fat as a source of energy because our bodies are using more energy than they are taking in. Staying within the guidelines in the PRISM program should result in a weight loss of approximately two to three pounds per week for most people, which is all most people can safely lose.

Calorie limits also establish a point of accountability. One aspect of the PRISM program is planning food intake carefully enough so that you do not go over the acceptable limit of caloric intake or under the minimum level required to keep your body operating in a healthy manner.

CALORIE VARIABLES

Although the PRISM guidelines regarding caloric intake are very specific, we recognize that not all bodies are created equal and that not all of us should consume the same number of calories. Allow for the following adjustments where they may apply:

- If a medical condition requires you to have more calories, be sure to add them. Note: We advise anyone beginning a weight loss program to consult his or her physician. If you are unsure of your caloric needs or have any other medical concerns, we urge you to get specific answers to your questions.

- If you weigh more than 250 pounds, add three hundred calories per day. This would mean a calorie range of 1,300 to 1,500 for women and 1,600 to 1,800 for men.

- If you do heavy physical labor or exercise intensely, add three hundred calories per day.

Although we advise you to save a substantial number of calories for your evening meal (five hundred calories for women, six hundred for men), if you have a medical condition that requires you to eat several times throughout the day, please do so. The PRISM program will work fine within those guidelines as well.

In order to succeed on the PRISM program, you must keep accurate count of the calories you consume. You must weigh, measure, and accurately count caloric values of any and all foods you select. To help you do that, we have included in the program two helpful tools: food journaling and food measuring.

FOOD JOURNALING

Participation in the PRISM program requires you to write down any and all foods you eat and their caloric value on a food journal sheet every day.

This completed food journal sheet will be turned in to your leader—whether in a small group or through correspondence—every week.

Many people rebel at the thought of writing down everything they eat every day they're on the PRISM Program. It sounds tedious and overwhelming, and some might complain that it requires too much focus on food. But in actuality, food journaling takes the focus *off* food and frees you from thinking about it all of the time.

Here's how. For those of us who have battled overweight, food is constantly on our minds. We wake thinking about what we might eat and lay down feeling guilty for all we ate during the day. This is far more tedious and overwhelming than taking a few moments to jot down your food intake at each meal. Living a life obsessed with thoughts of food has been a problem for you as long as you have battled the problem of overweight.

Writing down the things you eat while on the PRISM program offers two tools that aid in the transformation process. First, it offers accountability. We cannot cheat ourselves along the road to transformation. Writing down what we eat forces us to take an honest look at the food we're eating and confirms us in our decision to eat to live and not live to eat. Second, it helps you identify what type of eating patterns you have developed and allows you to see that you have, indeed, eaten enough for the day.

In order to help you correctly journal the food you eat every day, the PRISM program requires you to measure accurately what you eat daily.

FOOD MEASURING

Through the PRISM program you will learn to view the weighing and measuring of your food as a tool to make sure you consume the right number of calories for you. This is another area where people tend to rebel. Measuring every thing you eat sounds tedious, but it is an effective way to maintain perfect accountability, and it prevents you from cheating yourself and thereby growing discouraged and falling off the program.

Weighing and measuring is also a way to learn what right portions look like. After years and maybe decades of overeating, sometimes we are surprised to find we can eat a small portion-controlled amount of food and be satisfied. Oftentimes in anticipation of not being satisfied, we begin to guess at our one-half cup of oatmeal or three-quarter cup of rice—and just pour an amount we think is right. Without the accountability of measuring, this guessed-at portion oftentimes doubles in a matter of weeks as we subconsciously attempt to grant ourselves more food.

Prepare for success and for a transformed lifestyle. Get the tools immediately so this won't be a stumbling block. The best way—indeed, the *only* way—to find simple success in the PRISM program is by purchasing or locating these tools for weighing and measuring food:

A complete calorie counter. The best versions of calorie counters are in paperback and can be purchased at your local bookstore for under $10. Look for one that lists foods alphabetically and not by category. Category listings often leave you wondering whether yogurt is a milk product or a dessert product or a snack food. In an alphabetical listing, you can flip to the "Y" section of your book and quickly and easily find yogurt.

A food scale. It is crucial that you have an accurate food scale. The best food scales have a large bowl for the food and an adjustable dial so you can add various ingredients without having to look for more bowls to hold them. You should be able to set the scale to "0," put in four ounces of tuna, set it to "0" again and add one ounce of chopped dill pickles, set it to "0" again and add three ounces of chopped carrots—all without emptying the bowl. These scales can be purchased for less than $15 at Target, KMart, Wal-Mart, or other discount stores. Gourmet cooking stores will also have them, but expect the price to be higher. Food scales and calorie counters may also be purchased from the PRISM Corporate Offices by calling 1-800-755-1738.

Measuring cups. If you don't have a complete set of measuring cups, or even if you do, this may be a good time to invest in a new set. They are inexpensive—usually less than $3 a set—and will make your daily task of measuring much easier. It is helpful to have two sets so that if one measuring cup is dirty, you won't be tempted to use a larger cup and guess at the correct quantity.

Measuring spoons. Although not needed as often as measuring cups, measuring spoons will make the difference when adding mayonnaise to tuna salad or figuring out how much salad dressing you can have for dinner. They also come in handy when measuring a tablespoon of peanut butter to spread on a rice cake.

Once you have these tools, you will not be able to excuse yourself for falling off the program because you had no way of knowing how much squash was in a cup or how many calories there are in a piece of steak.

People who attempt the PRISM program without these tools almost instantly find that they have sabotaged their efforts. When you have spent an entire day guessing at the quantities and calorie amounts of your food, you inevitably begin to err on the side of excess. This can happen in a matter of days and will leave you feeling discouraged and unsure of yourself.

Discouragement will usher in the voices of self-defeat.

You probably ate too much today.

You must have a few calories left—after all, you probably guessed too high at breakfast. Another bowl of yogurt couldn't hurt.

A week of this, and you will very likely find yourself giving up completely.

The exciting truth is that you can refuse to listen to the voices of self-defeat and overcome your problem with overweight. Through the PRISM Weight Loss Program, you will not have to be a food addict anymore. You will break your chemical addiction; then you will break your emotional addiction. In the process, you will be transformed into the person you were created to be, the TRUE YOU. And this will be a person whose eating habits and thoughts about food have changed completely.

It is important that you understand fully the reason you may not eat certain foods on the PRISM program and why certain other foods will help you break food addiction. It all starts with eliminating refined sugar and flour. In the next chapter, we will address the nutritional aspects of weight loss and food addiction.

PRISM SUCCESS STORY

SUE ANN WAS SIX YEARS OLD when she became aware of her size. She was not a heavy girl, but she was tall. In a single moment her life's focus was defined. It was the first day of school, and as she walked toward her classroom, two other girls approached her.

"What grade are you in?" they asked.

"First."

The girls' mouths dropped, and they began snickering and pointing at Sue Ann. "You're too big to be in first grade. Look at her! She's too big for first grade."

From that moment on, Sue Ann wanted desperately to be small. Shorter, thinner, smaller-boned. "I equated tall with big and ugly. I would watch television and dream of being small and slender like the girls on the TV shows."

The dieting cycles that would take Sue Ann through most of her life began in earnest when she was in junior high. She would skip breakfast, eat an apple or a bag of peanuts for lunch, and then pick at her dinner. It was an unhealthy existence, and her parents didn't approve. Still, she was driven to be thin, and this seemed the only way for her to achieve her goal.

In high school Sue Ann began taking mail-order diet pills—an assortment of colorful tablets that were basically nothing more than uppers that sped up her metabolism and made her heart race. She stopped taking them a year later when she began reading about their dangerous side effects.

"It was always something," she remembers, "because no matter what I weighed or what I looked like, I could always stand to lose a few pounds."

This became more evident as Sue Ann's compulsion with the scale took over. As long as she was working toward losing weight, she weighed herself at least once a day, sometimes more. The number that appeared would give her permission to have a good day or to condemn her to an awful one. The scale dictated what she would wear, how she felt, whom she would see, what she would do, and where she would go. If it was a "fat" day, she wore large clothes and skipped social engagements. If it was a "thin" day, she would take extra time getting ready and wear an outfit that showed off her accomplishment. Her emotions soared at the thrill of attending social outings on "thin" days.

Once the diet pills were out of her system, Sue Ann began to smoke and drink coffee to avoid weight gain.

"It's amazing I'm as healthy as I am," she says now. "I was willing to do whatever I had to in order to stay thin. I really put myself through torture, all because of my obsession with food and weight."

After the birth of her daughter, Sue Ann tried several legitimate programs and weight loss clinics. Once in a while she would put herself on a wacky cabbage-only diet or some other such thing. She didn't feel good or look good, but she was within fifteen pounds of her goal weight.

On a trip to Cancun, just as the plane took off, Sue Ann learned that her mother had died. During the ensuing time of emotional pain and loss, Sue Ann did what so many overeaters tend to do. She ate to take away the hurt.

"I knew there'd be consequences for what I was doing to myself, but still I didn't stop," Sue Ann recalls. "I just couldn't stop eating. I didn't know what else to do, so I went to the blanket of comfort food."

Twenty pounds heavier and gravely disappointed in herself, Sue Ann tried packaged meal replacement drinks from the supermarket. But after several weeks and no weight loss, she was struck by the thought that the only way God could help her lose weight was if she was willing to eat the foods he'd created. She examined the ingredient list on the meal shakes and found dozens of items she couldn't even pronounce.

That week she saw a notice in her church bulletin about the PRISM program. She talked it over with her husband and decided it would be a wonderful opportunity.

Sue Ann was excited and desperately desired to start the program, but she was also frightened. "I knew I was going to do this, but that first week I was really afraid. This was a huge commitment, not just to a program, but this time to God. And there's no hiding from God."

The first day on the program came, and after that there was no turning back for Sue Ann. "I flew high for the first two weeks; then I was asked to give up the scale. That petrified me."

Sue Ann put away her scale and continued on, taking the program one day at a time until eventually she reached her "right weight."

"I am a new person today, a different person," she says now. "I've learned so much about myself on the PRISM program. I didn't know how addicted to the scale I was. Now it's just a huge relief. I don't need a scale to tell me I'm all right or that I look good. My food addictions are gone, too."

Now Sue Ann stays on the PRISM maintenance plan, not because of what the scale says, but because it's the right thing to do. "Besides," she says, "it feels great."

9

DISPELLING SOME DIET MYTHS

The Nutritional Aspects of PRISM

A LOOK AT THE FAT-FREE FRAUD

Nutrition experts and health researchers are beginning to question a theory that became widely accepted in the early 1980s. The fat-free theory teaches that we can reduce our weight by reducing the amount of dietary fat we consume. Fewer fat grams in our diets would mean less fat on our bodies.

This theory had it that Americans in particular were fat because they ate too much fat. Studies were done at a cost of millions of taxpayers' dollars to prove that the average fat consumption in the United States far exceeded the recommended 30 percent of our daily intake of calories.

Dozens of diet programs came on the scene touting low-fat foods. Diet gurus surfaced and showed us how common lard in our foods produced a buildup of common lard in our arteries. This, they said, was the problem with Americans' diets. Too much dietary fat meant too many fat people.

The food industry quickly fell in line.

Overnight, it seemed, we began seeing a fat-free or low-fat version of all our favorite foods. We had low-fat crackers, cookies, pastries, and ice cream. Even peanut butter was produced in formulas that contained less or no fat.

Scientists predicted the results would be significant. They believed we would see fewer overweight Americans, less heart disease, less illness as a whole, and a massive decrease in the number of people trying to lose weight.

But what has happened since then?

Instead of the number of obese Americans decreasing, it is increasing, seemingly by the year. In the past decade, the percentage of overweight Americans has increased from 50 percent to its current rate of around 70 percent. Research over the past twenty years has shown that we have done three things that seem to have greatly contributed to this startling situation.

First, we have stopped moving. As computers have mainstreamed into the workplace, our jobs have involved less physical exertion. At the same time, we seem to be working more than ever. Loss of time and opportunity have resulted in an overall reduction in the amount of exercise we get.

Second, we have increased our eating. Studies show that we have turned more frequently to eating as a means of recreation, a way of entertaining ourselves.

Finally, and perhaps most importantly, we have shifted our diets away from fatty foods to foods that consist primarily of carbohydrates. The problem with that shift is that excessive refined carbohydrate intake translates directly to an increase in insulin, the hormone responsible for storing body fat.

We have become increasingly aware of dietary fat—counting fat grams, eliminating what has become the dreaded egg, and sticking to fat-free dairy products. In many cases we have nearly eliminated fat from our diets. We are eating non-fat cereal covered with non-fat milk and consuming "healthy" non-fat crackers, low-fat cookies, and desserts with little or no fat. We are avoiding red meat and are eating potatoes, pastas, and no-fat rice in record quantities. Besides being low in fat, these foods are all high in carbohydrates.

But instead of losing weight, we are getting fatter and fatter.

Something must be wrong with the theory.

The fat-free movement has not only failed to reduce the number of overweight Americans and improve their health, it has led to an increase in eating disorders. As many as 20 percent of all overweight women suffer from depression, either as a condition that led to their overeating or because of their excess weight. These women often develop eating disorders because they are desperately seeking a (false) sense of control over their weight problem.

It seems we have debunked two incorrect theories.

First, as we learned earlier, food addiction and friendships with food are indeed real. If there were no food addictions, only a fraction of the public would suffer from excess weight and the medical problems associated with it.

Second, the fat-free frenzy has not helped solve our society's problem with overweight. In fact, it may even have made it worse. We are still addicted to highly refined carbohydrate foods, and we are gaining more and more weight with each passing decade.

Now, let's take a more in-depth look at our carbohydrate intake, particularly simple carbohydrates in the form of white sugar and white flour.

ELIMINATING REFINED WHITE SUGAR AND WHITE FLOUR

Another aspect that sets the PRISM program apart from other weight loss plans is its elimination of refined sugar and white flour products. Because so many of us are addicted to highly refined carbohydrates, long-lasting success can be found only by completely ridding our systems of these foods, which have bound us in the past. The PRISM program is based on the belief that it is crucial to eliminate white sugar and white flour from our diets in order to experience complete transformation.

You may wonder why the PRISM program does this when other, seemingly successful, programs allow all foods in moderation. Some will even say that God created all foods to be enjoyed, and that no one should stipulate what a person can eat. This may be true for some people. But when many people who have struggled with overweight for years try eating half a brownie or three bites of a cream puff, although they may get by with it for a while, they eventually become chemically addicted to refined carbohydrates and end up binge-eating.

For those of us who are food-addicted, it is time for discipline. Discipline is a biblical concept. When Jesus desired to draw close to the Father, he fasted forty days and forty nights because he wanted nothing to distract him from his purpose and mission.

If food has come between you and the Lord; if it has come between you and those you love; if it has been a barrier between you and living an abundant, joyful life; then you probably need the discipline offered in the PRISM program. Within the guidelines of this program is a kind of glorious freedom unlike any you might enjoy by eating half a candy bar or nibbling on a few cookies in place of dinner.

Now let's look at how we become addicted to these foods and why we must eliminate them from our diets.

REFINED SUGAR: OUR POISON OF CHOICE

Since the early 1970s, dietitians have decried the evils of sugar. Current research connects white refined sugar with a number of ailments including many weight- and health-related problems. Some conditions directly related to sugar intake are overweight, excess insulin production, weakened immune system, hyperactivity, learning disabilities, poor nutrition, and cancer. We will examine these conditions individually.

OVERWEIGHT

Most people in the nutrition and health industry believe that sugar stimulates our appetites. In other words, when we eat products that contain sugar, our bodies scream for more food, even though we should be satisfied. This then leads to excess eating, and excess eating leads to overweight.

Most of us can remember eating a sugar-filled breakfast and then wandering around the kitchen an hour later wondering why we were hungry. In some ways, our stomachs felt full. Yet there we were, rifling through the cupboards and refrigerator, desperate to meet our body's cry for more.

One of the most amazing results you will see on the PRISM program is a drastic reduction in your appetite. Before starting PRISM, most of us ate amazing quantities of food. Of course we hid much of our eating, but most days our caloric intake must have been at least three times the normal amount.

It takes the body approximately three days to eliminate the chemical effects of sugar. During that time, you may still strongly crave refined carbohydrate and sugar. But once your system is free from the effects of overeating, your appetite will drop way off. Usually by the end of the first week, even small quantities of food will satisfy your hunger. This is because sugar creates a false hunger by causing a chemical imbalance in our brains that makes us demand more food—even when there is no physical need for it.

Replacing a diet high in refined carbohydrates with whole, healthy foods satisfies our body's physical need for nutrition. This then acts to eliminate our unnatural cravings for refined carbohydrates.

EXCESS INSULIN PRODUCTION

Studies in the past ten years have given us a better understanding of our bodies' chemistry. For years we were told to consume primarily carbohydrates and that as long as we monitored our fat intake, we would be fit and healthy. The reality is that we have turned into a society that consumes far too many carbohydrates—especially the simple carbohydrates found in white sugar and white flour.

Why is that a problem?

Simply put, the more refined sugar and white flour we eat, the fatter we are prone to get. Refined sugar and white flour have no fiber, nothing to slow down their absorption into the body. When we consume these foods, the simple carbohydrates found in them work in two ways to make us overweight and keep us there. First, they increase our appetites so that we eat far more than our bodies need. Second, they cause our bodies to convert excess blood sugar to fat and store it.

The carbohydrates we consume are converted into blood sugar to provide our bodies with the energy we need. However, consuming too many refined carbohydrates floods our bodies with excess blood sugar. This in turn causes a release of the hormone insulin. Insulin protects the body from high blood sugar by directing it to convert excess amounts of carbohydrate into fat, which is then stored as body fat to be used as an energy source when needed.

This God-designed system is a brilliant one, but combined with our current eating habits, it is causing us to gain weight at alarming rates. Since sugary foods make us want to eat more, we constantly flood our bodies with too many carbohydrates. These are then converted into fat to be used as energy later. But "later" never comes because we quickly fill our bodies with yet another high-carbohydrate meal.

Whereas it was once thought that dietary fat caused overweight, now many doctors and dietitians blame excess insulin—the fat-storing hormone.

The good news is that not all carbohydrates are metabolized the same way. Complex carbohydrates—those found in fresh fruits and vegetables and whole-grain products—contain fiber and are metabolized more slowly, allowing blood sugar to be released gradually into our blood streams. Since insulin is released only when our bodies detect a sharp increase of blood sugar, complex carbohydrates rarely cause the release of excess insulin.

WEAKENED IMMUNE SYSTEM

Although there are different explanations as to why, there seems to be a direct connection between the consumption of refined sugar and a reduced immune system. Currently the most common understanding is that in addition to causing us to store fat, insulin—especially excessive insulin—will cause our bodies to be more susceptible to illness.

There are three times a year when colds, flu bugs, and other viruses run rampant. The first is spring, the second is fall, and the third is during the Christmas holidays. Think back over your medical history and that of your immediate family. Remember when you were a child? Isn't it true? Isn't that when you were most often sick?

Our parents explained this by saying that people got sick when the seasons changed. The sun comes out in spring, temperatures rise, and our bodies, unable to cope, break down, and we suffer illness. Same thing in the fall. As for the Christmas season, we assume that we wear ourselves out shopping and preparing and get sick as a result.

There may be some truth to that, but let's look at another possible scenario.

Spring is when we celebrate Easter, and along with the cherished remembrance of our Lord's Resurrection, we purchase pounds and pounds of candy. Even people with no religious convictions observe this holiday with bountiful baskets overflowing with candy eggs, chocolate bunnies, jelly beans, and other sweet concoctions. For many of us, the Easter candy stays around for weeks. Made up almost entirely of sugar and butter, it makes its way into our mouths every day, even several times a day.

According to current thinking in medical circles, such excessive sugar intake compromises our immune systems and we become sick. Less able to fight off the germs that circulate constantly around us, we fall prey to colds, flu, and even serious bacterial infections.

Fall is much the same as we celebrate two sugary holidays—Halloween and Thanksgiving. For years, my children were sick the week after Halloween and susceptible to colds and flu bugs right on through Thanksgiving. The supermarkets make it easy to extend this sugar-filled period by placing huge displays of low-cost candy at checkouts. We buy candy early, open it early, and eat it early. Then when not enough trick-or-treaters show up to empty the ten bags of candy bars we purchased, we have leftover candy. Not only do our children have bags of candy from harvest festivals or other parties, there are also ample leftovers in bowls sitting about the house. The candy runs out about the same time we start baking pumpkin pies and frosting pilgrim cookies. No wonder we wind up sick in the fall.

Then comes Christmas. We bake from the beginning of December and, as the season wears on, we receive many homemade cookie platters as gifts.

For the first eight years after having children—which naturally gave me an excuse to bake Christmas cookies—I was sick on Christmas morning: sniffling, sneezing, wheezing, and coughing while I tended to the fevers and sore throats around me.

This year was no different for my oldest son, who has his mother's sweet tooth. But I refused to eat sugar as a way of celebrating Christ's birth. Yes, there were times when the frosted Christmas tree cookies and fudge brownies brought in by well-meaning friends beckoned. But for the most part, my husband and children sampled these and days later tossed out the stale leftovers.

My oldest boy, though, celebrated at school and Sunday school and choir. Every time he got a sugary snack in honor of Christmas, he ate heartily. Although he has no problem with weight, the sugar compromised his immune system. On Christmas Eve we spent several hours at the hospital worried that his sore throat and 104-degree fever might be an indication of spinal meningitis. It wasn't. It was strep throat, and he wound up on antibiotics through the holidays.

I can't believe that some inexplicable weather change every year around Christmas causes us to grow ill mysteriously. Rather, along with many people currently investigating the theory, I believe that sugar is to blame. We overeat sugar, insulin is released into our bloodstreams, and our immune systems are compromised. As a result, we get sick.

HYPERACTIVITY

There are several conditions running rampant among children today. They are generally associated with what used to be called hyperactivity, or a lack of concentration and attention. Certainly there are situations when a child truly has a disorder, one that can be treated successfully only with medication and is not linked to diet or discipline. However, many times there are ways to treat these "disorders" that have nothing to do with medicating a child.

I have a friend whose son was diagnosed with a hyperactivity disorder. In school he was having difficulty concentrating at a third-grade level, and he was hyperactive at times when he was required to sit still. It seemed to my friend and to the school staff that he might require medicine and perhaps even special classes in order to help him learn to sit still, listen, and ultimately learn.

But before resorting to medication, my friend researched hyperactivity disorder and found that occasionally the condition is linked to a sensitivity to sugar intake. She thought about the breakfasts, lunches, and dinners her son generally ate. Breakfast was whatever favorite cereal the cartoon commercials were touting—cereal in sugary shapes, consisting of cookie dough and frosting. A quick check of the ingredients confirmed her suspicions. These cereals were little more than camouflaged desserts topped with milk. In most cases, her son would have had the same nutritional start to his day by eating a handful of cookies for breakfast.

Lunch always included a prepackaged, processed dessert and a fruit drink. When she looked more closely at the labels, my friend learned that her son's favorite drink was only 10 percent juice. The rest was sugar and water.

After school snacks were often candy, cookies, and sometimes a soda pop. Dinner was nutritious, but dessert—candy or cookies—almost always followed, and the next morning the routine began again.

My friend decided to try an experiment. Although it was a drastic step, she cut out sugar in her son's diet for one week. She was stunned at the difference. After the second day, her son was able to sit still in class and listen to directions. He was a very bright boy, and once his head was clear of the effects of high blood sugar and excess insulin, his class work and homework quickly reached a neater, more complete and accurate level.

"I see you've gotten your son on medication," the teacher commented at the end of the week. "I think it's for the best. He's a different child."

My friend waited until the woman finished and then gladly told her the truth: There was no medication involved, simply an elimination of sugar.

This test may not surprise those of you who have been parents for years. Parents often used to joke that after birthday parties kids would be "wired" and need to play to "work off all that sugar."

Physiologically, an intake of sugar causes an increase in energy almost immediately. Twenty minutes later, this same intake causes a drop in blood sugar, which results in a loss of energy. The scenario is fairly easy to put together. Children eat sugary foods at breakfast and come to school severely hyperactive. Before the first hour is up, they are suffering the sugar lows and appear to have an attention problem. What does the teacher conclude? A hyperactivity disorder with an inability to pay attention. The pattern repeats itself after snack time and again after lunch. In essence, sugar reacts in the systems of many children much like a drug. It sends them sky high and then drops them below ground level.

Children and adults alike function better with an even, consistent blood sugar level. This is another reason why, for optimal health, you must avoid refined sugar.

LEARNING DISABILITIES

Sugar intake has also been linked to learning disabilities in both children and adults. Again, there are many genuine cases that have nothing to do with diet and must be diagnosed by professionals. However, as with hyperactivity disorders, there are instances when someone we take for a slow learner is really a person suffering from a diet far too high in sugar.

POOR NUTRITION

Many times we overeat because our body is craving sustenance. We have fed ourselves foods void of nutrients so that even though we have actually consumed more calories than we need, we are still "starving." When we eat a diet high in sugar, we inevitably lack the vitamins and minerals found in vegetables, fruit, and protein foods. As a result we feel "hungry" and may suffer conditions or symptoms linked to poor nutrition. A few of these include:

Tooth decay. Excess sugar intake does not always manifest itself as a weight problem. Rotting teeth with weak or diseased root systems can sometimes be evidence of a diet high in sugar.

Weak or brittle hair. Since hair is made up of follicles that are a living part of the lower layers of skin on our scalp, our hair will only be as healthy as we are. The condition of our hair is a visual indicator of our health and the adequacy of our diets. All the hair products in the world and the most expensive treatments from beauty salons and spas will never make up for hair that is naturally beautiful. It gets that way when we eat more of the foods God created and less of those that man has refined.

Thin, flaky fingernails. Fingernails are also an indicator of our internal health and nutritional state. If a diet high in sugar takes the place of one filled with high fiber, vitamins, and minerals, our fingernails will suffer.

Poor skin quality. There are some cases where skin problems are the result of an underlying disorder or heredity factor. But many times our skin is yet another indicator that what we are eating is not good for us. A diet high in sugar and saturated fat will result in skin eruptions for most people. Although hormones play a role in the production and extent of acne, pimples can also be caused by eating a diet high in sugar. If you suffer from occasional skin eruptions, or even a chronic case of acne, try eliminating sugar. Almost always, as your overall nutrition improves, so will your skin.

Poor vision. The old belief that carrots are good for your eyesight may have more merit than we realize. Our vision is clearest and most accurate when we eat a balanced diet with the proper amount of not only vitamin A, but also other vitamins, minerals, complex carbohydrates, and protein. When we disturb the nutritional balance of our bodies by eating a daily diet that includes sugar, our vision will suffer. This might explain why our vision troubles us more on some days than on others.

Lack of endurance. Physical endurance and achievement are closely related to our nutritional status. When we eat diets that are balanced and healthy, we find ourselves able to compete longer and at a higher level whether walking with friends during lunch breaks or playing a game of pick-up basketball with the guys from church. Our desire and ability to participate in regular exercise is directly related to our nutrition or lack thereof.

If we consume large amounts of sugar on a daily basis, we may feel uninspired, drained, tired, lethargic, and chronically fatigued. Many of us are trapped in such a cycle even now. We wake up drained of energy and resort to a quick, sugary breakfast and caffeine to provide us with the energy we need to get through the day. But with each intake of sugar, the feeling of fatigue grows stronger, and it's all we can do to complete our daily tasks. Exercise is completely out of the question.

On the PRISM program, you will eliminate refined sugar, and within a few days you will notice a dramatic increase in energy. This will lead you to a place where you will feel strong enough to want to exercise. Then, once exercise is a regular part of your weekly life, your energy will increase even more. You will wonder why you once had barely enough energy to do the breakfast dishes.

CANCER

Cancer has long been linked to a weak immune system. Virtually everyone has cancer cells somewhere in their bodies, but under normal circumstances our bodies fight the cells, destroy them, and leave us unaware of the miraculous unseen battle that goes on daily inside us.

But for reasons still being explored, our immune systems sometimes break down, and cancer cells are not destroyed. Instead, they begin to multiply and cause the growth of tumors, which, in many cases, leads to death. To date, cancer is one of the leading causes of death in the United

States, and although scientists continue to search for ways to stop its destruction, there are still no surefire cures.

It stands to reason that if cancer can be linked to a weakened immune system, it might very well be linked to sugar intake, as well. In fact, recent studies have been fairly conclusive that people who daily consume excessive sugar may be at a higher risk for certain kinds of cancer.

A study completed in January 1999 followed hundreds of thousands of women over a ten-year period in order to determine if dietary fiber intake was related to incidents of colon cancer. In fairly shocking results, scientists determined that, while fibrous vegetables and fruits are obviously healthy for the body and clearly help reduce the cases of mouth cancer and other cancers, they did not directly impact the number of colon cancer cases.

Instead, the study revealed a very different direct relationship. The more refined sugar the women consumed daily, the more likely they were to contract colon cancer. It was not clear whether sugar intake causes the bowels to become sluggish and constipated, or whether the elimination of products containing refined sugar simply disturbed the colon to the degree that cancer was sometimes the result.

Either way, the study firmly established the link between sugar intake and cancer, and many people who had previously only speculated about the connection had their answer. Those of us at PRISM will not be surprised if in the next decade more studies confirm such a link.

Obviously, if we want our bodies to be at their "right weight," if we want to be healthy physically, emotionally, and spiritually, if we hope to be able to sit through an hour-long Sunday school class, and if we desire strong immune systems, we would do well to eliminate refined sugar. Given the previous list of possible problems associated with sugar intake, a chocolate candy bar looks more like a piece of hazardous waste than a treat.

After a week on the PRISM program you will feel like a new person because you have eliminated sugar and increased your consumption of high-quality foods. When that happens, you will wonder why you ever fell into the sugar addiction and compromised your body in so many ways. And you will be that much more determined to remain sugar-free for years to come. Perhaps for the rest of your life.

Prism Success Story: Linda McCrary

Weight loss: 28 pounds

PRISM group leader

LINDA HAS HELPED MORE THAN 2,000 PEOPLE find freedom from food addiction and overweight through the PRISM Weight Loss Program. Her Albany, Oregon, group meets weekly and averages 150 people at each meeting.

When Linda talks about her motivation for being the leader of one of the most successful PRISM group meetings in the country, she is painfully honest.

"I was terribly addicted to food, trapped in a horrible bondage to overeating," she says. "I needed help, and this is the only program that has ever worked for me. It rescued me from my destructive eating habits and brought me closer to the Lord at the same time."

Linda remembers that for much of her life she would wake up discouraged with her overweight—even when she didn't have much weight to lose. The discouragement would trigger an attack of overeating that caused her to cram food down her throat all day long.

If the scales showed a five-pound weight gain, she'd starve herself for an entire day. But the very next day she'd be discouraged again and binge on vast amounts of food from morning to night.

"I'd lie in bed, disgusted with myself for eating nine million calories that day and pray to God, begging him to help me."

In response to her prayers, God sent a woman Linda likes to call "a little angel." This woman sent Linda information about the PRISM program and asked her if she'd be interested in starting a group in Albany.

At the same time, a friend at church began asking Linda if she'd ever heard of PRISM.

"It was coming at me from all sides," she says. "I gave in reluctantly and agreed to start a group, mostly because I was desperate to get my own extra weight off and be done with my food addiction. That's how it all started."

That was three years and 2,000 people ago. Five percent of those who've been through her group are from her church. The others are from all parts of Albany. Word of mouth has brought people to Linda's PRISM meeting from all walks of life—business people, busy mothers, lawyers, doctors, teachers, and overweight teenagers.

"For a lot of them, their biggest need is to have a Savior. They've tried everything else and nothing's worked. They may have lost weight for a while but they can't keep it off. "With God, the PRISM program is transforming hundreds of people in Albany, Oregon."

10

STRIKING A NEW BALANCE

A Different Approach to a Balanced Diet

TIMES WERE WHEN OUR ANCESTORS—as recently as just a generation or two ago—worked primarily on farms. It was hard work, and it lasted from sunup to sundown. They worked hard, and they fueled up daily on meals that included creamy whole milk, real butter, eggs, beef, pork, and chicken, along with fresh garden vegetables and fruits. Each of these foods was whole and unprocessed—just the way God made it.

According to today's theories, their high protein, moderate fat diets should have led to high incidences of obesity, heart disease, and an assortment of other nutrition-related ailments. But that generally was not the case. Although life expectancy was shorter in the 1800s and early 1900s, it can be attributed mostly to a lack of vaccinations and cures for common ailments. People died from tetanus, polio, measles, and, because there were no antibiotics, from bronchitis, strep throat, and other simple bacterial infections.

But generally they did not die from cancer and heart disease. In fact, these two ailments, which are among the most common killers today, were virtually unheard of a hundred years ago.

In the past five years, doctors and scientists have begun to link this curious fact to a simple conclusion. Perhaps there is nothing wrong with a high-protein diet that contains moderate amounts of fat. Studies were undertaken, and almost overnight the markets were deluged with books touting the power of protein and the necessity of including meat, fish, and poultry in our daily diets.

The PRISM program promotes a balanced diet, and that includes an adequate amount of dietary protein. Let's take a look at the importance of protein in our diets.

THE WAYS OUR BODIES USE PROTEIN

Protein is essential to build and maintain a healthy body. Our bodies use protein in several ways:

To Build and Maintain Muscle Mass. We must eat an adequate amount of protein each day in order to maintain our body's muscle, or lean body, mass. Muscle is made entirely from protein. When we eat a high-carbohydrate, low-protein diet, we often force our bodies to use existing muscle tissue in order to meet the body's demand for protein.

To Maintain Healthy Organs. Body organs are made up almost entirely of protein. We must eat a certain amount of protein each day in order to keep our organs working at optimal levels.

To Promote Healing. Protein is also necessary for our bodies to heal themselves. When we suffer illness, injury, or recuperation from an operation, it is essential that we have an adequate intake of protein.

RECOMMENDED SOURCES OF PROTEIN

One of the best features of protein is the length of time it takes to digest. Whereas simple carbohydrates—white sugar and refined flour—digest almost instantly and flood the bloodstream with sugar, protein digests very slowly. Therefore, foods high in protein keep our blood sugar at a moderate level and eliminate the wild hunger that comes when we are in a sugar addiction cycle.

As strongly as the PRISM program discourages the intake of refined sugar and flour, it encourages the consumption of foods high in lean protein. These foods include:

- Poultry (chicken, turkey, etc.)

- Fish

- Lean beef

- Lean pork

- Eggs/egg whites

- Shellfish

It should be noted that while dietary protein plays an important part in weight loss on the PRISM Weight Loss Program, vegetarians can successfully participate. The recommended protein requirement may be met by eating soy products, tofu, and combinations of foods such as beans and lentils. A person wishing to participate in PRISM while eating a vegetarian diet should purchase a book on complete proteins.

WHAT ABOUT THE FAT?

You may wonder why it is necessary to eat lean protein foods if creamy milk and butter didn't pose a problem for people a hundred years ago. The reason is twofold. First, those products were not processed back then. They were "whole" foods, just the way God made them. Second, our ancestors were far more active than we are today. They worked all day long, moving barrels, digging holes, pulling plows, sweeping floors, etc. They were able to consume more calories and because they burned them off, only a small percentage of them ever had weight problems.

Today it takes effort to make room in our busy schedules for exercise. Some days the most activity we might get could be the walk from our kitchen to our parked car. Instead of spending several hours a day in aerobic activity, we do well to make time for it several hours a week.

Because of our reduced level of activity, we must also have a reduced level of caloric intake. Although eating fat may not cause a direct buildup of fat in the body, it is high in calories and must be limited in order to stay within the calorie guidelines of the PRISM program. This is why the lean protein foods listed above are recommended during each of the program phases.

In the previous chapter, we explained that the real problem with the American diet hasn't necessarily been too much fat intake, but rather the consumption of too many "simple" carbohydrates, such as those found in foods containing large amounts of white sugar and white flour.

It is important that you not think that the PRISM program's inclusion of protein and elimination of simple carbohydrates is a reason to get rid of carbohydrates altogether. There are diets that encourage this, and they lead to quick weight loss. However, when our bodies are starved for carbohydrates—the most important source of energy we have—they will also regain weight quickly. I know many people who have tried to lose weight in just a few weeks' time by eating only protein foods. They lost weight at first, but soon began suffering a severe drop in energy. Not long afterward, most ended up returning to their former habits of high-carbohydrate eating. These people regained their weight quickly and generally wound up heavier than when they first started.

The key to the PRISM program is a balanced, healthy diet. You may eat high protein foods—perhaps at every meal—but each day you will also eat two or more servings of whole-grain foods and several servings of fruits and vegetables, the sources of complex carbohydrates. In addition, you will also consume an adequate amount of dietary fat, which is as essential for good health as protein and carbohydrates. When you do that, you will find yourself replete with energy and endurance, able to get the most out of life. The results will be worth the effort required to make the change.

There is one more thing we at PRISM recommend that you do when you are on the program: Remember to take your vitamins!

VITAMINS AND OTHER NUTRITIONAL SUPPLEMENTS

We at PRISM strongly recommend that in addition to striking a balance among protein, carbohydrates, and fat in the foods you eat, you take quality vitamin and mineral supplements. Vitamin supplements can be a great help to people who want to make sure their diets are healthy and balanced, and that is vital as you begin your weight loss program.

Vitamins work to maintain cellular health and are crucial in the body's process of utilizing energy. When you are on the PRISM program, it is essential that you take a multivitamin and a calcium supplement. In addition, we recommend that you take any or all of the supplements listed below in order to ensure proper nutrition, metabolism, and overall health. All of these vitamins can be found in supplement form in various health food stores, nutrition centers, and other outlets.

We have done our best to list the foods that supply these vitamins so you will see the importance of eating a healthy, balanced diet—the kind prescribed on the PRISM Weight Loss Program. Remember, you should always consult your physician before taking any vitamin or mineral supplement. Some vitamins can cause serious interactions if taken with certain medications.

VITAMIN A

This fat-soluble vitamin must not be taken in excessive doses since it accumulates in the body's fat stores. However, it is important that you get enough because it is essential to many of the body's functions, including the immune system, the ability to heal, healthy skin, and proper vision. Vitamin A has been shown to safeguard against cancer.

You can find vitamin A in eggs, milk, and in a nutrient called beta carotene. Beta carotene does not build up in the body's fat stores and so is not toxic. It has been shown to have some benefit in lowering the risk of many kinds of cancer. Beta carotene can be found in leafy green, yellow, and orange vegetables.

B-COMPLEX VITAMINS

The B vitamins are most closely linked to energy release in our bodies. They help manufacture red blood cells and aid in the breakdown of carbohydrates, fat, and protein. These vitamins have also been used to treat premenstrual conditions and, because of their ability to help the body utilize oxygen, to treat fatigue and boost energy levels. The best food source for the B vitamins are legumes, whole grains, organ meats, and brewer's yeast. This vitamin is not fat-soluble, but always remember to follow the recommended dosage on the bottle.

VITAMIN C

The best-known of all vitamins, vitamin C, is water-soluble, and what the body doesn't use, it eliminates. Vitamin C is best known for its ability to maintain a healthy immune system. There is still much debate about the benefits of vitamin C and whether it actually aids the body's healing process. Information available today suggests that it may help lower cholesterol levels. Supplemental vitamin C is recommended in the PRISM program. Foods that contain this vitamin include citrus fruits, potatoes, and dark green vegetables.

VITAMIN D

Known for its ability to strengthen bones and teeth, this vitamin is fat-soluble and must not be taken in excessive amounts. The body uses vitamin D along with calcium and phosphorus in a balanced manner. Generally, our need for this vitamin can be met by including tuna, salmon, and milk in our diet, and getting some exposure to sunlight each day.

VITAMIN E

Another fat-soluble vitamin, this one is helpful in fighting free radicals in our bodies and is considered an antioxidant, a popular term that means something that aids our body's immune system. Vitamin E can be found in leafy vegetables, whole grains, beans, and vegetable oils.

GARLIC

Many people, especially in areas outside the United States, use garlic as a form of antibiotic. Tests have clearly shown that garlic helps ward off illness and bring about speedy healing. Garlic has also been linked with reducing the risk of heart disease, lowering cholesterol, and a host of other health benefits. Be sure to get the odorless capsules. Your friends and family will thank you.

CALCIUM

Most of the calcium in our bodies is found in our bones and teeth, which are made and kept hard through dietary calcium. Because calcium is not readily absorbed from common food sources—milk, yogurt, leafy green vegetables—it is very important that you take a calcium supplement. After the age of twenty-five, we especially need this mineral to ward off the possibility of osteoporosis.

CHROMIUM PICOLONATE

This mineral aids in the conversion of carbohydrates into energy and helps the body maintain even blood sugar levels. Tests have shown that many Americans are deficient in this mineral. Recently, chromium picolonate has been packaged to look like a modern-day diet pill. Although tests have not shown to the degree to which our metabolisms benefit from this mineral, there is certainly some benefit in taking it— with your doctor's permission, of course—while you are on the PRISM Weight Loss Program.

MULTIMINERAL SUPPLEMENTS

There are many minerals and trace minerals that tend to be lacking in the diet of average Americans. Even following the PRISM Weight Loss Program, your diet may not include enough of the right kinds of foods to assure you get the proper amount of a given mineral. For that reason, it may be helpful to find a mineral supplement that will provide you with everything your body may lack.

THE BENEFITS OF BALANCE

Remember, you are on the way to finding the TRUE YOU. You will look different and feel different when you eat differently on the PRISM program. An adequate intake of protein, carbohydrates, and dietary fat—as well as taking your vitamins—are an important part of the formula.

Balanced diets—those that include protein, fruits, vegetables, and dairy products but remain low in simple carbohydrates and saturated fats—inevitably result in more energy and less illness. When our diets are balanced, our metabolism speeds up because it must work longer and harder to break down the protein in our system. Almost immediately we find it easier to lose weight and to keep it off because we are completely satisfied with our healthy, wholesome, balanced food choices.

But there is another balance that must be achieved before success can be complete: the balance between mind and body. In the next chapter we will look at winning the battle of the mind. And this, more than anything else, will make the difference in lasting success.

FOR MANY YEARS, TOM HALSEY AND HIS SON Peter had a habit of stopping at the local Dairy Queen. Not once in a while, but every day. Every afternoon as the day wound down, they went to Dairy Queen, bought high-calorie, sugar-filled desserts, and drove to a spot overlooking the freeway for good conversation.

"We'd eat our treats and watch the cars pass by," Tom says. "It seemed like good quality time to me, but it really made an impact on our health. A bad impact."

Tom and his wife, Sharon, were raised in families that ate in excess. They brought poor eating habits to their marriage and it wasn't long before extra weight began piling on.

Over the years they tried several weight loss plans, often they went on the diets together. They'd lose some weight for a while, but, like so many other people, eventually they'd gain it all back.

Meanwhile, Peter was in a special education class and struggling with the pangs of adolescence while carrying around nearly a hundred excess pounds. "He was sick all the time with colds, flus, and other illnesses. His energy was very low, too."

Tom and Sharon vaguely understood that sugar was somehow related to their failure to lose weight permanently. It seemed there was no way to eat fewer sugar-filled items. Every time the Halsey family allowed foods with sugar into their diets, it was as if the floodgates had been opened, and there was no end to their overeating.

Two years ago the Halseys saw a notice on the church bulletin board about a PRISM Weight Loss Program meeting. They met with the group leader and were very encouraged.

"She told us there was a freedom in this program that she hadn't seen with any other weight loss plan. She said it was something that would last," Tom recalls. "The spiritual aspect was a huge draw. I wanted that back in my life, a closer walk with the Lord."

Tom and Sharon discussed the PRISM program and decided it was something they wanted to do together. The idea that the PRISM program eliminated sugar was a big factor in their decision.

"We knew we had to get away from the stuff. It was ruining our health and our lives. Eventually it would have killed us," Tom says.

Progress for the Halsey family has been steady and encouraging. Their combined weight loss is more than most adult men weigh. Peter has enjoyed much success at school as a result of losing so much weight—especially in physical education class where his teachers are impressed with his increased stamina and energy.

"It's like he's a whole new person," Tom says.

And as for their father-son afternoon conversations, the Halsey men still get together at their spot overlooking the freeway.

"Only now we bring along fruit-sweetened yogurt or something healthy, something good for us," he says. "To tell you the truth, we feel great, and we don't even miss our trips to Dairy Queen."

The Halsey
Family

combined loss
of 213 pounds

35
pounds
lighter

Bev
Passwaters

11

A Body-Mind Balance

Winning the Behind-the-Scenes Battle

THERE IS MORE—SO MUCH MORE—to the PRISM Weight Loss Program than a list of guidelines concerning what foods you may eat, how much of them you can eat, and when you can eat them.

The goal of the Prism program is to transform not only how you view food, but the way you take care of your body and mind. That is what this chapter is all about.

We strongly recommend to people who choose to take part in the PRISM program that they do two things we believe will help ensure their success: Get plenty of exercise so your bodies can become strong, fat-burning machines, and learn to take control of your thoughts when it comes to food and weight loss.

Let's take a look first at the benefits of regular exercise.

Exercise: PRISM's Powerful Ally

For many people, "exercise" is the dreaded "E-word" they hope never to read in a book about weight loss. It can feel almost like a betrayal: "Hey, wait a minute, I thought I was going to lose weight by changing my eating habits, and now you throw in all this exercise. Who needs it?"

Let us state up front that the PRISM Weight Loss Program will be successful in transforming your life and breaking your problems with eating whether or not you exercise. The weight will most likely take longer to come off without exercise, but it will come off.

That said, we want to examine the numerous benefits of exercise as you work to reach your "right weight." Not only can regular exercise cut down the amount of time it takes for you to reach your "right weight"—in many cases by as much as half—you will also enjoy the benefits of improved muscle tone, shapeliness, increased metabolism, and added energy.

Exercise is clearly something you will want to incorporate into your new healthy lifestyle. And there is no better time to start than just a few weeks after you begin the PRISM program. The energy you will have will make you that much more likely to be successful.

Now let's talk about the different types of exercise and how you can benefit from them. Note: Remember to consult your physician before beginning any exercise program.

Aerobic Exercise

Aerobic literally means "in air" or "with air." Aerobic exercise involves elevating the heart rate to force us to take in extra oxygen in order to meet our body's demand. It is generally agreed that twenty minutes of aerobic exercise is the minimum amount necessary in order for the body to reap any benefit. Many take this a step further and claim that only after the twenty-minute mark do our bodies begin to burn stored fat efficiently.

Any activity that elevates your heart rate to seventy-percent of its maximum level—the level at which your body begins to burned stored fat—and that can be sustained for twenty or more minutes is considered aerobic. You can find your maximum heart rate by subtracting your age from 220 then multiplying by .70. For example, if you are thirty-five years old, your maximum heart rate would be 185. Multiply that by .70 in order to find your "target heart rate," the rate at which your body most efficiently burns fat. If you are thirty-five, then your target heart rate is betwen 129 and 130.

There are literally dozens of ways to get aerobic exercise, including walking, running, cycling, tennis, roller skating, stair stepping, rowing, water aerobics, dancing, swimming, cross country skiing, pool exercises, jumping rope, ice skating, trampoline rebounding, and stationary bicycling.

You will have the most success in your weight loss program if you *develop a regular exercise routine*. You should strive to do an aerobic exercise for at least twenty minutes, four times a week. Advanced fitness would likely entail forty to sixty minutes of aerobic exercise, five days a week.

Obviously you can't expect to develop this type of routine immediately. Later in this chapter, we will discuss how to begin and stay motivated as you work to make your body stronger, healthier, and more fit. This is an important part of the transformation process—replacing your former favorite pastime of overeating with exercise. You will almost always feel better, look better, and be healthier as a result. Remember, it's time to get excited about a future free from overweight, a future full of life and energy and hope.

RESISTANCE TRAINING

Resistance training builds muscle tissue, and a continuous program of this type of exercise will bring about three beneficial results:

An increased metabolism. Muscle tissue requires more energy to operate efficiently. Therefore, the more muscle mass we have, the more rapidly our bodies burn energy and the faster we lose excess fat.

A more defined body. Muscle will add tone and definition to our bodies. We will look different when our body makeup contains a greater percentage of muscle. You may reach your "right weight" without ever participating in a resistance-training program, but you will never lose the infamous wobbly-arm look without it. Neither will you find your abdomen flat and toned without working the underlying muscles that have in many cases been stretched and weakened by time, overweight, and child-bearing.

Strength. Resistance training will almost always make you stronger overall. You may discover that as you train you will be able to leap out of your chair, bound up the stairs, and run alongside your children through hours of outdoor play. In most cases, knee pain and even back pain will diminish or disappear as the muscles that support those areas grow strong enough to carry more of the body's weight. This type of strength is most noticeable when a resistance-training program is used along with regular aerobic exercise. You will also notice increased energy as you faithfully train.

There's little doubt that you can benefit from making resistance training part of your approach to the PRISM program. But what types of exercise constitutes resistance training? The most popular kind is weight lifting. Here are some pointers.

WEIGHT LIFTING

Your weight lifting program should be designed by a professional trainer. As with other diet or exercise programs, it should be approved by your doctor or medical team. You can obtain additional information on weight lifting from a variety of places, including your local library, bookstore, or the Internet. Research may turn up pointers as well as specific exercises for your individual needs.

Here are some general guidelines to follow when weight lifting, unless your doctor or personal trainer directs otherwise:

Do ten to fifteen repetitions. Choose a weight that can be lifted ten to fifteen times in a row with some exertion but without straining.

Do three sets. Choose several arm exercises and several leg exercises that work the specific muscle groups you want to strengthen. Then do three sets of repetitions. As we mentioned earlier, each set should probably include ten to fifteen repetitions. Be sure to rest a minute or so between sets.

Maintain correct posture. Be careful to maintain good posture and form. For example, if you are lifting a three-pound weight to strengthen various arm muscles, be sure to stand with your feet slightly apart and your knees slightly bent. This will usually protect your back from injury or strain. When you are doing knee bends or squats for various muscles in your legs, be sure to keep your chest lifted and use your knees as little as possible. Also, try not to lower your body beyond what would represent a sitting position. This can be very hard on the knees.

Lift three or four times a week. Muscle tissue is built and strengthened after it has been torn down and healed. Lifting tears down, resting heals and builds. Be sure to limit your program to no more than three or four days a week so your muscles can rest.

Increase weight increments gradually. You may start by lifting a light amount of weight, one pound or perhaps two. After several weeks of consistent training three times a week you will probably be able to increase that by one or more pounds. The more weight you lift, the stronger your muscles will become. However, unless you want to have the look of a bodybuilder, you will probably not want to lift much more than ten pounds per hand. Again, this is a general rule, and limitations and requirements will vary for each person.

Make the muscle do the work. With each repetition be sure that you are allowing the intended muscle to do the work. In general, you must squeeze your muscle, focusing on forcing it to lift the weight. For instance, if you are trying to work out your biceps, you should grip the weights lightly in each hand and curl your arms so that your wrists rise to meet your shoulders. Try this without a weight and see if you can notice the difference when you focus on squeezing the bicep muscle versus when you merely move your arm. You will need this type of focus in order to truly work your bicep and eventually make that muscle stronger and more defined.

ABDOMINAL CRUNCHES

When we work many parts of our body, we may use our body weight as the force of resistance to build and strengthen the muscle. Abdominal crunches are one of these exercises. Using the weight of your upper body, crunches are generally best performed when they are done as a half sit-up. Basically, this exercise is performed when you raise your head and shoulders up off the floor enough to feel a contraction in your abdominal muscles. Technique is very important because people who are not careful may injure their backs or do this exercise for weeks with no results.

The following are a few suggestions regarding abdominal crunch technique; however, as we mentioned before, be sure to check with your doctor before starting any exercise program. In addition, there are many books and videos available that offer other advice or techniques. The best approach is to find what works for you and continue it on a regular basis.

Protect your lower back. Crunches are intended to strengthen your torso, abdomen, and back. As you do them, you should feel less back pain and more overall strength. However, if you are not careful, you can injure your back and end up worse off than when you started.

Lie flat on the floor for almost every type of sit-up. Consciously focus on pressing your lower back into the floor as you perform each repetition. Be sure that you do not arch your back as you raise your torso since this is how injuries often happen. By keeping your lower back on the floor—almost as if it were pinned to the floor—you will force your abdominal muscles to work harder, and you will alleviate nearly all pressure on the lower back.

Protect the neck. Depending on how strong you are, you will probably want to perform your crunches with your hands clasped behind your head to support your neck. What you must not do is lift with your hands. Doing so will take the work away from the abdominal muscles and work the arms instead. It can also put undue stress on the neck. Many people have performed crunches for weeks by using their arms to pull the head and shoulders up. When there are no results, they usually become discouraged and give up, although the problem was their technique, and not their inability to gain strength in their abdominal muscles.

Link your hands behind your head and keep your elbows open so that the entire upper body is lifted by the abdominal muscles.

Don't rush. Because of the higher number of repetitions, it is easy to hurry through a set of sit-ups. For example, if you start with fifteen sit-ups, you may be tempted to lift only slightly and hurry through this number in a matter of seconds.

Focus on contracting the abdominal muscles. Keep your abdominal muscles tight until you lower your upper body back to the floor. You should feel each repetition so that the muscles are truly worked by the set, whether you start with five or twenty-five.

Remember to breathe. It is important when performing sit-ups or any weight-training exercise that you remember to breathe out with every exertion. This keeps the oxygen flowing evenly throughout your body and allows you to get the most out of each repetition.

Work each section of the abdominal muscles. The abdominal muscles are broken into several areas and weave their way like so many ropes across the middle torso. You will want to include several slightly different crunches in your regular routine in order to strengthen the entire abdomen. Again, there are books and videos that offer a variety of exercises to help you accomplish this, but in general, your program should strengthen the upper abdomen, lower abdomen, and oblique—or side—muscles.

SQUATS OR KNEE BENDS

Squats or knee bends work the leg muscles by making them lift the body's torso weight. The following suggestions will make your squats more effective:

Maintain posture and form. As with all weight-training exercises, it is crucial that you maintain correct posture and form. Never completely straighten your legs. Straight legs will increase the risk of injuring your back—particularly your lower back.

Keep your chest up. Keep your chest up so that the buttocks and upper legs do the work. Try to imagine you are sitting in an invisible chair. Lower yourself to the point that you are in a sitting position, then rise with your knees slightly bent. This will constitute a single squat and will work out your upper leg and buttocks.

DEVELOPING A ROUTINE

For many people, this information may seem overwhelming. Perhaps the last time you lifted a weight was when your college-age son was an infant. Perhaps the only aerobic activity you participate in each week is restocking the pantry with groceries. If this is the case, please do not be alarmed. The exercise program discussed above is a goal to work toward, or if you are already at that level of fitness, a suggested routine.

Your first step is just to get started. If you have never had a regular exercise routine, or if it has been too long to remember the last time you elevated your heart rate, then it is time to begin.

Examine the list of aerobic activities above and choose something you feel you might enjoy. Wear loose clothing and do your chosen activity for five minutes. Repeat this at least four times a week, increasing the duration as you feel able.

It is important to remember that in the past, you have used food to comfort, tranquilize, reward, and entertain yourself. Look at the list of aerobic exercises again. Isn't it possible that one or more of those activities might bring you comfort when you are feeling down? Don't you think thirty minutes on a treadmill might help ease depression on a day filled with the blues? Wouldn't a game of tennis or a walk around the block bring you more reward than fifteen seconds of chocolate followed by an entire day of guilt? Isn't it more entertaining to spend a day playing outside with your family or golfing with your friends than to overeat and bury yourself deeper in your problem with overweight?

The PRISM program will work for you as you uncover the reasons you have overeaten in the past. As part of the transformation you will undergo, you will replace prior destructive patterns with new beneficial patterns. Exercise is one of those patterns.

As you begin, it is crucial that you take a new look at exercise and the ways it can benefit you emotionally as well as physically. Once you've started, allow yourself time to adjust to the exercise program you've chosen. You'll notice results more quickly than you ever thought possible.

Exercise is a huge weapon in the battle against overweight. But there is another weapon that is every bit as important in your endeavor to find success in the PRISM program. It is the weapon of taking your thoughts captive.

WINNING THE BATTLE OF THE MIND

You have heard the phrase, "you are what you eat," and for many of us, this has been our life story. Nearly everything we have discussed proves the truth of that statement. However, there is a similar phrase that is less popular but also true: "You are what you think you are."

What we think makes a tremendous impact on what we are and how we handle various challenges. Joining the PRISM program is a huge undertaking, one that cannot be successful without the support and guidance of our loving heavenly Father and his perfect Word, the Bible.

Once we have these tools, we must take a careful look at the battle of the mind. Scripture teaches us to take every thought captive to make it obedient to Christ (2 Corinthians 10:5). If we don't take a thought captive, we can wake up on day four of our most recent diet effort and immediately begin complaining to ourselves.

Why am I doing this?... I haven't lost any weight anyway....I might as well eat what I want.... I'm wasting my time.... I'll never be thin.

After an hour of unchecked negative self-talk, you will find yourself in the kitchen browsing through foods you aren't even supposed to be thinking about. As you stand there, you mull over your choices, searching for a reason to continue but sabotaging yourself more intensely by the moment. You allow more negative self-talk, and the situation gets worse.

It's been four days since I've had any cookies. What does everyone think? That I'm some kind of saint? What's one cookie going to hurt?

The thoughts come at alarming speed and with increasing insistence until you finally give in and eat a cookie. Then the voice changes. It's no longer in first person; it's from the viewpoint of the enemy of our souls, the enemy of every good thing we might ever do in the strength of the Lord.

What a loser you are! Now you've done it. Gone and blown your entire diet. Can't you do anything right?

Don't stop at one. You've already blown it.

Ten cookies and a major wave of depression later, you are feeling desperate, hopeless, and weak. If there were a contest for ultimate losers, you would win hands down. At least that's what you tell yourself. You wonder what went wrong. How was it you could be so successful for three days only to forget it all on the fourth?

The average diet lasts just four days because people allow their minds to entertain wrong thoughts. Sometimes we practically invite them into our minds, putting them up as regular houseguests. This self-defeating habit must be done away with if you are to find lasting success in the PRISM Weight Loss Program.

There are two key aspects to changing negative self-talk.

First, you must identify this habit, catch yourself in the act, and forbid any further negative self-talk. Since this is difficult to do, you must learn to do a second thing. You must replace the negative thoughts with positive ones that will encourage your right eating habits and the transformation taking place.

The PRISM program has devised several tools to help you in this area. They are the following:

THE TRUE YOU MIRROR

Early in the first phase of the PRISM Program you will be asked to locate a photograph of yourself when you were at your "right weight." The photo must be no more than five years old and must be a full-body pose. If you have not been at your "right weight" in the past five years, or possibly never, you will be asked to search magazines and catalogs looking for a body image that resembles the one you picture you will have when you reach your "right weight." You must not pick out a swimsuit model or any other unrealistic, computer-enhanced image. Women whose bodies taunt us with the ultimate perfect look almost never look that way in person. Computer imaging is able to erase inches off the waists even of supermodels. If their bodies are not good enough without computer enhancement or editing, then it would be wise to refrain from cutting the picture of such a body out of a magazine and pasting it on the TRUE YOU mirror.

There are, however, many catalogs that will contain photographs of average people of normal weight whose body images are real and attainable. Find one who is similar to your build in bone structure and height. Be sure to paste your face over the model's face so that you begin to connect a normal weight with your face and personal image of yourself.

The TRUE YOU mirror is wonderful not only because it gives you a goal to shoot for, but because it helps you reconstruct your image of yourself as you begin to lose weight. Many people have spent years desiring a thinner, healthier body but somehow have always stopped themselves before reaching their goal. This may be caused by fear or an inability to see yourself at your "right weight." This pieced-together picture or photograph of you at your "right weight" will then be glued to the TRUE YOU mirror, which is provided in the phase one workbook.

You will be asked to look at this TRUE YOU mirror at least twice a day, so put it where you will see it often. As you look at this image, you will say: "This is the size I was created to be. I am a lovable, worthwhile, and successful person. I am thankful for these truths."

Right now, if you have not yet begun the PRISM program, you may think this is a strange or silly idea. But Scripture teaches us that we must be transformed by the renewing of our minds (Romans 12:2). The PRISM program gives you hope because it addresses the mind, which is the place where temptation and self-doubt take root, the place where negative self-talk undermines your determination to change.

As time passes, the TRUE YOU mirror will seem less a foreign idea and will become something you will depend on. You must be able to visualize where you are headed, the reason you are weighing and measuring your foods at each meal. The TRUE YOU mirror gives you that light at the end of the tunnel, the prize to look forward to. It also shows you that your transformation is a present truth, rather than some wistful, way off, unattainable goal.

Next, let's take a look at PRISM's second tool to help you keep your thoughts where they need to be.

DETERMINING YOUR "RIGHT WEIGHT"

After you visualize what the TRUE YOU will look like, you must also decide on a number that will reflect your "right weight." This number is obvious for most people who have either been at that weight or are familiar enough with their bone structure and body composition to know what it is. However, some people will be unsure of this number. If you are one of those people, you can use one of several means to determine your "right weight."

BMI (Body Mass Index). This is a formula that determines your right weight.

Life insurance charts. These are sometimes too general, but if they include bone structure allowances, you can use them.

Doctor's advice. Sometimes your doctor will be able to help you find your "right weight." Ask the next time you're at the doctor's office or as part of your checkup prior to starting the PRISM program.

You will be asked to repeat a statement to yourself every day, twice a day or more. The statement is this: "_____. This is the 'right weight' for my body."

REEVALUATING YOUR "RIGHT WEIGHT"

You must reevaluate your weight between PRISM phases. Even with all the available tools, you may still have to reconsider the number you've chosen as you near your "right weight." The number you have chosen may have been too high or too low. Either way, your goal is not to weigh as little as possible. Rather, you want freedom from food addiction and a healthy body that weighs the amount God intended it to weigh. That number is your "right weight." By stating this number over and over throughout the day, you plant a new image of yourself in your mind. Eventually you will no longer see yourself as having a weight problem, but as working toward a goal. The goal is not to be "skinny," or even thin, but to have a healthy lifestyle.

AFFIRMATION TAPE

PRISM gives participants an audiocassette tape when they register in a PRISM small group. This tape includes many of the affirmations you will be asked to recite to yourself during your time on the program. The statements include the following:

"I am a unique, one of a kind, original. I am the creation of a loving God."

"I am open to God's truth, and the truth sets me free."

"I am honest with myself and unafraid of the success I can achieve through this program."

"I am no longer a slave to any behavior—I have taken the keys and am working toward lifetime freedom!"

"Today is a new day—a clean slate with no mistakes on it."

So often we are our own worst enemies when it comes to weight loss. Since this is a journey to complete transformation, and since you will be given the keys to break food addiction for a lifetime, it is essential that you replace years, maybe decades, of negative self-talk with affirmative statements. We realize this may seem odd to some of you. But the truth is that if you have failed at weight loss before, if you are food-addicted, you have an entire vocabulary of negative self-talk statements. These must be replaced if you are to be permanently transformed.

Having the right mindset is crucial in one other area—shopping. Armed with the right thoughts, traveling the aisles of the supermarket is easier. But it helps to have a list. The following chapter will cover what foods you will need to buy and provide sample daily menus that may simplify the journey to transformation.

PRISM Success Story: Nancy Benedict

Weight loss: 59 pounds

Halfway to "right weight"

WHEN SHE WAS GROWING UP, NANCY NEVER WORRIED about her weight. She was thin no matter what she ate and never gave her size a lot of thought. Even during her pregnancies she never gained enough to truly worry about.

For that reason, when she had a hysterectomy and her metabolism changed, she was not ready for the weight that began accumulating. Before she realized what was happening, she was finding it difficult even to bend over and tie her shoes.

"When I started gaining weight I was frustrated and began eating more for comfort. It was the only thing I could really control, but I ate to the point of being addicted."

Nancy delivered mail during that time in her life, and she often found herself eating extra food between meals out of boredom or frustration—because it was something to do, a way to pass the time on her long route.

The PRISM Weight Loss Program was making an impact in her town, and she came home one evening to find an article about the organization on the front page of the local newspaper.

"I had reached a point where I knew I had to do something about my weight," she says. "And then I heard about PRISM. I had a friend who was losing weight on the program, and finally I knew it was my turn, my time."

Nancy began having success on the PRISM program immediately. She was especially thankful for the fact that PRISM is based on Scripture and finding strength in the Lord.

"Obviously I wasn't able to do this on my own," Nancy says. "I needed help, and everything about PRISM not only helped me lose weight, but change the way I think about eating."

These days Nancy is still working toward her "right weight," still following the PRISM lesson plans. But she can bend over and tie her shoes a lot more easily.

"And I've gone shopping for all new clothes," she says. "That's more fun than eating for comfort any day."

HEADING TO THE SUPERMARKET

Grocery List and Sample Menus

IN ORDER TO ASSURE SUCCESS ON THE PRISM PROGRAM, it is crucial for you to stick to the food guidelines as laid out for you in chapter 8. This will most likely mean a major change in how you shop for the foods you will be eating.

In this chapter we want to offer some help in doing those things. For your convenience, we have included a suggested grocery list, menus, and recipes to help you get started on the PRISM program.

Here's a list that will help you know what to buy at the grocery store.

SUGGESTED GROCERY LIST

VEGETABLES AND FRUITS

Fresh vegetables and fruits are a great source of needed vitamins and nutrients, which are important when you are on the PRISM program. All fresh vegetables are allowed, including but not limited to the following:

Broccoli	Lettuce	Cucumbers	Onions
Celery	Tomatoes	Squash	Green Beans
Carrots	Cauliflower	Peas	Spinach

Remember, potatoes are not allowed in the first phase of the program. ALL fresh fruits are allowed. Some we recommend are:

Apples	Pears	Bananas	Plums
Grapes	Berries	Peaches	Nectarines
Melons	Cherries	Pineapple	Citrus fruits

FATS

Dietary fat is an important part of any diet, including yours when you are taking part in the PRISM program. Avoid oils that have been hydrogenated or partially hydrogenated, and use the following in moderation:

Extra virgin cold pressed olive oil
Canola oil
Light mayonnaise (to keep calorie totals lower)

GRAINS AND CEREALS

Whole grains and cereals must be monitored carefully during phase one of the PRISM program, and bread in any form is not permitted. In the second phase of the program you can reintroduce bread—but only 100 percent whole grain or whole wheat sandwich bread. Here are some good, healthy grain/cereal foods that are allowed in moderation during all phases of PRISM:

Oatmeal	Brown rice
Shredded wheat	Cream of rice
Brown rice cakes	

Any other whole grain, sugar-free cereals.

MILK AND DAIRY PRODUCTS

When you purchase milk and dairy products, make sure they are low fat or nonfat items. Here are some examples:

Milk—low fat or nonfat
Yogurt—low fat with sugar substitute or natural fruit sweeteners
   (Be sure to read the labels carefully because many brands have
   sugar added.)

Cottage cheese—low fat or nonfat

Cheeses—all kinds (But be advised that cheeses are high in calories unless you choose a low-fat brand.)

Sour cream—Light or low fat will have fewer calories

Natural butter (high in calories, but allowed with care)

Note: Avoid margarine products or butter substitutes. They have been hydrogenated.

MEAT/PROTEIN

Protein intake, in the form of meat or other products, is an important part of any balanced diet. Here are some great sources of dietary protein:

Chicken, preferably boneless breasts	Fresh fish fillets
Tuna—packed in water	Lean ground beef
Lean pork	Beans or legumes
Lean luncheon meat slices from the deli	Soy products (tofu, etc.)

Eggs and/or egg whites (Avoid highly processed, chemical egg substitutes unless otherwise advised by your doctor.)

Natural peanut butter—no sugar added, no hydrogenated fat

BEVERAGES

When purchasing prepared beverages, be very careful to avoid buying those with added sugar. You can have:

Natural fruit juices with no sugar added

Natural vegetable juices with no sugar added

Purified, bottled water with fresh lemon or lime

Sparkling mineral water—sugar free

Tea—herbal or regular

MISCELLANEOUS

When in doubt about an item, consult your PRISM group leader. The rule of thumb: If you don't get an answer and you are still in doubt, DON'T EAT

IT! Here are some miscellaneous foods that are allowed in the program:

Fruit spread—no sugar added (for rice cakes)
Salad dressings—no hydrogenated fats

Salsa	Lemon juice (for cooking)
Dill pickles	Parmesan cheese
Balsamic vinegar	Multivitamins with iron

Microwavable entrees are acceptable, but they are highly processed. Use only when there are no other alternatives. Look for entrees low in fat, and during phase one remember to choose entrees with no pasta or potatoes.

CANNED FOODS

When grocery shopping, fresh food is always best. Shop the outer aisles of the grocery store for fresh produce, meats, and dairy products. If you can't obtain fresh fruits and vegetables, choose frozen rather than canned. Remember, the less your food has been processed, the more nutrition and fiber it retains. Be adventurous! Don't be afraid to shop in health food stores or at local farmers' markets. However, when you have no other choice, these canned items will work in the program:

Canned fruit—no sugar added
Canned vegetables—no sugar added
Soup—no pasta, potatoes, or sugar added
Chili—no sugar added
Tuna, chicken, turkey, or other lean meat product—water-packed only

OTHER FOODS

- *Soups.* Health food stores will have powdered soups in cardboard cups. These soups are a healthy alternative to homemade and need only to be mixed with boiling water to be ready to eat. Most of them vary between 150 and 220 calories for a large serving. Be sure there are no potatoes or pastas during phase one.

- *Dried fruits (no sugar added)*. These can be good for variety and are packed with nutrients and fiber. For example, ten dried apple slices have roughly a hundred calories and make a good snack. An unsweetened dried date has between fifteen and twenty calories and will add flavor to hot cereal or yogurt. Be careful, though, as dried fruit has a higher natural sugar content than fresh fruit and is therefore higher in calories.

- *Raw, unprocessed nuts*. These are healthy and allowed, but be careful because their calorie content is high.

In addition to the grocery list, we want to provide you some sample menus. The recipes for these menu items can be found in appendix B.

SAMPLE PRISM PROGRAM MENUS

Planning menus is another important aspect of the PRISM program, especially in the early phases. You must plan ahead in order to succeed during the first week. It is crucial that you have on hand food items from the suggested grocery list so you will have no trouble making up meals that are healthy and easily within your calorie limits.

For some people, this will mean planning out meals a week ahead of time. For others, it will simply mean having the right foods available so you can make healthy choices with little thought.

The best way to stick to your menu is to purchase the right foods ahead of time and then plan in the way that best suits your lifestyle.

For those of you who enjoy having a menu plan, we have created the following sample menu for a one-week period in phase one of the PRISM program. These menus include calorie contents and daily totals so that you will have an idea of how much food you may eat and the variety of foods you may include at this early stage of the program.

Remember, this is just a sample. You may use it any way you wish. Read it and store away the information; or follow it exactly or in any combination of the options. The menus that will work best for you may be these, or they may be something entirely different. Plan your meals around foods you feel comfortable preparing and enjoy eating.

Success is simple when the food and menu choices you make are those that work best for you within the program guidelines.

SAMPLE MENUS FOR WEEK ONE

Day One

Breakfast:	Wonder Omelet (see recipes)	250
	Sliced orange	50
Lunch:	Crunchy Chicken Salad (see recipes)	250
	1 rice (preferably brown) cake	
	with fruit spread—no sugar	50
Dinner:	5 oz. New York Steak	288
	1 cup steamed acorn squash	82
	1 cup corn	180
	1 cup nonfat milk	90
Total:		1240

* * * * *

Day Two

Breakfast:	1 cup Cheerios	110
	1 cup nonfat milk	90
	1 hard-boiled egg	80
Lunch:	Chicken Caesar Salad (see recipes)	215
	1 cup red bean soup—instant	135
	2 rice (preferably brown) cakes with	
	1 tbs. natural peanut butter	150
Dinner:	6 oz. piece broiled swordfish	210
	1 cup steamed brown rice	160
	1 cup green beans	40
Total:		1190

Day Three

Breakfast:	Scrambled Eggs a la Mushroom	
	(see recipes)	240
	1 grapefruit	44
Lunch:	2 cups Grandma's Chicken Soup	
	(see recipes)	190
	1 cup steamed brown rice	160
Dinner:	Fiesta Mexicana Salad (see recipes)	320
	Bubba's Baked Apple (see recipes)	70
	1 cup corn	160
Total:		1184

* * * * *

Day Four

Breakfast:	Susan's Famous Oatmeal	
	(see recipes)	300
	1/2 cup 1 percent milk	50
Lunch:	Crunchy Turkey Salad (see recipes)	250
	10 dehydrated apple slices	110
Dinner:	Chicken Parmesan (see recipes)	310
	1 cup steamed rice	160
	1/2 cup applesauce—no sugar added	60
Total:		1140

* * * * *

Day Five

Breakfast:	Cowboy Creamed Wheat (see recipes)	320
Lunch:	4 oz. sliced fresh turkey	140
	1 cup vegetable beef soup—no pasta	
	or potatoes	160
	2 rice (preferably brown) cakes	
	with fruit spread	100

Dinner:	Broiled chicken breast	140
	1 cup steamed brown rice	160
	1 cup yellow squash	82
	1 cup diced melon	80
Total:		1182

* * * * *

Day Six

Breakfast:	Susan's Famous Oatmeal	300
	1/2 cup light vanilla soy milk	60
Lunch:	Crunchy Tuna Salad (see recipes)	250
	1 cup steamed zucchini	50
Dinner:	1 cup low fat cottage cheese	200
	1 cup chopped apple	50
	2 rice (preferably brown) cakes	
	with 2 tbs. natural peanut butter	230
Total:		1140

* * * * *

Day Seven

Breakfast:	Scrambled Eggs a la Canada	
	(see recipes)	325
Lunch:	2 rice cakes	70
	4 oz. tuna, 2 tbs. light mayonnaise	190
Dinner:	Rib-Sticking Chili Con Carne	
	(see recipes)	300
	1 cup corn	160
	1 large sliced apple	75
Total:		1120

This menu provides for a healthy, balanced diet for the first phase of the PRISM program. In appendix B, we'll provide some quick and easy recipes for some of the items on this menu.

PRISM Success Story: Lilly Thompson

Weight loss: 77 pounds

Inches lost: 79

From a size 26 down to a size 12

BY THE TIME SHE FOUND THE PRISM WEIGHT LOSS program, Lilly had been obese for all of her adult life, and she was at the end of her rope. Her back was in chronic pain, and she had tried every diet on the market within her budget.

The pounds started piling on during Lilly's first pregnancy. "I had always been thin until then, and no one told me what might happen," she says. "I gained fifty pounds, and before I had time to lose it I was pregnant for the second time."

Over the next several decades she failed on a series of diet plans.

"I tried everything, but nothing treated the problem," she says. "Eventually I began taking drastic measures, even starving myself to lose the weight."

Lilly slowed her metabolism down so severely that her body refused to lose even a few pounds. She worked with elderly people, and her excess weight combined with the lifting and physical labor involved with her job made life unbearable.

With each passing year, the pain in her back grew worse, and she didn't know how she could survive much longer. It was at that point in her life that she ran into a friend at church who had lost weight.

"I asked her what she was doing, and her entire face lit up," Lilly says. "She told me she was on the PRISM Program and that she'd been praying for me to start coming to the group meetings."

Lilly prayed about the opportunity. When everything fell perfectly into place, she knew PRISM was the program for her.

"That first day I saw the list of foods we could eat and I thought, Oh, no! Where I worked they made everything deep-fried with lots of homemade bread," Lilly remembers. "But then I thought about what the Bible says. I can do all things through Christ who gives me strength."

Lilly rested in that truth, and for the first phase of PRISM—six weeks—she was careful not to eat a bite of or taste anything that wasn't on the PRISM program. She also took the water requirement very seriously. Each morning she would fill a jug with the equivalent of six glasses of water and carry it with her everywhere she went.

"I drank two of those jugs every day," she says. "I started feeling different almost immediately."

The weight that had stayed on so stubbornly for more than thirty years began melting away, and at the end of phase one she had lost twenty pounds.

"I was on my way," she says. "By Easter I had lost six dress sizes."

Today she is on the PRISM maintenance program and feels wonderful.

"My back doesn't hurt; I walk the mall and jump rope. My body is healthier than it was when I began having children," she says. "PRISM changed my life, and I will always be grateful. I look like a new person, and I praise the Lord for every inch I lost."

13

NEW LIFE AWAITS YOU!

The Encouragement to Begin and to Persevere

YOU'VE REACHED THE POINT WHERE YOU ARE ARMED with every tool to ensure your success on the PRISM Weight Loss Program. You have read and related to the stories of food addiction and overweight in the lives of others. You have come to the realization—if you hadn't before—that you have a food addiction, or at the very least a problem with overeating. Otherwise, you would have found a way to gain control over your binge-eating, overeating, and excess weight before now. But somehow food has been more important than reaching your "right weight."

You have explored the guidelines of the PRISM Weight Loss Program and seen in them something different than you've ever tried before. You have thought about what it would mean to be transformed in your approach to eating—and not just temporarily lose weight. And you have read in this book story after story from people like yourself who finally refused to allow the problem of overweight to rule their lives. You have been inspired beyond words with their stories.

Now it is your turn.

There is no time like now to make a commitment to join the PRISM Weight Loss Program. How many years have you tried to lose weight only to gain back all you lost and more? How many times have you promised to start a new eating plan on Monday only to have the plan dissolve by Wednesday? How often have you wondered where you will shop for clothes in the coming years if you continue to gain weight as you have in the past?

It is time to stop asking yourself these questions and start asking yourself one very simple one:

Why not start PRISM now?

Imagine life free from addiction to food and the struggles of over-weight. Imagine what it would be like to wear chic clothing and feel healthy and full of energy. Imagine the hope you would offer to others in your family and circle of friends. What freedom there will be for you and others like you once you have made the decision to rid yourself of the problem of overeating and overweight!

If you are like most people who choose to begin the PRISM Weight Loss Program, the following statements will very likely be true for you one day:

- You will be transformed in the way you think about food.

- You will be transformed in the way you think about yourself.

- You will be slender, fit, energetic, and healthier than before.

- You will be able to wear a new wardrobe.

- You will be free from addiction to food, especially sugar and white flour products.

- You will understand what triggers food binges, and you will have learned ways to prevent them.

Are you excited? Are you brimming with enthusiasm about the changes that are about to take place in you?

This is the beginning of a changed life for you. It's time to make a decision that will help you for a lifetime take care of the one body you've been given for this lifetime.

Remember, there are two weeks of lesson plans at the end of this book. If you have already purchased your food scale and calorie-count book, you may decide to start tomorrow. You can sign the Agreement of Resolution in appendix C and get started. Tomorrow! How wonderful to know that change and transformation and lasting weight loss are so close at hand.

If this is you, if you are ready to begin, then please make the call to PRISM so you can get connected with a local group. That number is 1-800-755-1738. You will need six weeks of lessons in order to complete phase one of the PRISM Weight Loss Program. And, as you have already learned, the workbooks will be issued upon registration in a PRISM small group. To find out the location of your nearest PRISM small group, call PRISM at 1-800-755-1738.

In the meantime, let's get started!

SPECIAL ENCOURAGEMENT FOR SPECIAL CASES

For the person who is more than one hundred pounds overweight, the PRISM program does something many programs cannot do: It offers hope.

If you are such a person, you may think of yourself as a failure. You may have tried every weight loss program available, only to remain in bondage to overeating and overweight. We want you to know that it is possible to stay with a program that will transform your eating and your thinking. It is possible to find freedom from overweight and food addiction.

First, you must realize that the PRISM program is not exactly like any other program. Even now you may be thinking that PRISM sounds good but would never work. You may find yourself silently saying, *Oh, that's too much work. I can't write down what I eat.... A workbook lesson? That'll be too hard.... I could try it but it will never work....*

These are the voices that will keep you trapped in an overweight body. They will keep you at the mercy of the problem of overweight. We have been there, and we know the discouragement that accompanies excessive overweight. You have trouble fitting in an airplane seat, and the restroom is out of the question. You worry that even the big-women and tall-men stores will not have your size, and you fear you may have a heart attack the next time you have to climb a flight of stairs.

For you, losing weight is not merely a matter of becoming the TRUE YOU and reaching your "right weight." It is a matter of life or death.

One woman who lost nearly a hundred pounds on PRISM put it this way: "I had learned that I could not succeed at any program for any length of time. I could not be successful. Then I found the PRISM program. I learned how to think differently about myself, how to believe it was possible to reach my goal. And finally, after years of despair, I had hope. My weight loss is a victory, but by far the greatest victory is that I don't think about food and dieting all the time. I have hope again. With God's help, I can beat my food addiction and find freedom for a lifetime."

While we have faith that you will find freedom through PRISM, there are some program alterations that may help you experience greater success. Your journey to transformation is longer, so it will inevitably take more time. We want to give you encouragement—and some crucial advice—that will help you find success in what will be the greatest months of your life.

STICK WITH THE PROGRAM!

Success on the PRISM program is always found by sticking with the guidelines. This is true for all people on the program, and we want to give special encouragement to those who have more than one hundred pounds to lose. If you are such a person, remember that the guidelines are your ally, your help. Sticking with them is something like getting on a train. You will almost certainly reach your destination, as long as you don't step off the train.

Many people with excessive weight to lose have found success in PRISM by viewing it as a rehabilitation program designed to change their approach to food and maybe even save their lives. You can view it as one step short of checking yourself into an inpatient rehab center, and that way of thinking could help motivate you to stick to the program the way a drowning man holds fast to a life preserver.

ADDITIONAL PHASES

Each phase in PRISM is six weeks long. Typically, when a person finishes the workbook for phase four, he or she continues the program using additional resources provided by PRISM. This will work for many people regardless of how much weight they have to lose. However, there are other options for the person with more than a hundred pounds to lose. Discuss these with your small group leader. In addition, the following material provides tips for those with a significant amount of excess weight. The PRISM program will be successful for these people, but there are certain ways they can be more assured of success.

CHART THE VICTORIES ALONG THE WAY

It is important that you stay encouraged. Since it will take longer for you to reach your destination and find total transformation, you must look for victories along the way.

When you are victorious, when you achieve a goal in PRISM, make sure you celebrate. At the end of each phase or after repeating phase one, buy yourself something special—new clothes or a piece of exercise equipment, maybe a journal so you can write down the new attitudes you are developing. If you have a hobby, buy supplies, take a few hours with friends or by yourself, and focus on that activity. Celebrate! Treat yourself to a facial or a massage. It is important that you don't wait until the end of your journey to acknowledge the progress you are making.

FIND ENCOURAGEMENT IN SCRIPTURE

When you are in the midst of something difficult and worthwhile like losing more than one hundred pounds, we believe it is crucial that you find hope and encouragement in the Scriptures. When you come across a verse that particularly speaks to you as you journey toward transformation, memorize it. Repeat it over and over during that week or that phase. You will be amazed at the strength and staying power available to you through God's Word.

USE YOUR TIME WISELY

One of the adages that always seems to help people who have a longer journey of weight loss is that time will pass anyway. You must choose whether you will use time to transform your eating habits and help you become the person you were created to be, or whether you will allow time to slip by while you continue in your problem of overeating and overweight.

TAKE IT A DAY AT A TIME

For most people in this situation, failure has been such a part of their lives that they can no longer bring themselves to trust in another weight loss plan. Equally depressing for such a person is that it may take more than a year for them to reach their "right weight."

If you fall into this category, you may be viewing the road ahead in a way that exhausts you. All those days, all those weeks and months, maybe even a year or more. *Impossible!* you tell yourself. *Impossible!*

Thoughts like those have caused you to give up hope in the past, but it doesn't have to be that way anymore. In the PRISM program you will take one day at a time. You will not be allowed to read ahead in your workbook, nor should you ever skip a lesson. In this way, the days and weeks and even months will never seem ominous. There is too much attention given to the day at hand to have time to worry about next week.

Finally, no matter how many times you have failed or fallen off a previous plan, take the attitude that this time will be different. You will not only be changing what you eat, you will be changing your entire approach to food and the way you think about yourself and your eating habits. All the while you will have the support and encouragement of those in your group. You are not alone.

It is time to stop the negative self-talk and set your mind on the truth. You are a successful, intelligent person who has it within yourself to make a decision, once and for all, to change your eating habits and maintain that change for a lifetime. It is a matter of choice and absolutely within your ability to make those changes, starting now.

If staying with the PRISM program is like getting on a train that will take you to the destination you've only dreamed of, then listen closely. I think I hear a train whistle in the distance. Isn't it time to get on board?

IF YOU SHOULD STUMBLE...

Because of the Agreement of Resolution and the success available in accountability, it was difficult to decide whether to include this section in the PRISM book. We chose to include it because we are all human and, because of that, we fail rather consistently.

We believe you will be successful on the PRISM program if you stay within the guidelines. One of those guidelines states that you are not permitted to have one bite of the foods not allowed in any given phase.

Let's look at a few scenarios where that could happen.

Say you begin the PRISM program, and your first week in phase one goes something like this:

Day one: You read workbook lesson; eat within food and calorie guidelines; drink plenty of water.

Day two: You skip workbook lesson; eat within food and calorie guidelines; drink plenty of water.

Day three: You do Day two and Day three workbook lessons; run out of time and fail to write down the food you ate; guess that you are probably within the calorie guidelines.

Day four: You skip workbook lesson; avoid writing down the food you eat; guess at calories and realize you are probably over the program limits.

Day five: You attempt to catch up on the workbook; skip breakfast in a hurry to get to work; succumb and eat three slices of pizza at lunch time.

If this is how your first week on phase one looks, you are not ready for the PRISM program. Perhaps you need to take time alone to think over your past problems with overweight and dieting. Maybe your problem isn't as bad as you first thought. Maybe you have only five pounds to lose and really need only to increase your activity level in order to maintain your "right weight."

But most likely, you are simply not ready to face your food addiction.

If you are more than 20 percent over your right weight and are unable to get through a successful first week on phase one, you need to discontinue your efforts. Next you need to take a look at your commitment level—how badly you want real and lasting change in this area of your life.

Let's look at another scenario.

SITUATIONS BEYOND YOUR CONTROL

Let's assume you have stayed on the PRISM program successfully for two complete phases, but midway through the third phase, you have a week that is fairly crazy. Let's take a look at such a week and how it might affect your commitment to the PRISM program.

Day one: You do the workbook lesson. Midway through the morning you get a call saying that your father in California has suffered a heart attack and is in the hospital. He is in critical condition. You make quick travel arrangements, dress, pack for you and the kids, and hit the red-eye flight to Los Angeles by 10:35 that evening.

Day two: You forgot your PRISM workbook in your haste to get the family out the door and to the plane on time. You pray for strength and find some scrap paper to keep track of your food and caloric intake. Since you want to be at the hospital by 9:00 A.M., you skip breakfast and set out for a long day's bedside vigil. Amidst the sorrow of tending to your sick father, you eat two meals at the hospital cafeteria. Eggs and toast for breakfast and chef's salad for lunch. You choose carefully, selecting whole wheat toast and avoiding the croutons in the chef's salad.

Day three: You have lost the scrap of paper on which you scribbled your daily food intake and decide to keep track in your head. After all, you've been doing this for quite some time and can probably do it in your sleep. You reason that there are more pressing matters at hand and that whatever you wind up eating this week will not end your PRISM experience, nor your transformation. That day you have again eaten in the hospital cafeteria. You eat a hamburger for lunch, remove the bun and add an apple to your plate. Dinner offers two choices: spaghetti or chicken with an unfamiliar sauce. Since spaghetti has pasta—made with white flour—you opt for the chicken and hope there isn't anything too bad in the sauce. Just in case, you scrape off much of it. You avoid the cheesecake and pastry rack and stick to drinking water instead of sodas.

Day four: Your father takes a turn for the better. It looks like he will recover after all, and you and the kids are thankful. You spend the day at the hospital again, and you eat a cheese quiche, removing the bottom crust, and a bowl of beef stew which doesn't seem to have any flour products. That night you and the kids catch another red-eye back to Chicago, arriving at 6:00 A.M.

Day five: It's Friday, and a neighbor offers to take the children so you can sleep. You wake up at two that afternoon and realize you're out of the eggs and oatmeal you generally like to eat for breakfast on the PRISM program. Instead you have a bowl of cereal and assess the situation. You decide to take an hour and make up your missed workbook lessons, filling in the food sheet to the best of your memory. In doing so, you commit to telling the truth and look forward to being back on track.

You did not intend to disregard the PRISM program guidelines. You were bombarded by circumstances that went way beyond your regular routine—and your control—and as a result, you had a blip on the screen of progress.

Had you chosen during that time to throw the program out the window and eat cakes and pastries and all manner of sugar-laden, highly refined carbohydrate foods, it would have been a willful choice to break the program guidelines. Instead, you ate from the choices available to you at the hospital and were unsure if the food you consumed had any forbidden ingredients. Still, in your heart you knew you had made the healthiest choices available, and you were ready to jump right back into the program guidelines the moment you returned home to your normal routine.

Breaking program guidelines is a heart issue—a matter of intent versus circumstances that are out of our control.

It is important that we do our best to avoid situations where we break the PRISM guidelines, but certainly there are times when we cannot do so. Illness, busy days, houseguests, vacations, and other life events interrupt our usual schedules and must be taken into consideration in planning for the PRISM program. But these expected interruptions must not be used as excuses to willfully deviate from the program guidelines.

Remember, if you find yourself slipping out of the program guidelines, be sure to take stock of the situation and get back within them as soon as possible. Your group leader will almost always be able to advise you how to be ready for unexpected interruptions in life. If your leader is unsure, she may contact the PRISM corporate office at any time.

Your leader or accountability partner are there to help you if you have willingly chosen to break the program guidelines but want to be more serious in your commitment to change.

PREPARING TO SUCCEED

Since most PRISM groups begin a new phase every six weeks, if you take yourself off a phase of the program, you may have to wait a while before starting PRISM again. During this waiting period, it is important that you gear up for success. Analyze why you were unwilling to stay within the program guidelines the first time. Then make corrections where they are needed. The following is a list of reasons why people sometimes choose to take themselves off a phase in the PRISM program:

- Failure to purchase the right foods prior to starting the program

- Failure to purchase a food scale, calorie guide book, or measuring cups

- Failure to devote ten minutes each day to the workbook lesson

- Failure to pray about your commitment to the PRISM program

- Failure to take seriously the Agreement of Resolution

- Failure to get hooked up with a PRISM group in your area

- Failure to be honest about every aspect of your eating behavior

- Resorting to guesswork

Guessing about your calorie totals or food intake gives you the impression you have failed, even if that impression is false. Once you feel that you have failed, you will willingly eat the wrong foods. This progression starts with guesswork.

You Are Not a Failure!

Always remember that although you may have been sidetracked on your journey to transformation through PRISM, you are not a failure. You may have failed to adhere to certain aspects of the program. You may have failed to prepare for a successful start on the PRISM program. But you are not a failure. You are a treasure, a wonderful creation hand-knit by a holy God who does not make mistakes. The Bible says he has known you since before you were conceived.

Through God alone, you can find strength to pick yourself up, dust yourself off, and start again. He created you to be free from overweight and to have a "right weight." You must learn to identify with that image, the one he has for you, as you gear up to start the PRISM program again, this time with a deeper commitment.

Here are some ways you can give yourself a better chance at success the second time around with the PRISM Program:

Purchase the correct foods, scale, and calorie guide book ahead of time. Do not put this off. Once you have chosen a day to begin the PRISM program, take that date seriously and have the items in place that will help assure success.

Always avoid guesswork. Use the calorie book, scale, measuring cups, and measuring spoons. This is so you will *know* that you are staying within the program guidelines. When you guess, you have the feeling of failure. Feelings like that lead to reality. Don't guess!

Make your workbook time a priority. If you are too busy to fit the workbook lesson into your schedule, get up ten minutes earlier. You are worth the extra time and attention to detail you will need to put forth. One lesson per day will go a long way in keeping you on your journey to transformation.

Pray about your commitment and remember to read your Agreement of Resolution every day. If you feel you are being tempted to break your commitment, read your agreement twice a day. Also remember to use your TRUE YOU mirror and your "right weight" statement. The battle against overweight is won in the mind first.

Get connected with a PRISM group before starting the program. Your connection with this group must be in place when you begin. That way you will have the encouragement of and accountability to a group of people who are also going through the transformation process. You will also have a leader who will help you with any concerns, questions, or feelings of doubt you might have.

Finally, be honest with yourself. You have used food as a friend for so many years that it is time to get brutally honest. Do not allow yourself to lie about the foods you eat or the way in which you are adhering to the program guidelines. If you cannot be completely honest with yourself and your PRISM small group, then you are not yet ready to solve your problem with overeating. A very small percentage of people in this group may actually need professional counseling, outpatient eating disorder help, or admission to an inpatient eating clinic. Check with your doctor to see if this applies to you.

DESIGNED FOR SUCCESS

So you see that although the PRISM program has been designed for success, it is possible to be ill-prepared and get off to a clumsy start or have unexpected events detour you along the journey. Either way, there is still hope for you. Make a choice to get serious about your commitment to break your food addiction. Choose to take a few weeks off and then start again, this time prepared for transformation.

Whatever you do, don't give up. The PRISM program covers every aspect of weight loss so that this time you will find success, freedom, hope, and the new life you've always dreamed of.

You are done with the past; finished making excuses. Finally you are truly ready to take that first step toward lasting change.

We at PRISM are excited for you! And we look forward to hearing your success stories. E-mail us at: rtnbykk@aol.com or prism@pwlp.com.

Remember, we'll be praying for you.

Appendix A

FREQUENTLY ASKED
QUESTIONS ABOUT PRISM

AS I HAVE WORKED WITH THE PRISM WEIGHT LOSS PROGRAM for the past year and talked about it with many people, I have been asked the same questions over and over. People are curious about my change in appearance and interested in how I lost the weight and how I'm keeping it off. Of course, this is also true for Toni Vogt and the staff at the PRISM corporate office.

There are a handful of questions we are asked on a regular basis. For that reason, we thought it best to anticipate those questions and provide answers in this appendix. Naturally, you may have questions that are not covered in this chapter, but we will assume that you will find the answer somewhere in the text of this book. If not, you will want to call the PRISM corporate office for additional or special information that will make your transformation that much more successful.

Can I begin the PRISM program without the workbooks?

The strength of the PRISM Weight Loss Program is not in the calorie limits or food guidelines, although these are both excellent aspects of it. The strength is in the workbooks. Most of us who have ever tried to lose weight know that 1,200 calories is a safe amount that will result in a reduction of pounds and inches. Likewise, when you cut out sugar and refined flour, you will not feel the chemical addiction that has caused you to overeat in the past. These are not necessarily new ideas.

The workbooks are.

In the workbooks you will uncover destructive patterns and negative self-talk, behaviors that sabotaged your previous weight loss attempts and kept you addicted to food. The workbooks will help you examine these issues, unravel them, and replace them with actions that will help develop the TRUE YOU, the one God created you to be. Although the workbook lesson will take only about ten minutes each morning, the truths and helps you will discover during that time will stay with you for the entire day.

In other words, yes, you can follow the PRISM Weight Loss Program without the workbooks, but you will not experience true transformation and the power to continue in the PRISM program without the workbooks.

How do I get the workbooks?

Workbooks are issued when you register in a PRISM small group. Find out where your nearest PRISM small group is by calling PRISM at 1-800-755-1738. Two weeks of workbook lessons have been included at the back of this book to get you started.

Do I have to belong to a small group?

No, but it is the surest way to accomplish lasting transformation through the PRISM Weight Loss Program. Small groups offer encouragement, advice, and accountability. They help you know that you are not alone in your battle against overweight, and they celebrate with you your victories on the road to transformation. If you are not able to join an existing group, PRISM offers a correspondence option. Call the PRISM corporate office for details.

How do I find out if there's a PRISM group meeting in my area?

The way to get hooked up with the PRISM Weight Loss Program is to call PRISM at 1-800-755-1738 and ask if there is a PRISM group meeting near you. If so, you will receive phone numbers and other information so you can locate the group meeting and begin attending. If not, you will be given several options.

First, you may choose to start a new small group at your church by seeking permission from the minister, pastor, or priest, and by having six people, including yourself, willing to begin the program.

Second, you can start or participate in a new group of two or more (including yourself) that meets at your home or work. In this situation you will still meet once a week, but the setting will be more intimate.

Finally, you will have the option of a correspondence plan whereby you will talk weekly with a PRISM representative, but otherwise work on your own.

It is important that we take a moment to recall the importance of a group meeting—even a group of two people. There is accountability in numbers that would not be there otherwise. When you know you will have to report to your group leader, coworkers, or one or two very close friends, you are much more likely to stay within the program guidelines.

Of course, ultimately you are accountable to the Lord. The agreement you make as you begin the PRISM program is one that is between you, your PRISM group leader, and God. Prayer will make a world of difference, as will memorizing various suggested Scripture readings offered in the PRISM workbooks.

God gave us each other.

The best way to experience the power of the PRISM Weight Loss Program and the transformation that will follow is to have someone to share with each week.

Why can't I have snack foods?

Snacks are always allowed on the PRISM program. Apples, carrots, cheese sticks, and other foods allowed on the program may be very important for people with hypoglycemia. Snack foods, however, are forbidden for a very specific reason. Generally we eat snack foods for all the wrong reasons, including out of boredom, to have something to do, as a way of celebrating, from habit, or to have an activity to share with a friend.

You can see that these reasons have nothing to do with hunger and nourishing the body God has given you. Because you have probably been addicted to man-made foods, sugar-laden foods, and foods high in processed or refined flour, it is crucial that you step back and take a fresh look at food and the reasons you eat.

We do not live to eat. Eating is not a valid recreational pastime, nor is it healthy to eat merely to have an activity to share with a friend. While on the PRISM Weight Loss Program you will examine these issues in detail and discover that it is enough to watch a movie without mindlessly passing your hand from a popcorn bowl to your mouth for an hour or longer.

You will learn new habits, find ways to occupy your time, and plan activities to share with a friend that will have nothing to do with food and everything to do with making healthy choices. It is part of the transformation process. From now on you will eat to live. You will enjoy your food because it is making you healthier and stronger and because it is the food God created for you to eat.

You tell me I can't have brownies and other sugary desserts when I'm on this program, but didn't God put those here for us to enjoy?

There is a misconception currently making its way around dieting circles—especially among Christians—that if we would only allow the Lord to tell us when to stop eating, we could eat anything we want. "Moderation is the answer," we're hearing. "God wouldn't have put ooey-gooey brownies on Earth if he didn't want us to eat them."

Is this so? Did God really put those brownies here?

We believe brownies have nothing to do with God. He created very specific foods for us—foods that build our health and cause us to truly enjoy life. Foods such as fruits, vegetables, 100 percent whole wheat and whole grain products. Each of these things can be found growing from God's rich earth. Protein is also on the list. God himself told man to "kill and eat" the animals among us. No animal is unclean, Scripture tells us, but is put here for our benefit.

Brownies, however, are made of hydrogenated fat, processed chocolate, refined sugar, and refined flour. *Refined* and *processed* are two words that mean, in essence, that man has tampered with it. In fact, man has changed these products so drastically that the end result looks nothing like the original. Fiber, vitamins, minerals, and health-giving goodness has been stripped from these items. In place of God's goodness, man has laden these foods with chemical additives.

Ask yourself this: Would God want us to eat man-made items that have been linked to disease and overweight—two side effects of such foods?

In fact, the best way to know whether a certain food is on the PRISM food guidelines is to ask yourself this question: Did God make it, or did man make it?

Man-made foods have left you sick, tired, overweight, and addicted to food. God-made foods will restore your health, your energy, and your body to the way God created it to be.

If I can't have brownies, isn't the PRISM program too rigid?

On the lists of foods that can be eaten on the PRISM program are hundreds of varieties and thousands of combinations. You will find that you can create plates of food with bright colors and wonderful textures and still eat a different meal each night. Check the menu section of this book.

After you have been on the PRISM program for a while, you will notice that you are no longer as concerned about eating that brownie you once craved. Your appetite will have adjusted, and your body will be free from the addiction to sugar that has kept it in bondage for so long. As this happens you will find that sometimes you want to be creative and fix something amazing for dinner. Other times a salad, chicken breast, and squash will be very satisfying—even if it isn't all that original.

Remember, food will no longer be your source of excitement. In light of that truth, brownies will lose their appeal, and you will start to consider them harmful. Bring on that crunchy cold apple, and get ready for the PRISM Weight Loss Program! Foods God created will make your weight loss journey a very satisfying one.

Many people—even many Christians—talk about program guidelines and restrictions as if they were ungodly or even sinful. To the contrary, the Bible has many references to walking the narrow road in an effort to live a godly and righteous life. While Christ did away with rules as a means to salvation, we are still admonished to treat the body with care because it is the temple of the Holy Spirit. We are taught that self-control is a fruit of the Holy Spirit, the evidence that he is indeed living in us.

Therefore, changing our diets to replace man-made, chemical-filled, sugary, flour-based foods with fruits, vegetables, whole grains, and dairy products—foods that God has made—is hardly against God's will for us.

Rather, it is one way we can incorporate self-control into our daily lives to make ourselves stronger, healthier, and more effective in our service for God's kingdom.

Won't I be thinking about food all day long if I'm asked to keep a journal of everything I eat?

Many people who begin the PRISM program have suffered from over-weight for a large portion of their lives. For these people, there is no doubt that they will actually think of food far less than they used to. Whereas once they thought about food virtually nonstop from sunup to their final conscious moments before drifting off to sleep, now they only think of food when they are preparing a meal or writing in their workbooks.

You may notice that more time is needed at first to consciously train yourself to eat and desire the foods that will make your body healthy and fit. But then it is important to realize that you are a child of God, well worth the extra time needed to develop habits that will last for a lifetime and set you free from destructive patterns and overweight.

It encourages me to step on the scale and see the progress I've made. Why are we asked to put the scale away on the PRISM program?

Many of us have lived for years in bondage to the bathroom scale. Our wardrobe, attitude, menu, and outlook on life fluctuate with the gains and losses we see when we take that frightful step onto the scale each morning.

You will be in the process of transformation, becoming the TRUE YOU, the person God created you to be. No longer will you need a scale to validate your efforts or your appearance. You will find encouragement by staying within the program guidelines and feeling your clothing grow looser. Encouragement will also come from looking at the picture of the TRUE YOU. Imagine how good it will feel when you look like you did before you gained weight, or like you know you can once you've reached your destination.

The scale is one reason you have not been successful until now. When the scale showed a significant weight loss, you used this as an excuse to give in to food binges or unhealthy eating habits. One bite led to one day, one day led to one week, and one week led to just one more diet failure. At the same time, when the scale showed no weight loss or even a dreaded weight gain, you also gave yourself permission to overeat. *Why bother?* you asked yourself. What was the point if you weren't going to lose weight anyway? According to the scale you'd probably never lose weight at all. Why try?

This mental torture comes as a result of the scale and the number you have associated with yourself every day for years, maybe even decades. It is time for transformation; time to do away with the bathroom scale. You'll be amazed at the freedom you'll feel as a result.

How do I know what my "right weight" is?

There are many ways to discover your "right weight." First, you may be a person who lived at your "right weight" for a period of time before gaining weight. In this case you will only have to remember that number or one near it. You might also come up with what you think is your "right weight" and talk it over with several close friends. Pray about the number, and ask God to show you whether it is realistic or not.

Another method would be to have a physical trainer perform a body composition analysis on you. This can then be used in a formula that will determine a "right weight" or a "right weight" range for you. From that range, you can choose a "right weight" number.

The most important thing is to check with your family doctor once you've decided on a number. He or she will be able to help you decide whether it needs to be adjusted.

You will also find that when your transformation process is well under way, your idea of your "right weight" may change. Some people in my small group found they had estimated too high. When they got closer to their goal, they realized they could lose another ten pounds and have an even healthier body.

Others had estimated too low. When the bones in your face and neck begin jutting out, and you still feel you need to keep your calories limited in order to reach your "right weight," then most likely you have set an unrealistic goal.

As one woman who was successful on PRISM put it, "As I got closer to my 'right weight' I didn't need the scales to tell me how I was doing. My clothes fit better, and I looked better overall. The mirror was my way of knowing when I reached my 'right weight.' And now it's my way of maintaining."

If the scale is not important, why do I need to choose a "right weight" at all?

Although the scale is not important in the process of transformation while on the PRISM program, a "right weight" number is necessary. This is because you have long identified with a number that does not represent the TRUE YOU. This number is higher than you'd like and discouraging. Attaching it to your self-image is a negative thing to do and you must stop doing it.

Instead, look at your "right weight" picture several times a day and repeat the number out loud. You will eat and think and see yourself as a person who has one number attached to your body image—the number of your "right weight."

Therefore the "right weight" number is part of the transformation process—the part that helps you replace negative self-talk and develop a new understanding and reality in the way you view yourself, your food, and your eating habits.

I want to start the PRISM Weight Loss Program, but I have a graduation coming up, and two weeks after that I'm in my friend's wedding. The next month I'm scheduled for knee surgery. Should I wait until I have a stretch of time with no major events to distract me from my weight loss efforts?

No! If you feel motivated, there is no time like the present to start the PRISM program. The only waiting you should do is to allow yourself time to determine whether you are serious about losing weight and keeping it off. You also need time to prepare by purchasing the right food and tools necessary to follow the PRISM program. Once you have made the decision, you must connect with PRISM to find out if there is a group meeting near you. Then you must start. You owe it to yourself. After months and years and sometimes decades of living at the mercy of overweight, buried under pounds of excess weight, it is finally time to break free.

As for the social events on the horizon, they will always be there. Birthdays, anniversaries, special celebrations, promotions, holidays—the list is endless. If you wait for a time when nothing out of the ordinary is happening, you will wait for a lifetime.

How am I supposed to survive these special events and still remain on the PRISM program?

The workbook lessons will help you understand that the reason we gather with friends and family for celebration is not because of food. Although our society has made food the cornerstone and sometimes the centerpiece of such celebrations, that is not the way you will view special events in the future.

You will learn how to strike up special conversations and engage in interesting discussions. Making memories with loved ones will become more important than getting an extra helping of Grandma's chocolate cake. This may be difficult to believe if you are currently trapped by the problem of overweight. But you will feel amazing freedom once you are able to look forward to the people and not the food at a special event. When you are able to enter the room with a burst of energy and stylish new clothing, you will wonder how Grandma's chocolate cake ever held you captive for so many years.

On a practical note, here are some tips that will help you keep your focus while you celebrate with friends and stick to the PRISM program:

Bring a vegetable tray. So often this item is overlooked at parties, but it is always a hit. Find a tasty low-calorie dressing and place a decorative bowl of it in the center of a tray. Surround it with carrot sticks, celery sticks, and more exotic items such as olives, dill pickles, jicama root, bell peppers, radishes, raw green beans, cauliflower, broccoli, or mushrooms.

Hold your conversations in rooms where food is not the main attraction. Most parties or get-togethers involve action in several rooms. You must make a point to spend your time around the upstairs pool table or share in discussion on a comfortable sofa in the living room. If the weather is nice, be one of the guests that finds a breezy spot outdoors to visit with others.

Whatever you do, don't wind up anchored at the food table chatting. Remember, this is your old spot, the one from where you could watch what everyone ate and manage to sneak twice as much food as the others simply because you had no distance to travel to reach the food trays.

Suggest a game. When gathered together with friends and family— especially at events that have previously centered around food—take a chance and suggest a game or activity. Perhaps everyone would be interested in a group word game or board game. If the weather is nice, suggest a friendly game of softball, Frisbee, or tennis. If there are children involved, perhaps the group would be interested in tag or hide-and-seek. When an outdoor game doesn't seem appropriate, suggest a walk around the block. Sometimes the most memorable conversations take place during a walk—a walk you would have missed if you were anchored at the food table.

Prepare yourself. You must think about the special event beforehand in order to remain successful. Think about what might be served, what might have previously tempted you, and what might still be tempting.

For instance, if it is a wedding, you can almost be sure that wedding cake will be served. If cake is a food that has triggered overeating in the past, plan to avoid this moment as best as possible. Perhaps when you see that the cake is being served, you can take a few minutes to freshen up in the restroom. Maybe you can choose that time to dance with your brother—something you may not have done for years. If you do not choose to be away from the table, at least you will be ready.

Sometimes you will have to bring food to such an event. Carry a purse or bag large enough to contain a ripe apple or rice cakes with a tablespoon of natural peanut butter spread on each. That way, when the cake-serving moment arrives, you can pull out a healthy food choice or even a piece of gum.

See beyond the event. Part of why we tend to break diets at a celebration or special event is because we forget that there will be countless celebrations to follow. We somehow convince ourselves that there will never be an opportunity like the present to have that wedding cake or homemade dish.

We must remember that the item tempting us is only food. If it were good food, God-made food, you could eat it and still be within the PRISM guidelines. But if it is not food your body needs, food that is not permitted on the program, you should substitute the food you brought when you planned ahead of time.

Make special requests. You may have trained yourself to believe that special requests are for picky people. Perhaps you do not believe that making special food requests is necessary—even while on a life-changing program like PRISM. This is a way of thinking that will disappear as the transformation process takes hold in your life.

You are worth every extra step it takes for you to be successful on the PRISM program. You do not need to be pushy in order to make requests that pertain to your way of eating. Be polite, friendly, humble, but firm. Your entire life will improve as a result, and nothing is more important right now than walking in obedience to what God has set before you in this marvelous program.

While at a hospital, for instance, you can choose virtually every aspect of your meals. When traveling by air, you can call ahead and order a special meal. Restaurants often serve lower-calorie foods that may not be listed on the menu, and they generally have calorie values available. Ask for your chicken to be cooked over a flame instead of fried. Order vegetables without butter or oil. Request that the breading on a piece of fish be left off.

Remember, it is your body, your life. You have decided to take the step to start the PRISM program and to change your life. It is crucial that you also take the time to make special requests whenever possible to ensure your adherence to the PRISM guidelines.

What about fast foods on the PRISM program?

The PRISM program is designed to be a part of your everyday lifestyle. It does not include prepackaged meals or powdered drinks. Rather, it teaches you how to eat correctly in any situation. Still, it is crucial that people just starting out on PRISM avoid fast-food restaurants. Many people with excessive weight to lose enjoy eating fast foods—especially with one another. If you have more than a hundred pounds to lose, you probably have many food memories and poor habits associated with fast food. Therefore, it is essential that you avoid all fast-food stops while you are still more than one hundred pounds from your "right weight." Remember, you are in a self-imposed rehabilitation program, which, thankfully, allows you to live at home with your family. If you treat the PRISM program that seriously, you will not even desire to eat fast food. You may, however, dine out at quality restaurants with menu items allowed on the PRISM program. These items include broiled chicken, fish, or beef without breading or sauces, steamed vegetables, and salad without croutons.

For many people, even this type of dining out may cause difficulty in the early stages of PRISM. Perhaps the bread basket and after-dinner dessert tray are too tempting. Know yourself well enough to avoid this type of dining if it is a problem for you.

You must protect yourself and your place in the PRISM program.

What can I do if I want to eat out at a nice restaurant?

Obviously there will be times while you are on the PRISM program when you will eat out. You will find better success in this if you follow these guidelines:

Plan your menu ahead of time. If it is a familiar restaurant, try to get a calorie count figured out so there will be no guesswork once you are seated at the table. Japanese, Mexican, Chinese, and American Grill type restaurants will be the best for finding food choices within the PRISM program guidelines.

Eat chicken or fish. Most boneless breasts of chicken are less than 200 calories as long as it is charbroiled and no sauce has been added. Fish is also low in calories as long as it is not breaded or fried. Ask the waiter how many ounces of fish or chicken are in your portion. Most restaurants have this information easily available and an accurate weight will help you make an accurate calorie total.

Eat salad with light dressing on the side and no croutons. The more greens the better. Not only do they fill you up, they also give you a way to eat in a social setting without looking different or odd because you are on a program.

Ask for fresh steamed vegetables. You will not be able to eat potatoes on the first phase, and none of the phases allow white bread or starchy side dishes. Because of this, you need to ask for substitutes. Be sure to ask that the steamed vegetables be free of butter or oil. Some come with butter unless you ask them to leave it off.

Eat shrimp cocktail. This is basically jumbo shrimp on ice, and it has very few calories and almost no fat. Skip the tangy sauce, which has sugar, and use lemons instead.

Is it better if I stay away from restaurants altogether?

Again, the best rule of thumb for people with excess weight to lose is to avoid fast food completely and dine out only on special occasions. Whatever you decide, know your strengths and weaknesses and stay away from what is too great a temptation. For now, the most important thing is realizing the TRUE YOU and your "right weight."

Do I need to be religious in order to be successful on the PRISM Weight Loss Program?

Toni Vogt, president of PRISM, and writer Karen Kingsbury are Christians. Both feel very strongly that any transformation that is lasting and life-changing will ultimately include God. However, the workbook lessons are designed to work for everyone. Whether you have a faith or not, these lessons will work for you. Each lesson includes suggested topical Scripture readings for that day. Although these are optional, they are highly motivational and have the power to bring you closer to God and give you a greater, God-given strength than you would otherwise have.

Do I need to be a praying person in order to be successful on PRISM?

It is not required that you pray for your success. However, if praying is something you have never done, it might be worthwhile to give it a try. God is listening, whether you're talking to him or not. It seems logical that at this moment—a crucial crossroads of your life—you might actually want to talk to God.

Bev Smallwood

60 pound weight loss

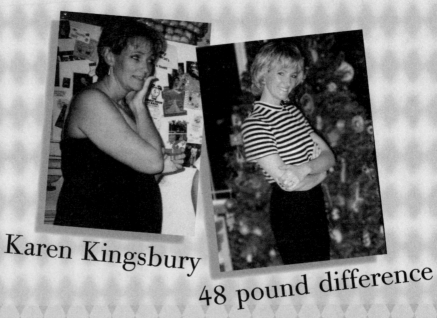

Karen Kingsbury

48 pound difference

Appendix B

THE ADVENTURE OF COOKING WITH PRISM

THOSE OF US WHO HAVE BEEN ON VARIOUS weight loss programs before PRISM usually have strong preferences about recipes. Others look forward to the recipe section and rely on it to find success on an eating program.

When I finally had the chance to put all my personal weight loss experience and the wonderful transforming truths from the PRISM program into a book, I did not plan to include recipes. This is mainly because I am not one to spend much time in the kitchen. I am a wife, mother, PTSA volunteer, writer, and spokesperson. I am thankful to be married to a man who doesn't mind having sliced turkey sandwiches for dinner a couple times a week.

Still, I drew on my experience with the PRISM program and the helpful tips from other PRISM members and was able to pull together a handful of recipes that should get you thinking about what you will be eating.

MEASURING ACCURATELY

When you use the recipes in this section, remember to measure accurately all the ingredients and the serving sizes.

With a few exceptions (mostly in the section covering recipes from the PRISM Weight Loss Cookbook), most of these recipes are designed for single servings and will match the calorie totals given in chapter 12. These recipes can be prepared in larger quantities, but I expect it would be much more difficult to determine caloric amounts that way. In that case, make sure you measure serving sizes accurately.

I suggest that you cook your food portions separately as much as possible. For example, rather than make a casserole with multiple chicken breasts, a jar of pasta sauce, and a cup of shredded cheese on top, prepare foods separately. If you have six in your family, cook six chicken breasts. Cook the sauce separately on the stove top and when both are ready, use a measuring cup to dole out the sauce on your piece of chicken. Measure your cheese the same way and dish up the other plates after that.

Cooking on the PRISM program can be as adventurous as any other type of cooking. By experimenting with spices and food combinations (being careful to keep track of the caloric values of the ingredients you use), you can make cooking and eating both enjoyable and rewarding.

FIVE-MINUTE RECIPES

The following recipes are simple, and most of the dishes take less than five minutes to prepare and cook. This is what works best for my lifestyle, but you can work them into your own schedule in whatever way works best for you.

For example, if you prefer fresh kidney beans in your chili, put your beans to soak the night before, and proceed from there. Being busy and desiring to spend as much time as possible with my family, I tend to open a can of kidney beans, drain the juice and measure.

It's up to you to tailor this part of the program around your interests, schedule, and preferences. Some days you may want to soak your beans; on others you may reach for the can opener, wondering why there isn't a faster way to get them from the can to the stove.

Also, feel free to substitute or be creative within these recipes. So long as you stay within the PRISM program guidelines, you may use these recipes just to get you thinking; from there, create your own recipes.

For instance, if you like hot cooked barley instead of wheat, adjust the caloric values and use barley. If you like water chestnuts instead of celery in your tuna salad, use water chestnuts and adjust the caloric values. Chopped dates instead of bananas also add fiber and sweetness to hot cereal—again adjust the caloric values. The possibilities are endless.

Wonder Omelet   Calories: 250

A friend at my local PRISM meeting told me about this recipe. She said she ate it every day for several weeks and it seemed to virtually eliminate her sugar cravings for the remainder of the day. It also took away her appetite. I made it several times on Phase one. It's a wonderful, high-protein omelet that fills an entire plate and is a great way to start your day.

Although it looks complicated at first, it's very simple and can be prepared in about seven minutes.

Ingredients:

2 eggs

2 oz. lean sausage

2 egg whites

3 tbs. chopped onion

1 slice nonfat cheese

(handwritten: 140, 72, 28, 35, 275)

(handwritten: 2T. light cheddar)

In a bowl, mix the two eggs and two egg whites with a hand-mixer and set aside.

Spray a frying pan with no-fat nonstick vegetable spray and cook over medium heat. Add chopped sausage and onion. Sauté until onions are clear. Set the mixture aside.

Pour the egg mixture into a hot empty skillet so that pan is covered evenly. When eggs are partially cooked, add sausage and onion. Tear nonfat cheese slice into strips. When eggs begin to look cooked through, take sliced cheese and spread evenly over half the egg mixture. Flip half of the egg mixture over so that the inside is covered. Cook to desired doneness.

* * * * *

Crunchy Chicken Salad   Calories: 250

Sometimes, especially when you first begin the PRISM program, you will feel as though you want to spend some time chewing. This is probably because your food intake has suddenly been cut in half, and although you will absolutely NOT be hungry on the PRISM Program, you may occasionally want to eat something more substantial than a rice cake.

Crunchy Chicken Salad (and its cousins, Crunchy Turkey Salad, and Crunchy Tuna Salad) are perfect for those days.

Also, sometimes it's nice to have a lunch that takes longer than five minutes to eat. This one takes a while and is incredibly good for you.

You can follow this recipe or add dozens of different crunchy chopped vegetables to make this a filling, healthy meal that takes as long to eat as some of your binge-meals of old.

On the days I ate this salad, I felt I could run three miles after lunch— and sometimes I did.

Ingredients:

    4 oz. diced cooked chicken

    1 tbs. lowfat mayonnaise

    2 tbs. mustard (spicy mustard is good)

    1 finely chopped medium apple

    2 chopped dill pickles

    2 chopped baby carrots

Mix all ingredients in a bowl. Serve on a bed of chilled lettuce or spinach greens.

* * * * *

Chicken Caesar Salad   *Calories: 215*

This is another tasty, satisfying salad recipe.

Ingredients:

    4 oz. cubed cooked chicken breast

    2 hard-boiled egg whites, chopped

    2 tbs. light Caesar dressing

    1 tbs. Parmesan cheese

Mix all ingredients in a bowl. Serve on chilled lettuce or spinach greens.

Scrambled Eggs à la Mushroom   *Calories: 240*

When I was growing up, back when I vied for a seventh of all the
gooey sugary foods my family ate, my mother cooked scrambled eggs
one way only: with lots of butter. The theory was this made the eggs
moist and tender.

The fact is, while butter leaves a slippery oily substance on the surface of the eggs, it definitely does not make them softer.

I learned the REAL way to have tender scrambled eggs from my
mother-in-law, Phyllis Cummins, who is quite the cook.

"The trick is water," she once told me.

I took her advice—and not just because she is my mother-in-law—
and voilà! Incredibly tender scrambled eggs.

Another tip: Don't overcook.

Ingredients:
    2 eggs
    1/2 cup chopped mushrooms
    2 egg whites
    1 oz. lowfat mozzarella cheese
    3 tbs. water

Whip eggs, egg whites, cheese, and water. Set aside. Spray a skillet
with nonstick spray. Cook over medium heat. Add mushrooms and
sauté until cooked. Turn down flame. Add egg mixture and cook to
desired doneness.

* * * * *

Fiesta Mexicana Salad   *Calories: 320*

Every now and then it's nice to eat something a little different. The PRISM
program allows for this because it is designed for a lifetime. While there
are many ways to eat Mexican food within the PRISM program guidelines,
here is one option. It's a quick one, too. Preparation time: less than five
minutes (unless you feel like making your own homemade refried beans).

Ingredients:
>   1 cup refried nonfat beans
>   2 oz. chopped chicken
>   1 cup canned tomatoes—no sugar added
>   1 oz. shredded lowfat cheese
>   3 cups salad greens

In a microwave-safe bowl, mix all ingredients except for the cheese and salad greens. Place in microwave and heat. Spread 3 cups of salad greens over a serving plate, spoon out the bean mixture over greens, and sprinkle shredded cheese on top.

* * * * *

Bubba's Baked Apple   *Calories: 70*

When you want the smell of baked apples without the traditional pie, this is a family favorite. It's extremely low in calories, but warm, sweet, filling, and filled with vitamins and fiber.
Ingredients:
>   1 large Rome apple
>   1 tsp. cinnamon

Core the apple without splitting the fruit. Sprinkle cinnamon on the outside and inside of the apple. Wrap in foil. Place in a casserole dish lightly coated with nonstick spray and bake at 400 degrees for forty minutes.

* * * * *

Chicken Parmesan   *Calories: 310*

This is a filling, nutritious item that is great for your evening meal. It's also incredibly quick and easy to prepare (unless, of course, you make your own sauce).

Ingredients:

    1 cooked chicken breast—4 oz.

    1 cup pasta sauce (If you purchase the sauce, make sure there is no sugar in it, unless it's listed fifth or further down on the ingredient list.)

    1 oz. Parmesan cheese

Place steaming hot chicken breast on a serving plate and cover with hot pasta sauce. Sprinkle Parmesan cheese on top.

* * * * *

Susan's Famous Oatmeal   Calories: 300

This oatmeal is perfectly balanced in protein and carbohydrates. The recipe makes a very large bowl, and although you may be unable to finish it at one sitting, it is only 300 calories and a favorite at my home.

My sister Susan, who is also finding amazing freedom and success in the PRISM program, invented this recipe. She used to cook it in the microwave—until the day of the "Oatmeal Adventure."

That day she accidentally left the oatmeal and egg whites cooking in the microwave for fourteen minutes instead of four. When she pulled it out, it looked like a miniature piece of plastic play food. She stared at it long and hard and finally poked her fork into it. It exploded all over the refrigerator, walls, cupboards, as well as her clothes, face, and hair.

Thankfully, no one was injured, and she now cooks her oatmeal in a saucepan. (Even so, you may choose to microwave it. Send your humorous stories to our e-mail addresses.)

Ingredients:

    1/2 cup oatmeal

    4 whipped egg whites

    2 cups water

    1 medium chopped banana

    1 tsp. cinnamon

    1 tsp. vanilla

Spray a saucepan with nonstick spray. Add the water, oatmeal, chopped banana, cinnamon, vanilla. Bring to a boil. Stir constantly for two minutes. Add the whipped egg whites, or, to save time, unbeaten whites directly to the oatmeal. Bring to a boil. Stir for one more minute. The oatmeal will have the texture of tapioca pudding and will leave you feeling full way past lunchtime.

* * * * *

Crunchy Turkey Salad   Calories: 250

A favorite during the holidays or any time.
    Ingredients:
        4 oz. diced cooked white turkey
        2 tbs. lowfat mayonnaise
        1 tbs. mustard (spicy mustard is a good option)
        4 chopped black olives
        1 chopped dill pickle
        1/4 cup chopped sweet onion

Mix all ingredients in a bowl. Serve on chilled lettuce or spinach greens.

* * * * *

Crunchy Tuna Salad   Calories: 250

You may recognize some similarities between my chunky salads. If so, then you've been paying careful attention.

During the first phase of the PRISM program, it is important to find variety where you can get it, and these three salads offer variety—albeit very little. For a creative change, try mixing and matching the extra ingredients and allow yourself some creativity (see list below). Be certain to vary your protein foods as well. This keeps you from getting in a rut that may lead to self-sabotage.

Ingredients:
    4 oz. white tuna—packed in water
    2 tbs. lowfat mayonnaise
    2 tbs. capers
    1/4 cup chopped celery
    3 chopped baby carrots

Mix all ingredients in a bowl. Serve on chilled lettuce or spinach greens.

Other ingredients that may be added to the crunchy salads are:
Broccoli   Cauliflower
Sweet peppers   Mushrooms
Grapes   Other fruit or vegetables
Sliced raw almonds or walnuts

If you add these ingredients, be sure to count the calories, however few.

* * * * *

Scrambled Eggs à la Canada   *Calories: 325*

Ingredients:
    2 eggs
    2 egg whites
    2 oz. diced ham
    3 tbs. water
    2 oz. lowfat mozzarella cheese

In a bowl, beat eggs and add water, ham, and cheese. Set aside. Spray a skillet with nonstick spray and cook over medium heat. Add egg mixture. Wait one minute, then reduce heat to low. Stir occasionally, cooking to desired doneness.

Rib-Sticking Chili Con Carne   *Calories: 300*

A couple I know, who together have lost far more than a hundred pounds, make this quite often. They multiply the recipe a dozen times, stir up a large, steaming pot, and then draw cupfuls each time they want a hot and hearty meal.

The advantage to this is that once it's measured and cooked, it makes a quick meal. The disadvantage is that there is really only one way to determine how many calories are in such a large batch. Count them all as they go in, then measure how many cups the entire pot holds. Simple division will give you the only accurate calorie count.

If you choose to make the following smaller batch, you can be certain of the calorie count without the added mathematical challenge.

Ingredients:

    2 oz. browned lean ground beef
    1/2 cup kidney beans
    1 cup canned tomatoes
    2 tsp. chili powder
    salt
    pepper

Mix all ingredients in a bowl and heat on stove-top or in microwave until steaming hot.

* * * * *

Cowboy Creamed Wheat   *Calories: 320*

I personally enjoy the oatmeal more, but when you need a change or a moment of variety, this is another favorite. You'll find that the texture is grainier than the oatmeal and that it takes longer to eat.

Ingredients:

    1/3 cup uncooked Grape Nuts
    2 cups water
    4 egg whites
    1/2 banana

1/2 cup applesauce
1 tsp. cinnamon
1 tsp. vanilla

Spray a saucepan with nonstick spray. Add water, uncooked cereal, banana, applesauce, cinnamon, and vanilla. Bring to a boil. Cook one minute, stirring constantly. Add egg whites (either whipped or straight from the shell depending on your time). Bring to a boil. Cook one more minute, stirring constantly.

PRISM WEIGHT LOSS COOKBOOK RECIPES

Here are some recipes from the PRISM Weight Loss Cookbook. If you are looking for more sophisticated recipes that work within the PRISM program, contact the PRISM office at 1-800-755-1738 and ask about the PRISM cookbook. It is filled with great ideas and delicious, satisfying recipes. Categories include: Appetizers; Soups; Salads; Meatless Main Dishes; Meats; Fish and Poultry; Vegetables; and Side Dishes.

Chili Relleno Casserole

*Calories: 216 per serving
(6.1 grams of fat)*

Eight servings
Ingredients:
    1 cup evaporated milk
    4 egg whites
    3 tbs. cornstarch
    3 4-oz. cans whole green chilies
    1 8-oz. can tomato sauce
    1/2 lb. lowfat jack cheese, grated
    1/2 lb. lowfat sharp cheddar cheese, grated

Preheat oven to 350 degrees. Spray a deep 1–1/2 quart casserole dish with vegetable oil cooking spray. Beat evaporated milk, egg whites, and cornstarch until smooth. Split open chilies and rinse to remove seeds; drain on a paper towel. Mix cheeses together and reserve 1/2 cup for topping. Alternate layers of chilies, cheese, and egg mixture in casserole dish. Pour tomato sauce over top layer and sprinkle with reserved cheese. Bake one hour or until done in the center.

* * * * *

Easy Chili

Calories: 257 per serving
(5 grams of fat)

Six one-cup servings
Ingredients:
    1 medium onion
    1/2 lb. lean ground beef
    4 cups kidney beans, cooked
    2 cups stewed tomatoes
    1/2 green pepper, diced
    Chili powder to taste
    Tabasco to taste (optional)
    Jalapeño peppers to taste (optional)

Sauté onion. Brown ground beef and drain. Mix all ingredients together and season to taste. Simmer for fifteen minutes. Serve hot.

This spicy dish is great with or without meat. To vary, add 1/2 cup cooked brown rice and 110 calories to your count.

Pizza-Baked Fish

Calories: 221
(8 grams of fat)

Two servings
Ingredients:
  1/2 lb. fresh or frozen skinless rockfish or red snapper
  fillets
  1/2 cup sliced fresh mushrooms
  1/4 cup chopped onion
  1 clove garlic, minced
  1/4 cup water
  3 tbs. tomato paste
  1/2 tsp. dried basil, crushed
  1/2 tsp. dried oregano, crushed
  1/4 tsp. fennel seed
  1/8 tsp. crushed red pepper
  nonstick spray coating
  4 green pepper rings
  1/2 cup (2 oz.) shredded part-skim mozzarella cheese

Thaw fish, if frozen, and set aside. For sauce, in a small saucepan combine half the mushrooms, the onion, and garlic. Add water, tomato paste, basil, oregano, fennel seed, and red pepper. Bring to a boil, reduce heat. Simmer, uncovered, for four minutes, stirring occasionally. Remove from heat.

Spray two shallow individual casseroles with nonstick coating. Cut fish into two equal portions. Place fish in casseroles, tucking under any thin edges. Measure thickness of fish. Pour sauce over fish. Top with remaining mushrooms, green pepper rings, and mozzarella cheese.

Bake in a 450 degree oven until fish flakes when tested with a fork. Allow five to seven minutes per 1/2 inch thickness of fish.

Mozzarella-Zucchini Medley

Calories: 243
(15 grams of fat)

One serving
Ingredients:
    2 tsp. olive oil
    1/4 cup thinly sliced celery
    1/4 cup minced onion
    1 small garlic clove, minced
    1 cup sliced zucchini
    1/2 cup canned crushed tomatoes
    Dash of oregano leaves
    Dash of pepper
    2 oz. mozzarella cheese, shredded

In small nonstick skillet, heat olive oil until bubbly and hot; add celery and garlic, and sauté until garlic is lightly browned. Add zucchini and sauté until tender-crisp; stir in tomatoes and seasoning; let simmer until zucchini is tender and almost all of the liquid has evaporated (about five minutes). Transfer zucchini mixture to microwave-safe plate, sprinkle with cheese and microwave until cheese is melted—about one minute on high.

* * * * *

Broccoli Casserole

Calories: 250
(5.5 grams of fat)

Four servings
Ingredients:
    4 oz. cheddar cheese, shredded
    1 cup cooked long grain rice
    1/2 cup drained canned sliced mushrooms
    1/2 cup diced onion
    1/2 cup skim milk
    1 tbs. plus 1 tsp. butter

2 10-oz. packages frozen chopped broccoli, thawed
1 tsp. salt

Preheat oven to 350 degrees. Spray a two-quart casserole with non-stick spray and set aside. In a three-quart saucepan combine all ingredients, except broccoli and salt. Cook over medium heat, stirring constantly, until cheese and butter are melted. Add broccoli and salt, stir frequently, and continue cooking until broccoli is heated—about two minutes. Turn into sprayed casserole and bake until tender—about 30 minutes.

* * * * *

Fluffy Egg Quarters   *Calories: 144*
                                                         (9 grams of fat)

Four servings
Ingredients:
    Nonstick spray coating
    6 egg yolks
    1/2 tsp. onion powder
    1/4 tsp. salt
    1/8 tsp. pepper
    6 egg whites
    1 14-1/2-oz. can stewed tomatoes
    1/2 medium zucchini (1/2 cup), quartered lengthwise and sliced
    1/8 tsp. pepper

Spray an 8x8x2-inch baking dish with nonstick spray; set aside. Beat egg yolks, onion powder, salt, and pepper about four minutes or until thick and lemon-colored; set aside. Beat egg whites until soft peaks form. Fold into egg yolks. Spread mixture evenly into prepared dish. Bake at 350 degrees for twenty-two to twenty-five minutes or until knife inserted comes out clean.

Meanwhile, combine undrained tomatoes, zucchini, and pepper. Bring to a boil. Reduce heat. Simmer, uncovered, for ten to twelve minutes more or to desired consistency. To serve, cut omelet into quarters. Top with sauce.

Appendix C

A Two-Week PRISM
Workbook Sampler

We have provided this two-week lesson plan from PRISM so that you can get started on the program and get a taste of the daily workbook lessons. These lessons will help you find the strength to continue with the program.

The best way to find true success in the PRISM program is to join a local group and continue through at least twenty-four weeks of workbook lessons, no matter how much weight you have to lose. Only by finishing the entire program can you have the best opportunity for complete transformation in the area of overeating.

These two weeks of workbook lessons have been provided to give you every opportunity to be succeed on the PRISM Weight Loss Program. During these next two weeks you should contact the PRISM office (1-800-755-1738) as soon as possible to find the location of the nearest PRISM group or to purchase workbooks.

Once you get started, you will repeat the two weeks of lessons provided in the following section. But since it is crucial to have a strong beginning with PRISM, repeating these lessons will help give you a sure foundation in the program.

Before you start, make sure you have a food scale and a calorie-count book, along with the correct groceries. With that in mind, you're ready to begin.

Phase One Guidelines

The PRISM workbooks were created to be a source of daily encouragement, teaching, and motivation. Although we have already covered this material, here is a summary of the PRISM program guidelines:

1. Read one unit per week; one lesson per day.

2. Read ONLY that day's lesson. Reading ahead is not allowed. You may, however, review past lessons.

3. Complete the entire lesson and all that is requested.

4. The weekly class lectures are very important, and attendance at a small group is indispensable for your success in this program. Your group will provide instruction, accountability, and support. Do not sabotage your efforts by allowing other activities to get in the way of attending. Set the time aside and resolve to attend all classes. Your participation will be beneficial to you and your fellow class members.

5. Call PRISM. The number has been given several times in this book. But here it is again so you will make the phone call and find out the location of the nearest PRISM group meeting: 1-800-755-1738.

In the meantime, the lessons in the following section will help you get started in the program. You will be repeating each of these lessons once you get started with your local PRISM group. So make the phone call. You will need workbooks for at least four six-week phases in order to experience a transformation in your battle with overweight and/or food addiction.

With that in mind, you have now made the decision to be all that you were created to be. You understand that we take your decision seriously and stand ready to give you the help, support, and direction you need. As you read this, you may have serious doubts about your ability to complete even one day of the program. Let us assure you that you have before you and within you all that you need to make your dream of freedom a reality. You must begin by recognizing some basic facts and putting them to work for you:

- You have little or no self-control where food is concerned.

- Deception has become a part of your lifestyle where your eating habits are concerned.

- How you see yourself is distorted by deception.

- You desire to be slender but are unwilling or unable to give up overeating.

- You have underestimated the impact of overeating on your total life.

- What you think of as nurturing your body through food is really self-abuse.

- You don't understand how God views the problem of overeating and how he desires to help you overcome it.

At this moment these facts may appear overwhelming and impossible to deal with all at once. That's why the program devotes the time and attention necessary to address each one fully. It is comforting to know you are finally involved in a program that is honest enough to address difficult issues and offer solutions to the problems of overeating. No more time, money, or effort wasted. You are going to discover the keys to unlock doors that have been standing closed between you and lifetime freedom far too long.

Your workbook and the responses in it comprise your personal journal. No one else will see it unless you choose to share it.

On the following page you will find the PRISM Weight Loss Program Food Guide. Please read it carefully. Be sure that you understand each point. If you are unsure about any portion of it, please go over it with your leader or someone at PRISM before you begin this program.

You will be accounting for your food intake on your food journal sheets. Two weeks of journal sheets have been provided in the following section; you will receive more in your workbook when you join your local PRISM group. Once you are part of such a group, you will turn in your completed food sheets to your leader on a weekly basis.

THE PRISM FOOD GUIDE

Phase One

8 TO 10 EIGHT-OUNCE GLASSES OF WATER,
MINERAL WATER OR HERBAL TEA PER DAY.

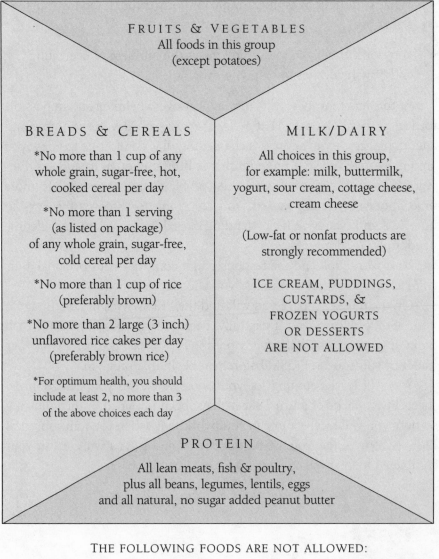

FRUITS & VEGETABLES
All foods in this group
(except potatoes)

BREADS & CEREALS

*No more than 1 cup of any
whole grain, sugar-free, hot,
cooked cereal per day

*No more than 1 serving
(as listed on package)
of any whole grain, sugar-free,
cold cereal per day

*No more than 1 cup of rice
(preferably brown)

*No more than 2 large (3 inch)
unflavored rice cakes per day
(preferably brown rice)

*For optimum health, you should
include at least 2, no more than 3
of the above choices each day

MILK/DAIRY

All choices in this group,
for example: milk, buttermilk,
yogurt, sour cream, cottage cheese,
cream cheese

(Low-fat or nonfat products are
strongly recommended)

ICE CREAM, PUDDINGS,
CUSTARDS, &
FROZEN YOGURTS
OR DESSERTS
ARE NOT ALLOWED

PROTEIN

All lean meats, fish & poultry,
plus all beans, legumes, lentils, eggs
and all natural, no sugar added peanut butter

THE FOLLOWING FOODS ARE NOT ALLOWED:
ALL CRACKERS, CHIPS, ROLLS, BREADS, POPCORN, WHITE FLOUR PRODUCTS,
SNACK FOODS, PASTAS

Phase One Food Guidelines Continued

1. Women may have no less than 1,000 calories and no more than 1,200 calories per day. No more than 700 calories should be eaten before the evening or main meal. Exceptions: There are exceptions for people with specific needs or health concerns. Also, if you are a woman who weighs more than 250 pounds, you may eat 1,300 to 1,500 calories per day. You may also have up to two servings of cereal as listed on package and count it as one bread/cereal exchange.

2. Men may have no less than 1,300 calories and no more than 1,500 calories per day. No more than 800 calories should be eaten before the evening or main meal. Exceptions: If you are someone who does physical labor, you may have up to 1,600 to 1,700 calories per day. You may also have up to two servings of cereal and count it as one bread/cereal exchange.

3. You must write down any and all foods you eat and their caloric value on a food journal sheet every day. This completed food journal sheet will be turned in to your leader at your local PRISM group each week.

4. You must weigh, measure, and accurately count calorie values of any and all foods you select.

5. Liquid beverage meal replacements are NOT ALLOWED.

6. Any food bars, breakfast bars, granola bars, etc., are NOT ALLOWED.

7. ALL dessert products are NOT ALLOWED, with the exception of sugar-free diet gelatin.

8. Sugars, brown and white, are NOT ALLOWED. Foods with sugar added are also not allowed. Some salad dressings or condiments with sugar as the fifth or later listed ingredient are allowed.

9. Other than those with sugar as a primary ingredient, condiments, diet sodas, coffee, tea, sugarless gum, artificial sweeteners are allowed. You must count their caloric value.

10. Gravies are NOT ALLOWED.

11. Popcorn, popcorn rice cakes, and white flour snack foods are NOT ALLOWED.

12. Vitamin supplements should be taken daily in the form of a multivitamin plus iron and a B-complex timed release.

13. You may have up to 1/4 cup of oat bran or wheat bran per day. You must count the calories.

14. Deep-fried or breaded foods are NOT ALLOWED.

15. Communion is sacred and part of worship. Bread for this purpose is allowed in all phases of this program.

16. If you are unsure about any food or any recipe you may want to try, please check it first with your leader or by calling PRISM.

17. If you have to ask yourself whether it's okay to eat it—don't!

Introduction Lesson

The KEY PRINCIPLES and guidelines of the PRISM Weight Loss Program have been designed to provide you with the best possible opportunity to complete your weight loss and help you become the person you were created to be. With that in mind, considerable thought has been given how best to help you solidify this new beginning with a strong personal commitment.

If you are like most overeaters, this commitment is a key point missing in your past efforts. You say you want to lose weight; you see the need to lose weight; you believe you should lose weight; and yet here you are.

Think for a moment. What prevented you from completing your last weight loss attempt? Wasn't it the moment you took your first bite of that food you had promised yourself you would not eat? The decision to take that first bite dictated failure in your ability to lose weight once again. When you say to yourself, *Just one bite of this won't hurt me* or *I'll go ahead and eat this tonight and get right back on my diet tomorrow,* you have sabotaged your own weight loss efforts. You must realize that you are not alone in this vicious cycle of dieting and overeating. Violating the guidelines on a diet has kept many people like you from success. Such violation not only robs you of the freedom from fat you long for; it also casts a dark shadow on your self-worth. Self-worth is vital to your motivation and the integrity you have in setting and achieving your goals.

Guideline violations must be removed from any serious program for change!

Optional Scripture Reading: No discipline seems pleasant at the time, but painful. Later on, however, it produces a harvest of righteousness and peace for those who have been trained by it. (Hebrews 12:11, NIV)

PRISM WEIGHT LOSS PROGRAM

Agreement of Resolution

I, _____, resolve my desire to change my eating behaviors and learn methods for continuing this control for my lifetime. I resolve that I will follow the food guide (including calorie levels), the guidelines, and KEY PRINCIPLES of this program exactly, without any deviation from its standards. I agree that there are no foods more important to me than becoming slender and reaching my "right weight." Even one bite of extra or prohibited food cannot compare with the freedom I will know when I take steps to become the person I was created to be.

I understand that in the event I decide to revoke this resolution through violation of the program guidelines and KEY PRINCIPLES, I will inform my PRISM group leader or my accountability partner of my decision.

I willingly submit myself to receive the support, strength, and guidance I will require from my leader, fellow class members, and God to complete this program.

Member signature _____ Date _____

Leader signature_____ Date _____

Personal Evaluation

1. Describe the feelings you have about beginning this program.

2. Do you believe that the Agreement of Resolution will influence your ability to succeed in the program? How?

3. What is different about this program compared to others you've tried?

4. What is your primary motivation for beginning this program?

5. How will your life change when you reach your "right weight"? How do you feel when you think about becoming the person you were created to be?

WEEK ONE

NEW BEGINNINGS

Week One–Lesson One

NEW BEGINNINGS

How many times have you gone out to dinner vowing to order the fish and salad and not even look at the bread—only to eat four rolls and then order the chocolate mousse for dessert? How often have you gone to a social function and spent the evening fending off offers of chips, dips, and pie— only to go home later and devour every leftover in the refrigerator? Can you even begin to count the Mondays you started a "diet" only to find by Thursday you had long forgotten your intentions? *The weekend is coming, after all, so why try? I might as well just get a fresh start again on Monday.*

You talked to a friend or overheard at a party about "this new diet"— heavy on the cabbage, fruit, or a liquid—that promised miraculous weight loss. You began the diet with a decision to stick it out NO MATTER WHAT! Alas, you gave in to the WHAT before you reached your goal. Instead of losing weight, you found yourself gaining back what little weight you had lost plus more. Like other members of the overeating world, you cling to the saying, "If at first you don't succeed, try and try again."

As you know, the creators of this program also followed the diet cycle of failure until they found a better way. A way which begins with:

"If at first you don't succeed, analyze what went wrong and try a new approach."

That is what this program offers you today:

A NEW BEGINNING!

You must put behind you all those Mondays and good intentions. Those failures must serve only as a valuable reminder of your past inability to realize your dream of being slender. You must not allow them to create roadblocks or instill fears that would deter you from becoming the person you want to be. No one has to tell you of the serious nature of this problem. You know it is not one to be downplayed or diminished. In that same measure you need to focus on the hope you have today of taking the appropriate steps to conquer overeating.

Say the following statement out loud:

> "TODAY I CHOOSE TO PUT THE PAST BEHIND ME
> AS I REACH OUT FOR WHAT IS AHEAD."

The first thing to reach out for is your commitment to the PRISM Weight Loss Program. You understand the food guide and the reasoning behind it. The guidelines are clear to you—now FOLLOW THEM!

Do not throw away this wonderful opportunity and hope of becoming slender and free. Do not rob yourself of experiencing the joys of a new life.

**YOU WILL NEVER AGAIN
WEIGH AS MUCH
AS YOU DO TODAY.**

Optional Scripture Readings:

And he that sat upon the throne said, "Behold I make all things new." And He said unto me, "Write: for these words are true and faithful." (Revelation 21:5, KJV)

And I shall give them one heart, and shall put a new spirit within them. And I shall take the heart of stone out of their flesh and give them a heart of flesh, that they may walk in My statutes and keep My ordinances, and do them. Then they will be My people and I shall be their God. (Ezekiel 11:19–20, NASB)

Week One—Lesson One

PERSONAL EVALUATION

1. Have you made a plan of what you will eat and when you will eat today? You can use your food journal sheet as a worksheet. How do you think this will assist you in remaining on the PRISM program?

2. What new foods would you consider trying that you do not normally eat while you are on a diet? Use your imagination!

3. In what ways will calorie counting and food journaling prevent you from repeating mistakes you have made on prior weight loss attempts?

4. How will being disciplined and following the first KEY PRINCIPLE benefit you?

5. Which of the above benefits are most important to you? Why?

This concludes Week One—Lesson One

Week One—Lesson Two

Let the Past Pass Away

Yesterday's lesson referred to analyzing what went wrong in previous attempts to lose weight.

You are probably aware of some of the "whats" of your past after only one day on this program. Even if you have gone grocery shopping, stocked your cupboards with "right" foods like an army bunker, and prepared for the diet battle in every way, you still may have awakened this morning ready to put out the white flag of surrender to food. The problem is, there will be no "peace treaty." As you have experienced in the past, the chains of guilt and condemnation just get heavier. The walls of the "fat prison" have just been reinforced. Remember, that is not what you really want or you would not have started this program.

TODAY IS A NEW DAY....
IT IS A CLEAN SLATE WITH NO MISTAKES ON IT!

One of the things that went wrong for you in the past was your inability to release your history of failure in overeating as you entered each new day. Regardless of the fact that you carry with you the "battle scars" of fat on your person, you do not have to carry along the defeats of yesterday. TODAY THE PAST HAS NO PLACE IN YOUR LIFE. Stop and think about that for a moment. Allow it to become a part of you.

Be concerned only for today. In your efforts to overcome, you are often so busy looking ahead that you miss the needs and opportunities you have today. You look forward to "the wedding," "the reunion," "the houseguest," "the end of the six weeks"...and in the meantime you neglect to prepare yourself for TODAY'S EVENTS!

You are accountable for TODAY, and today only. Tomorrow will take care of itself. Today is the first day of the rest of your life!

Say the following statement out loud:

"JUST FOR TODAY
I WILL LET THE PAST PASS AWAY—
JUST FOR TODAY."

Optional Scripture Readings:

> So don't be anxious about tomorrow. God will take care
> of your tomorrow too. Live one day at a time. (Matthew
> 6:34, TLB)

> Forget the former things; do not dwell on the past. See,
> I am doing a new thing! Now it springs up; do you not
> perceive it? I am making a way in the desert and
> streams in the wasteland. (Isaiah 43:18–19, NIV)

Week One—Lesson Two

PERSONAL EVALUATION

1. What are some of the things that may have caused you to give up on other diets?

2. What are some safeguards of this program that will help you in the above areas?

3. How does that encourage you for today?

4. In what ways can you let your past pass away, just for today?

This concludes Week One—Lesson Two

GETTING A GRIP ON NEW ATTITUDES

These last two days you have been making some challenging new choices in your eating behavior. No doubt you have already experienced reaching for that chip, then quickly pulling back. If you cook, you may have discovered how many "complete meals" you used to consume while preparing the actual meal. You must now be conscious of not tasting, sampling, or cleaning up those leftovers. You can begin to understand why you have put on weight and have been so helpless to take it off. There are so many hidden ways of overeating. It is important that you continue to recognize these behaviors as they surface. They will soon lose their influence over you!

The discipline of journaling your food choices is difficult to incorporate into your lifestyle. Remember, THIS WILL BE MUCH MORE EFFECTIVE IF YOU TAKE THE TIME TO COMPLETE YOUR FOOD JOURNAL SHEET BEFORE YOU EAT YOUR MEAL. You will thoroughly and completely weigh, measure, and accurately count calorie values of the foods you select. If you wait until you have satisfied your appetite, you will have weakened your motivation, awareness, and attitude.

Learning to use a calorie reference book or reading food labels can be compared to cleaning out a closet that has been a storage place for years—you are amazed at what you discover! You may be pleasantly surprised by this knowledge as it will explain many of your eating problems. On the other hand, you may resist this process and excuse your opposition to it by saying things like, "Oh, I am not good at this" or "This calorie-book is so confusing." In reality, YOU DO NOT DESIRE TO KNOW HOW MANY CALORIES ARE IN YOUR FOODS—ESPECIALLY YOUR FAVORITES. Whether or not you choose to acknowledge it, all foods do have caloric value! Ignoring this fact does not remove or cancel the way they affect you. If you truly want to attain lifetime freedom from overeating, you must face the truth about your misuse and misunderstanding of food. You must see food for what it really is—an energy source with varying values. Recording the calories of the foods you eat will give you knowledge of those values and provide new insight that will last a lifetime.

One of the major changes for you may be the elimination of certain food products. You have now been challenged to look differently at foods to meet your daily nutritional needs. You may have already discovered the vast world of foods that do not include white flour or sugars. Or you may be caught in the "poor me" syndrome. Avoid self-pity by recalling the positive features of this program, which allow for a wide range of food choices to meet your individual likes and dislikes. Are you willing to reach out, experiment, be bold, and change? Your success in the war with overeating may just depend on it! Check your attitude in this area of challenge and change. Ask yourself, "Is this an immature, childish attitude I have held on to?" If the answer is yes, acknowledge your adulthood and "grown-up" power of choice. It is likely it will mean the difference between victory and defeat.

Say the following statement out loud:

"I CHOOSE TODAY TO GET A GRIP ON
A RIGHT ATTITUDE
ABOUT THE POSITIVE CHANGES
I AM MAKING IN MY LIFE."

Optional Scripture Readings:

Therefore, whether you eat or drink or whatever you do, do all to the glory of God. (1 Corinthians 10:31, NKJV)

Determination to be wise is the first step toward becoming wise! And with your wisdom, develop common sense and good judgment. (Proverbs 4:7, TLB)

Week One–Lesson Three

PERSONAL EVALUATION

1. What attitudes about your eating behaviors have surfaced that you know will have to change?

2. How do you feel about these changes you will have to make?

3. As you make new food choices and journal them, do you find yourself amazed and surprised or resistant and angry? Why?

This concludes Week One—Lesson Three

Week One–Lesson Four

A BOOST FOR THE CLIMB

You may have arrived at a point on the road in your weight loss journey which appears mountainous in nature. Today's lesson will give you a "right perspective" which will boost you over what is really nothing more than a hump in the road.

It probably is accurate to say you have been unable to get past day four of any previous diet. Day four seems to be the "hump day" for many success-seeking dieters. Getting over the hump is especially important for you because you recognize now your problem far exceeds the need to lose weight. This may be evident to you through the physical and emotional pains you may be experiencing at this point. Physically, you may be having symptoms of withdrawal from the lack of sugars and white flour products. Emotionally, there are stresses and longings for the foods which were a daily part of your life. This creates a feeling of weakness as you face the thought of one more day without them. Looking for a reason to go on and get over the hump, you may have turned to your old friend, THE SCALE. Even if it tells you what you want to hear—which is that you have lost two or three pounds—it will not be enough to aid your climb over the hump. The pain may seem too great.

To move ahead, you must have motivational equipment which meets the need to overcome the potential for defeat you are facing. You must recognize your desire to bring back into your life what you mistakenly believe to be "control" or "choice." You long to eat what you WANT, when you WANT it, and how you WANT it. You have been programmed to believe that ACTING ON THOSE WANTS WILL GIVE YOU WHAT YOU NEED.

"WANT" is a necessary component of life. The word WANT actually means "to lack a need." When properly applied, it provides the mechanism to sustain yourself. However, the WANT FOR FOOD you are now facing is based on old habits, attitudes, and responses. These habits have produced in you the very things that motivated you to begin this program. It might be helpful for you to take a moment to recall some of the things that have been produced in your life through giving in to the WANTS of your past. Take a moment and use the space below to identify what they are and how they have affected you:

Look at what you have written. Have these results had a positive impact on your life? How might these results have differed if you had exercised self-control? The last three days you may have FELT "controlled" by the program rules. The fact is, they have given you back your freedom of choice.

The power and strength needed to get over the hump is fueled by the recognition that violating your Agreement of Resolution will simply add another peak to the climb on your road to success.

THE AGREEMENT OF RESOLUTION
IS THE LEAD ROPE OF YOUR CLIMBING GEAR.
USING IT
WILL INSURE YOU AGAINST THE FALL
AND BOOST YOU
OVER THE HUMP!

Optional Scripture Readings:

Look carefully then how you walk, not as unwise men but as wise, making the most of the time, because the days are evil. Therefore do not be foolish, but understand what the will of the Lord is. (Ephesians 5:15–17, RSV)

I will surely do what I have promised, Lord, and thank you for your help. For you have saved me from death and my feet from slipping, so that I can walk before the Lord in the land of the living. (Psalm 56:12–13, TLB)

This Concludes Week One—Lesson Four

Week One—Lesson Five

SMALL STEPS FORWARD PRODUCE GREAT LEAPS AHEAD

"Oh, the changes I have made this week! Counting calories, writing down food choices, saying goodbye to my sweets and my French bread, thinking about what I am putting in my mouth—it is almost too much to bear at once!"

Could this be what you are thinking? Are you truly amazed and even a little hopeful by the changes you have made this week? You have proven to yourself that you do have the ability to be disciplined and to achieve success.

YOU HAVE BEEN GIVEN THE KEYS
TO THE DOOR OF SUCCESS!

These small steps of discipline, seemingly insignificant in and of themselves, add up to a lifetime achievement when joined together with your will to persevere. Do not forget your co-travelers who are taking each step with you and stand ready to offer their support. Your class members and leader are or have been where you are. Reach out to them when even the small steps seem difficult. You may even help them in their journey!

Only a week ago you did not know you had the strength necessary to complete even four days on this program. Now you know you do! Could it be possible you have what is needed to really complete the journey this time?

YES! MILES ARE LOGGED THROUGH
SMALL STEPS FORWARD!

Optional Scripture Readings:

> Therefore encourage one another, and build up one
> another just as you also are doing. (1 Thessalonians
> 5:11, NASB)

> My son, keep sound wisdom and discretion; let them
> not escape from your sight, and they will be life for
> your soul and adornment for your neck. Then you'll
> walk on your way securely and your foot will not
> stumble. (Proverbs 3:21–23, RSV)

Personal Evaluation

1. What are some foods you have found particularly hard to give up this week? What do you think it is about those foods that makes them so hard for you to give up?

2. In the past, have you gone on "food binges" where you ate foods regardless of their appeal? Afterwards how did you feel emotionally and physically?

2. What habits are you looking forward to removing from your life for a lifetime? What are you doing today that will help you succeed?

3. What does the term "addictive eater" mean to you? What habits have you formed in the past which parallel this definition?

This concludes Week One—Lesson Five

Week One—Lesson Six

REHABILITATED ATTITUDES AND ABILITIES

One of the important things missing in most weight loss regimes is the goal of "rehabilitation" of the overeater. You may have submitted yourself to many balanced plans, lost weight, and soon afterwards found yourself returning to your old way of eating. Diet creators seem unable or unwilling to realize the roots of the problem and offer ways to make lasting change. One of the obstacles they face is the need to appeal to the overweight individual. Most want quick, instant success; not the slow, thoughtful work of lifetime discipline. You, on the other hand, are ready to get off the diet merry-go-round. You are now willing to lay down your HABITS and exchange them for new ATTITUDES which create the ability to achieve results. Those results will bring rehabilitation and successful weight loss!

An important part of rehabilitation is restoration. To "restore" means to return to an original, intended state. When you restore a piece of furniture, you do not create a new piece of furniture, but simply bring it back to its original form. You must first remove the layers upon layers of paint and varnish to reach the original wood. Then you must sand out all of the imperfections before applying the new finish. This is a long, slow process. If the wood could talk, it would tell you how painful the process is. In a similar way, you are submitting your body, mind, and spirit to the restoration process. This restoration will be complete to the extent YOU are willing to be rehabilitated.

Regardless of the amount of weight you desire to remove, you must form new ATTITUDES and recognize YOUR ABILITY to change as part of your lifestyle. This week you have begun to realize the extent and reality of weakness in your eating behaviors. View each new day as an opportunity to reinforce new behaviors and use your keys to success. Your attitude will become more positive and strengthen your abilities.

Your firm commitment to the program this week has started the restoration process. As the piece of furniture, your first layer is coming off. It hurts, doesn't it? That varnish has been there for a long time! This truly is a new beginning for you. You will never be the same—even if you discontinue the process today by an act of your will. Do you want to be a beautiful piece of furniture marred by an unfinished process? NO!

THROUGH REHABILITATION
YOU FORM NEW ATTITUDES.
YOU RECOGNIZE YOUR ABILITY
TO BE ALL YOU WERE CREATED TO BE.

Optional Scripture Readings:

> If you want to know what God wants you to do, ask him, and he will gladly tell you, for he is always ready to give a bountiful supply of wisdom to all who ask him; he will not resent it. (James 1:5, TLB)

> I weep with grief; my heart is heavy with sorrow; encourage and cheer me with your words. Keep me far from every wrong; help me, undeserving as I am, to obey your laws, for I have chosen to do right. I cling to your commands and follow them as closely as I can. Lord, don't let me make a mess of things. If you will only help me to want your will, then I will follow your laws even more closely. Just tell me what to do and I will do it, Lord. As long as I live I'll wholeheartedly obey. Make me walk along the right paths for I know how delightful they really are. (Psalm 119:28–34, TLB)

Week One—Lesson Six

PERSONAL EVALUATION

1. How do you feel about using the word "rehabilitation" in connection with your overeating?

2. People usually think of the rehabilitation process as needing to be confined or set apart from society for a time. How have you found yourself "confined or set apart" this week (i.e. turning down a dinner invitation, eating differently than friends or family)?

3. List three foods you can have on the program which are not normally connected with a "diet." (If you can't name three, call your leader for help.)

4. Which of these foods could you find in an average restaurant?

This concludes Week One—Lesson Six

Week One—Lesson Seven

Go Ahead...Get Excited!

This week you have really made progress on the road to a new life! You are putting the past behind you; recognizing and attaining new attitudes; realizing you have the abilities to really make the changes that will bring about lasting results.

ARE YOU EXCITED TO BE ALL THAT YOU CAN BE?

You might find this an astounding question. *Shouldn't the fact that I have followed the guidelines of this program all week speak of excitement?* No, it speaks of willingness, desire, and hope. The question is: "Are you excited?" Can you see the difference?

EXCITEMENT IS JOYOUS EXPECTATION!

There is a confident, free person under that extra weight. You may have seen that person before. Perhaps it has only been a fantasy, quickly extinguished. The keys to freedom are firmly within your grasp! THERE IS ABSOLUTELY NOTHING TO STAND IN THE WAY OF YOUR EMERGENCE!

THAT IS EXCITING!

Take a moment right now and experience how great it is that you are making steps to achieve the fullness of health and vitality you have always desired. You had almost given up hope completely. You were prepared to "live with it." However, you chose instead to give those dreams another chance. Look how far you have come!

That person inside you must be acknowledged and recognized. As you make steps to bring about the restoration of that person within, the TRUE YOU, you must believe it is possible. The TRUE YOU must exit the realm of fantasy and become a reality in every facet of your mind, spirit, and body. Next week you will be given the KEY PRINCIPLE behind this concept. You will say goodbye to that fat, unhealthy picture you have of yourself and say hello to all that you were created to be.

BE EXCITED!

Optional Scripture Readings:

> For, after all, the important thing for us as Christians is not what we eat or drink but stirring up goodness and peace and joy from the Holy Spirit. (Romans 14:17, TLB)

> It is good to give thanks to the Lord, and to sing praises to thy name, O most high, to declare thy lovingkind-ness in the morning, and thy faithfulness by night, with the ten-stringed lute, and with the harp; with resound-ing music upon the lyre. For thou, O Lord, hast made me glad by what thou hast done, I will sing for joy at the works of thy hands. (Psalm 92:1–4, NASB)

Week One—Lesson Seven

PERSONAL EVALUATION

1. Who have you told about your new food guide since you began the program?

2. How did they react?

3. How did this make you feel?

4. Do you feel this person or those close to you understand your problem and support you? In what ways do you feel supported?

5. In what ways do you feel misunderstood?

This concludes Week One—Lesson Seven

Week Two—Lesson One

THE PART OF THE MIND YOU TAKE FOR GRANTED

Below you will read the testimony of a PRISM class member. Read about how she saw herself before she began her weight loss journey. If personalized, could these words be yours?

"As I look back on my old, out-of-control self by viewing pictures and movies, it is so hard to believe that is me. I knew I weighed at least 220 pounds and was fat, but I had no idea how I looked. I am sure that had much to do with why I kept getting fatter and fatter. I had no real body image. I looked in the mirror and thought to myself, 'You are so disgusting!' Still, I did not see the extent of my size. When I began a diet I had no definite idea of what I would look like at my 'right weight.' I did not even know how the 'FAT' me looked. How could I know what the slender me looked like?"

Self-image distortion is common in society. Examine how that distorted image exhibits itself in the overweight person. Have you ever viewed people in stressful situations and asked yourself how they go on living like that? You may even have approached a person and asked the question directly, only to have him react with confusion or lack of response. You see, he does not view the problem in a realistic manner. Something inside of him has closed off the truth. It can usually be traced to one of two things:

It is too overwhelming to change immediately, or—

It is too painful to view with honesty.

Some people would rather live with the problem than confront it. Confronting the problem with action results in facing the truth, which is painful. Even though they would like taking positive steps to change, they would be taking the risk of having to live aware of the depth of the problem.

Look at how the above analogy is connected to your subconscious mind. Your mind's conscious thought relies upon the subconscious process much more than you realize. It protects you from becoming overwhelmed when faced with personal weakness. It enables you to find a livable "comfort zone" while within the depths of a difficulty. Although consciously you may be aware of the fact that this zone is not ideal, at least your life can continue seemingly unaffected. That subconscious thought contains excuses, justifications, and the MAIN roadblock to your success—bad HABITS. The subconscious must be acknowledged and renewed in order to produce right attitudes within the conscious, which results in positive actions. This week the program will take you through the next two KEY PRINCIPLES, addressing areas of weakness and bad habits you have developed through your subconscious mind. You will learn that you want neither a "fat" image nor a "skinny" image in your mind's eye. You need the TRUE YOU to be your image. You will be choosing a "right weight" and deciding consciously, perhaps for the first time, what you were created to look like.

**WHEN YOU KNOW WHERE YOU ARE GOING
ON THE ROAD TO THE TRUE YOU,
IT WILL BECOME LESS OF A STRUGGLE
TO FOLLOW THE MAP!**

Optional Scripture Readings:

> Do not merely listen to the word, and so deceive your-selves. Do what it says. Anyone who listens to the word but does not do what it says is like a man who looks at his face in a mirror and, after looking at himself, goes away and immediately forgets what he looks like. But the man who looks intently into the perfect law that gives freedom, and continues to do this, not forgetting what he has heard but doing it—he will be blessed in what he does. (James 1:22–25, NIV)

Show me your ways, O LORD, teach me your paths;
guide me in your truth and teach me, for you are God
my Savior, and my hope is in you all day long. (Psalm
25:4–5, NIV)

Week Two—Lesson One

PERSONAL EVALUATION

1. Below are seven subconscious justifications people use to protect themselves from the reality of being overweight. Put a check mark by the ones you have experienced in your life.

_____ Dream of being skinny while able to eat like a pig.

_____ Avoid full length mirrors or full body pictures.

_____ Wear jackets or coats to hide the fat.

_____ Avoid social situations where you will be the only fat person—OR situations where you will be out of place in the type of clothing you must wear (bathing suit or shorts).

_____ You find an "eating partner." This is a person who will always eat with you. You may choose a fatter person to soothe guilt or a thinner one to help reinforce the "skinny pig" fantasy.

_____ Compare yourself to others in terms of who is fatter. If there are people you view as fatter you don't feel so bad.

This concludes Week Two—Lesson One

Week Two—Lesson Two

SHEDDING LIGHT ON THE RIGHT BODY IMAGE

Yesterday's lesson discussed your subconscious body size and how it plays a key role in your weight loss. Today you will consider some of the reasons why a RIGHT body size must be placed within your subconscious to help you make the necessary changes to your body image.

You may now be involved in a vicious cycle of habits and rituals you have not been able to overcome. These habits may have become a part of you over a period of years, and now you must implant new actions to replace your old habits. The actions contained in this lesson will help you attain the life of freedom you desire. However, the value of the actions will soon diminish if you do not have a correct body image. Both the "fat" and "skinny" images must be dealt with. Each will cause you to overcompensate and actually work to maintain them. Here are some examples:

You see yourself now as fat and desperately want to lose weight. Assume you continue this program with amazing perseverance and find yourself at your "right weight." The scale speaks to you on a conscious level, but remember that is only a small part of your mind. The subconscious mind still maintains the "fat image." You will find yourself looking in the mirror and still seeing a "fat person." Likewise, as you feel this way, you will allow your eating habits to follow. With your eating habits again out of control, you soon find yourself conforming to that "fat image." You will continue in this state until you feel up to ANOTHER diet.

The "skinny image" is just as harmful. This is the opposite unrealistic view of what your "right weight" looks like. This comes from looking at models or people of different proportions than your own and believing that is the only way to look. If this image is not replaced, you will not be satisfied when you reach your "right weight." You will feel frustrated that you worked so hard and you did not succeed. It is this kind of frustration that causes you to fall back into undisciplined eating and weight gain.

Are you beginning to realize how important it is for you to have an established, realistic picture of what you were created to look like? This picture will reinforce your commitment to action and firmly implant the positive attitudes necessary for your success.

Have you been on diets and experienced reaching your goal? Have you come close to your "right weight" but never quite made it all the way? You may have always been overweight and have no idea what a "right weight" would be for you. In any case, you have probably asked yourself: *Why in the world did I ever allow myself to gain this weight back again?*

You were told how to lose the fat, but not how to feel comfortable and at peace about your size after the fat was gone. One of the keys to the door to freedom from fat was kept from you.

This program will not allow that to happen to you again. Think today about what your body size was created to be. There are different ways to approach this exercise, depending on your history of weight loss. You may have been at your right body size before and have the pictures to prove it. If so, your assignment is to go back through those pictures and find one of yourself at your right body size. Some rules to consider in this exercise are:

The photograph of you must have been taken within the last five years.

You need to choose a FULL BODY pose.

You need to find a picture that brings back happy and peaceful memories.

If you do not have a picture, you need to find one of a person similar to you in build, height, and coloring. Taking what you know to be true about your proportions, look through magazines and catalogs to find a person you want to mirror in body weight. Cut out a picture of YOUR face and place it over the face of the model. Cut the model's picture out of the magazine.

You will find a mirror frame in the back of this book. Place your TRUE YOU picture in the frame. THIS IS THE IMAGE YOU WILL PUT IN YOUR MIND. Now you have a body size reference. You will now begin to accept this as the only right size for you.

KEY PRINCIPLE NUMBER TWO:

EVERY DAY, TWICE A DAY (or more often if you like) LOOK IN THE MIRROR AND SAY THE FOLLOWING STATEMENT OUT LOUD:

"THIS IS THE SIZE I WAS CREATED TO BE.
I AM A LOVABLE, WORTHWHILE, AND SUCCESSFUL PERSON.
I AM THANKFUL FOR THESE TRUTHS."

This is to be done by ALL program members WITHOUT EXCEPTION. Should you decide you are unwilling to do this, you need to consider your Agreement of Resolution. This principle is a VITAL KEY to your weight loss success.

Optional Scripture Readings:

> Now the Lord is the Spirit; and where the Spirit of the Lord is, there is liberty. But we all, with unveiled faces, beholding as in a mirror the glory of the Lord, are being transformed into the same image from glory to glory, just as from the Lord, the Spirit. (2 Corinthians 3:17–18, NASB)

> For you created my inmost being; you knit me together in my mother's womb. I praise you because I am fearfully and wonderfully made; your works are wonderful, I know that full well. My frame was not hidden from you when I was made in the secret place. When I was woven together in the depths of the earth, your eyes saw my unformed body. All the days ordained for me were written in your book before one of them came to be. How precious to me are your thoughts, O God! How vast is the sum of them!" (Psalm 139:13–17, NIV)

This concludes Week Two—Lesson Two

What Does This True Me Weigh?

It seems that body weight—in terms of number—has been increasingly important to our society over the past fifty years. Some people place critical importance and personal value on the number that shows up when they step on the scale. You may or may not know what you weigh right now, but you obviously feel it is too much. You need to have a number you have chosen as your "right weight." Today's lesson will help you decide what that amount is. Later, it will discuss the scale and make some suggestions for its role in your life.

As you choose a "right weight," it is critical that you take time to consider what constitutes your body weight. In the past you may have considered the scale a measurement of how "fat" you are and nothing else. When you stand on that scale, you do not just place your fat on it. You place YOUR BODY on it. Organs, blood, bone, muscle, water, waste, skin and fat. ALL of these things have weight—not just the fat. What you must realize is that you are a unique individual. Other people the same height, structure, and age are not made exactly like you. YOU ARE DIFFERENT! Because of this your body weight will be unique.

You have probably worked from a chart to determine your "goal weight" or you have been told what you should weigh by someone who looked at a chart. Did you know that charts are made up by taking ten people of the same height and bone structure, totaling their weights, and averaging them? So which of the ten people are you exactly like? NOT ONE!

This does not suggest you should not have a weight amount to correspond with the TRUE YOU. That would work against correcting past justifications of undisciplined eating. You must have a standard of measure to assure you will stay accountable to your right body size. If you have no specific "right weight," you will have a "somewhere out there" number you will never reach. Now is the time for you to choose that definite number.

You may have experienced a body weight which you felt was maintainable. That is a good number to choose, especially if it corresponds to what you weigh in your TRUE YOU picture. Even if you weighed more in that picture than you have been told you should, it is what you weighed when you looked like that. This is unique to you.

You may have no idea what you should weigh. Because of the importance of having a number you feel is right for you, consider asking close friends or family if they are willing to help you with this. The second suggestion is to have a physical trainer do a "body composition analysis" to determine your ideal weight. The most important thing is to be true to yourself. Inside yourself you know what you should weigh. Do not underestimate your own ability to choose your "right weight."

When you determine a right body weight, you must be sure you believe it is right for you. Doubt will weaken the power of this next KEY PRINCIPLE. This is what you are to do with your right body weight amount.

KEY PRINCIPLE NUMBER THREE:

IN THE BACK OF THIS BOOK [the workbook] YOU WILL FIND ONE LARGE SCALE AND A SET OF FOUR SMALL SCALES. WRITE YOUR RIGHT BODY WEIGHT AMOUNT ON EACH ONE. REMOVE THE FOUR SMALL SCALES AND PLACE THEM IN AREAS YOU OFTEN LOOK (bathroom mirror, refrigerator, car dash, checkbook). WHENEVER YOU SEE THE SCALE SAY THE FOLLOWING STATEMENT OUT LOUD:

"_____. THIS IS THE "RIGHT WEIGHT" FOR MY BODY."

Every day, twice a day (or more often if you like) look at the scale in the back of this book and say the following statement out loud:

"_____. THIS IS THE "RIGHT WEIGHT" FOR MY BODY."

Optional Scripture Reading:

> So we fix our eyes not on what is seen, but on what is
> unseen. For what is seen is temporary, but what is
> unseen is eternal. (2 Corinthians 4:18, NIV)

This concludes Week Two—Lesson Three

Week Two—Lesson Four

Verbal Roadblocks to Positive Actions

Now that you have determined your right size and weight, it is time to look at some of the roadblocks that have limited your weight loss success in the past. As you read in Week One, "If at first you don't succeed, analyze what went wrong and try a new approach." This statement is true not only in terms of positive actions you can take, but of negative thoughts that can hinder your efforts. These thoughts are more dangerous than ANY action because of their subtlety.

Self-defeating statements may have been a part of you for so long you are unaware of their existence. You may not see them as mere words but accept them as truth. Statements like "I just cannot stay on a diet"; "This is too hard for me"; "I have no willpower"; "I am too dumb to figure this out"; and "I am too busy to take time to do this" have contributed to keep you from becoming the TRUE YOU. If you are unwilling to remove and replace these negative statements in your inner self, you can look at the picture and the scale for an eternity without result. There will still be that little voice that says, "What a dreamer you are; you will never look like that." You could even falsely justify these statements as "humility" or "protection from pride." That is just another self-set trap to keep you fat. You must accept that these statements are untrue and filled with errors. They have no good place in your life.

You need to remember that subconscious part of your mind. Consciously, you accept that you need to change, and you are making choices every day to be disciplined and follow the program as agreed. However, the old subconscious thoughts are still operating on past information contained within them. When you allow negative statements to come out of your mouth, you simply reinforce the validity of negative information. In a similar way, when you replace those statements with what is true, good, and lovely, you send a message of CHANGE to your subconscious mind.

If you are a Christian, you believe that Christ has provided you with the power of self-control; however, in the vast realm of your mind are many doors closed to this truth. These closed doors are barricaded by the negative statements you make concerning your abilities. These negative statements are an evil influence, not a result of godly humility.

Consider Philippians 4:7–9, which instructs us concerning the things on which we are to concentrate our thinking. This positive concentration of thought is the daily process of renewing our minds. God desires that we walk in true freedom from evil's influence in our lives. This freedom is obtainable to the extent we are willing to submit our minds to this process. When you sense a negative thought beginning to surface concerning your ability to succeed, STOP! REMEMBER THE POSITIVE ACTIONS YOU HAVE CHOSEN TO TAKE TODAY. Do not concern yourself with your tomorrow and forever after—they will take care of themselves. The daily renewing of your mind is a positive action that becomes a bulldozer to remove your verbal roadblocks on the road to the TRUE YOU.

Say the following out loud:

> **"I CHOOSE TODAY TO THINK ON MY**
> **POSITIVE QUALITIES.**
> **I AM RENEWING MY MIND DAILY**
> **THROUGH THINKING ON WHAT IS**
> **GOOD, TRUE, AND LOVELY.**
> **THESE THOUGHTS PRODUCE**
> **ACTIONS OF SELF-CONTROL."**

Optional Scripture Readings:

> And the peace of God, which transcends all understanding, will guard your hearts and your minds in Christ Jesus. Finally, brothers, whatever is true, whatever is noble, whatever is right, whatever is pure, whatever is lovely, whatever is admirable—if anything is excellent or praiseworthy—think about such things. Whatever you have learned or received or heard from

me, or seen in me—put it into practice. And the God of peace will be with you. (Philippians 4:7–9, NIV)

In the way of thy testimonies I delight as much as in all riches. I will meditate on thy precepts, and fix my eyes on thy ways. I will delight in thy statutes; I will not forget thy word. (Psalm 119:14–16, RSV)

Week Two—Lesson Four

PERSONAL EVALUATION

1. List below the actions you are taking today to stay on the road to the TRUE YOU.

2. What are some of the negative statements you say to yourself concerning your ability to succeed? How do these statements affect your daily commitment to the program?

3. How do you feel about your performance in the program to this point? What are you most pleased about?

4. Is it difficult for you to do things for yourself? Why do you think you often care for the needs of others before your own?

5. When you gain control of your eating behavior and lose weight, how will those close to you benefit?

This concludes Week Two—Lesson Four

Week Two—Lesson Five

THE POSITIVE RESULTS OF TRUTH

Consider today two lines in the book of Proverbs 12:18–19. The first says: "Some people like to make cutting remarks, but the words of the wise soothe and heal."

How often in your struggle or resolve to deal with your weight have you been the recipient of discouraging statements? Examples include: "You will never be thin, it is genetic" and "You'll just gain the weight back like last time, so why try?" Yes, some people make remarks that cut deep into your heart and mind. Like so many others struggling with eating problems, you bring with you years and years of these negative, damaging statements. They have become a part of your subconscious mind and they, too, must be exposed.

YOU CAN NO LONGER ACCEPT NEGATIVE STATEMENTS AS A BASIS TO ACT ON OR VIEW YOURSELF— LET THE PAST PASS AWAY!

Notice the second half of the proverb: "But the words of the wise SOOTHE AND HEAL." Hold on to and accept only those statements that bring healing and help to you. Initially, positive statements may not be comfortable for you to hear and may be difficult to accept. The key is that when you begin to "live out" these statements, positive results follow. These positive results are an integral part of your journey to becoming the TRUE YOU. If the result of a comment is destructive and keeps you bound to overeating and fat, it has no place in your life!

The second proverb is a good measuring stick for identifying thoughts and statements that are true: "Truth stands the test of time, lies are soon exposed."

You can live in deception for only a limited time before the evidence of it surfaces. How can you apply this today? First, recognize that you cannot play games with this program and remain undiscovered for long. Do not allow this thought of deception to enter your mind. It is negative and self-defeating. If you begin to deceive yourself, you will not stand the test of time. Do not listen to negative statements like "one bite won't hurt." The truth is one bite will hurt you as it has in the past. Hold on to what you know to be true. In time you will reap all the benefits and rewards of your commitment to the truth.

Optional Scripture Readings:

> If you hold to my teaching, you are really my disciples. Then you will know the truth, and the truth will set you free. (John 8:31–32, NIV)

> Prove me, O Lord, and try me; test my heart and my mind. For thy steadfast love is before my eyes, and I walk in faithfulness to thee. (Psalm 26:2–3, RSV)

Week Two—Lesson Five

PERSONAL EVALUATION

1. What are three things you know to be true about yourself that make you special and unique?

2. Referring to the list above, name an action or personal characteristic which exhibits each trait.

3. Have you ever received negative comments concerning the traits listed above? What do you think motivated the person to say something untrue about you?

This concludes Week Two—Lesson Five

Week Two—Lesson Six

THE DIFFERENCES BETWEEN "CONTINUING" AND "REGRESSING"

What makes a person who has worked so hard to reach a "right weight" or size suddenly turn and gain back the lost weight? As discussed previously the subconscious mind plays a part in this mystery through body size and "right weight" concepts. There must be more to why a person resumes eating in an out-of-control manner. Many people who have regressed tell stories of wild binges far exceeding any of their old habits. It seems they have a need to regress and to regain their weight as quickly as possible. Where have they gone wrong? How can you avoid this trap?

The answer again lies in your subconscious mind, this time in the area of your attitude. Attitude is a strong determining factor in any project. YOUR ATTITUDE ABOUT THE NEED TO CHANGE YOUR EATING BEHAVIOR FOR A LIFETIME IS EVEN MORE IMPORTANT THAN WHETHER OR NOT YOU REACH YOUR "RIGHT WEIGHT."

When you look at the TRUE YOU mirror and the "right weight" scales, your ATTITUDE must be one of complete acceptance and belief. As you progress toward realization of these objectives, your ATTITUDE will help them become a natural part of who you are. You will be free to respond appropriately to the changes that have become a part of your life. You will walk, talk, and eat like the TRUE YOU should.

CONTINUERS ACCEPT THEMSELVES AS "I AM FINALLY WHO I WAS CREATED TO BE!"

If you neglect to change your attitude, you will find yourself struggling with appetite and urges to overeat. Your subconscious is not convinced of your success and it will urge you to eat in order to regress again to your "fat image."

REGRESSORS SEE THEMSELVES AS "I AM FORMERLY FAT AND I HOPE I CAN KEEP IT OFF FOR A WHILE."

Do you see the difference between the two attitudes? Your appetite will parallel your belief in the regressor's statement. Your appetite will be as controllable as your belief in the acceptance of the continuer's statement.

YOU MUST BELIEVE THE TRUE YOU.
YOU MUST ACCEPT WHAT YOU WERE CREATED TO BE!

Optional Scripture Readings:

> You were taught, with regard to your former way of life, to put off your old self, which is being corrupted by its deceitful desires; to be made new in the attitude of your minds; and to put on the new self, created to be like God in true righteousness and holiness. (Ephesians 4:22–24, NIV)

> Put false ways far from me; and graciously teach me thy law! I have chosen the way of faithfulness, I set thy ordinances before me. (Psalm 119:29–30, RSV)

Week Two—Lesson Six

PERSONAL EVALUATION

1. When you have experienced appetite urges in the last two weeks, how have you dealt with them?

2. Will these methods stand the test of time?

3. Have you noticed any particular times of the day when you struggle with appetite?

4. Which time of day or night is it? What do you associate this with?

5. Look up the word "accept" in the dictionary. Write the definition below.

6. Look up the word "believe" in the dictionary. Write the definition below.

7. Look at the two definitions. Which one will contribute the most to a right attitude? Why? What actions are you taking today to support this attitude?

This concludes Week Two—Lesson Six

Week Two—Lesson Seven

Taking an Honest Look at the "Weigh" You Use the Scale

As you learned yesterday, one of the goals of the program is to help you continue in your new lifestyle through the renewing of your mind. You have begun to work on this using the TRUE YOU mirror and the "right weight" scales. Today you will be introduced to the key which unlocks your subconscious. You will also get a new assignment. THIS ASSIGNMENT MAY BE ONE OF THE MOST IMPORTANT THINGS YOU HAVE EVER DONE IN YOUR WEIGHT LOSS HISTORY. Read carefully and act immediately.

How much importance have you placed on what the scale says to you? More than likely you fall into one of two categories. You may be the person who weighs as often as you can every day, especially when on a "diet." You actually live or die by the reading on the scale. Regardless of how closely you have followed the program, no matter how careful you have been, if the scale says you have not lost weight then YOU or "this dumb diet" are a failure. This mass of metal and springs becomes a motivating force for you. You form an intimate relationship with a scale! It has incredible power, bringing joy or sadness through the simple appearance of a number. The scale is the dictator, and you have allowed yourself to be its subject. This ruler has much to do with whether you feel good about your appearance or fat and ugly. Has your personal worth and well-being been measured beneath your feet when you stepped on the scale? Playing your weighing games, you have also adopted the scale as a "permission slip" for your eating behavior. You nervously step on the scale hoping the "right number" will appear. If it reflects that right number, you justify continuing your current eating program. But, if the wrong number appears: REFRIGERATOR, LOOK OUT! This number (right or wrong) results in excitement and permission to overindulge OR depression and the desire to fill that emotional hole with food.

The second type of person is the one who is so afraid of the scale that he does not even OWN ONE! If you're in this category you may even avoid going to the doctor for fear of having to confront the scale. How many times have you said, "Doctors' scales always make me weigh five to seven pounds heavier"? Weighing tells you what you do not want to know: you are fat and eat far too much. You do not want to face the fact that the scale is one measurement of your size. You want to continue to live in a food dreamworld that allows you to eat and eat and never gain weight. This is the "skinny pig" fantasy. This attitude is as unhealthy as the compulsion to weigh referred to earlier. It is self-destructive behavior based on attitudes concerning the scale.

Are you beginning to see how the scale can be enemy number one to you in light of your commitment to change your eating behavior? It is in no way an accurate measurement of how disciplined you have been with the program. Weight loss is only one factor and is made up of many different variables. Your objective in terms of weight loss is simply to lose fat on your body. Fat content is not measured by the scale. The scale works in combination with the earth's force of gravity and the total mass of your body. Body mass includes bones, muscles, fluids, waste, organs, and fat. Fat normally constitutes less than one-third of your total body weight. The fact is you cannot measure fat loss using the bathroom scale. You measure the force (weight) of your total body mass, which in no way is a test of how successful you are in fat loss. Fat loss occurs by burning fatty deposits through balanced, low calorie eating. Your adherence to the program guidelines each day produces that necessary action. The measurement of this process is your healthy food choices and food journaling—not the SCALE.

Your attitude about the role of the scale in your eating behavior must change! An attitude of confidence in your "right weight" and body size based on actions of disciplined eating will result in a continuing healthy lifestyle. Beginning today, you will not weigh for the rest of this phase. PUT THE SCALE AWAY AND STAY OFF IT! If this will be difficult for you, ask a family member or friend to keep it in a safe hiding place for you. If you go to the doctor, explain that you are not to be informed of your current weight. It is important you realize that the same attitude about the other guidelines of the program also apply to this one.

NO VIOLATION OF THE PROGRAM GUIDELINES
WILL BE PERMITTED.

It may be hard to believe at this point, but the freedom you will experience as a result of this decision to put the scale away will be life changing. You are just going to have to have faith and trust. The only "right weight" you will have in your mind after today is the weight on your paper scales. Your "right weight" will become such a part of you and your attitude that all of your actions will support it. You will begin to see the actions and attitudes that supported the wrong weight fade away.

**AS THE ACTIONS OF THE OLD YOU FADE,
THE IMAGE OF THE TRUE YOU WILL APPEAR.
YOU WILL NO LONGER NEED
A SCALE AS A SOURCE OF VALIDATION.
THE REAL EVIDENCE WILL BE RIGHT BEFORE YOUR EYES!**

Optional Scripture Readings:

> Let us not become weary in doing good, for at the
> proper time we will reap a harvest if we do not give up.
> (Galatians 6:9, NIV)

> Of what value is an idol, since a man has carved it? Or
> an image that teaches lies? For he who makes it trusts
> in his own creation; he makes idols that cannot speak.
> (Habakkuk 2:18, NIV)

Week Two—Lesson Seven

PERSONAL EVALUATION

1. Which weighing behavior can you most identify with?

2. How has this affected your attitude about yourself and your weight loss efforts?

3. Describe a time that the scale has defeated you in a weight loss effort.

This concludes Week Two—Lesson Seven

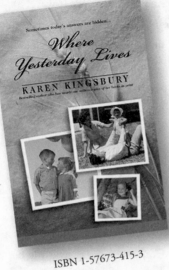

ISBN 1-57673-415-3

WAITING FOR MORNING
By Karen Kingsbury

A drunk driver, a deadly accident, a dream destroyed…

The scene seemed to unfold in slow motion, and from the diner where she stood, there was nothing Rae McDermott could do to stop it. The two vehicles careened toward the intersection, then collided. The impact was so explosive it was surreal, like something from a violent action movie. The Explorer spun off the ground in a cloud of dust and glass and shredded metal, and Rae watched it sail across the street and wrap around a utility pole a hundred feet away.

"Dear God," she whispered. She dashed across the diner, grabbed the telephone and dialed 9-1-1.

Only Jenny saw it coming. There was no time to scream, no time to warn the others…. One moment she was looking at Alicia, asking her about Mrs. Watson's English class, and the next, in a mere fraction of an instant, she saw a white locomotive coming straight at them, inches from Alicia's face.

There was a horrific jolt and the deafening sound of twisting, sparking metal and shattering glass. Jenny screamed, but it was too late. The Explorer took to the air like a child's toy spinning wildly and twisting unnaturally before coming to rest.

Then there was nothing but dark, deadly silence.

That night, somewhere between lying awake and falling asleep, Hannah moved her leg and in the process slid her foot under a section of the covers that was weighted down with a heavy book she'd tossed there earlier. Still, for an instant the weight wasn't a book at all. It was Tom, his leg comfortably stretched across the sheets just inches from her own. Hannah stirred and the weight remained. She enjoyed the feeling of Tom's leg on hers, heavy and warm. Suddenly a realization pulled at her. If his leg was here, that meant —

"Tom?" She sat straight up in bed and breathlessly peered through the darkness. Then slowly, as she had at least ten times before, she realized who she was and where she was and what her life had become.

She was a woman alone who had lost everything.

And tomorrow was Christmas.

Jenny narrowed her eyes and studied the stack of sweaters on the closet top shelf. She spotted Alicia's sweater almost immediately and took it gently from where it lay near the bottom of a stack.

She held it up and she could see Alicia, grinning and challenging her to a foot race at Winter Camp last year. Jenny took the arms of the sweater and pulled them around her neck. She held it that way for a while, desperately wishing that Alicia still lived inside it. Her fingers brushed over the soft blue cotton, and she felt the tears again. She folded the sweater gently, tucked it under her arm and moved quickly for the door, suddenly motivated to get to school and log onto the Internet. Her mind traced the electronic paths to the suicide web sites she'd found earlier. Information that would help her resume the most important task of her life.

Finding a way to join Daddy and Alicia.

The bottle was more than half gone, and Brian felt himself losing consciousness. The room was spinning faster, and he closed his eyes. Suddenly a loud noise pulled him from his stupor. This time when he opened his eyes, he saw something that sent a surge of bile into his throat.

Right in front of him was the blond girl and her father, their car wrapped around the utility pole. Only now the girl was crying and Carla was standing over her, trying to help her breathe. In an instant they all turned on him, glaring at him, hating him.

"Go away!" Carla shouted and she ripped the gold hoops from her ears. "You're a murderer and a liar and a loser. I hope you rot in prison."

As quickly as they'd come, they faded away and he could see more clearly.... There was a strange noise, like air leaking from a rubber tire. He tossed the bottle aside and looked up.

Demons filled the room before him.

Dripping blood and spewing venomous taunts and accusations, they crowded in around his face. He swung at them, shouted at them to stay away, but they drew nearer still, hissing and smelling of death and sulfur. They were carrying something, and Brian saw that it was a rusted, black chain. Before he could get up or run away or close his eyes, the demons bound his wrists and wrapped his arms tightly against his body.

He was utterly trapped, and the demons began hissing one word, over and over. Brian's heart beat wildly and he struggled to break free. What was the word? What were they saying? The noise grew louder, each word a hate-filled hiss.

Finally Brian understood.

Forever. Forever, forever, forever.

He was trapped. The demons had him and they would hold him forever.

He wanted to break free, to scream for help and chase the demons away before they killed him. But instead he felt his insides heave. Once, twice, and then a third time, until it seemed his stomach was in a state of permanent convulsion....

Brian woke up, face down in a puddle of pasty vomit, his entire body shaking violently from fear and alcohol poisoning. The room smelled like rotten, undigested food and urine. He noticed his pants were wet, and he realized he must have soiled them. His head throbbed and he recoiled as he touched his hand to his hair. It was matted with crusted vomit. Suddenly he remembered the hissing creatures. Using only his eyes, he glanced from side to side.

The demons were gone.

But they would be back. He knew with every fiber in his being that it was so. He struggled to his feet, wiped the vomit from his eyes and nose so he could breathe better, and staggered toward the phone.

It was time to call the Bible lady.

———

Matt faced the jury squarely and slid his hands into his pockets. His voice was strong, but Hannah thought his eyes looked damp as he continued. "What happened to Hannah Ryan could happen to me..." he met their eyes, "or you. Any day. Anytime. Anywhere.... It's time friends, please. Find Brian Wesley guilty of first-degree murder, and let's put an end to this madness now. Before it's too late."

The judge finished giving instructions, and the case was handed over to the jury. After just two hours the foreman notified the clerk.

They had reached a decision.

———

(You may purchase Karen Kingsbury's second novel, *Waiting for Morning*, through any retail outlet that carries Multnomah books.)

WHERE YESTERDAY LIVES
By Karen Kingsbury

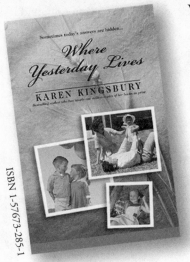

ISBN 1-57673-285-1

Ellen Barrett is a prize-winning journalist with an uncertain marriage, a forgotten faith, and haunting memories of her picturesque hometown and the love she left behind. The eldest of five siblings, Ellen longs for the time, long ago, when they were happy…when they were a family. Then tragedy strikes. Now Ellen's beloved father is dead and she must leave Miami and go back to her childhood home on the shores of Little Traverse Bay in Petoskey, Michigan. As she returns to a world that once was, an avalanche of memories is unleashed. And so Ellen's quest begins—a quest to make peace with the past, the people who still live there, the losses and changes that time has wrought, and the future God has set before her.

READERS COMMENT ON KAREN KINGSBURY'S FICTION

Where Yesterday Lives

What an excellent book! I couldn't set it down and I devoured chapter after chapter. I cried my eyes out and really felt myself relating it to my own life.
—Bobbi Terret

What a timely, loving message…. If I hadn't known better, I would have thought you had an inside line to my family…. I wept many times through it…. Hope and love flow through all the pages. I can't wait to read your next books.
—Kathy Glass

It's wonderful! I cried through the last five chapters.
—Katie Gause

Waiting for Morning

Waiting for Morning is one of the most powerful books I've ever read other than the Bible.
—JoAnn Lacy, author

I just finished *Waiting for Morning*. It was one of the most powerful books I have ever read. It felt like I was directly involved with this family. Please keep up the good work. I am looking forward to your next release.
—Denise Heckaman

I received *Waiting for Morning* yesterday and didn't put it down until I finished it last night. It is a wonderful story. I was in tears with a few audible sobs…. You were able to capture Hannah's grief in a way that I could truly feel her pain. In times when I want to minister to a hurting friend, I almost always go to the bookstore and try to find something there that would help. It is usually a book about dealing with pain or grief, or a book of comforting scriptures. *Waiting for Morning* will be my first choice now.
—Gail Miller

KAREN'S LATEST RELEASE
Coming March 2000

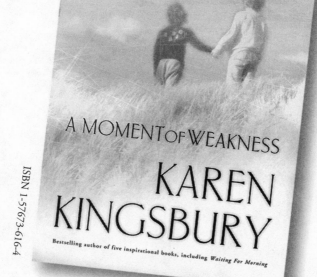

They found each other again that summer.
Then everything changed in...

A MOMENT OF WEAKNESS

KAREN KINGSBURY

ISBN 1-57673-616-4

Bestselling author of five inspirational books, including *Waiting For Morning*

Jade and Tanner were childhood friends until scandal drove them apart. Then one golden summer they found each other again. The days seemed endless as they shared their hearts and souls and dreams of forever. But in a moment of weakness they make a decision that will tear them apart for nearly a decade.

In their own separate corners of the country, Jade Conner and Tanner Eastman have become fighters for religious freedom. Now Jade's unfaithful husband wants to destroy her in a custody battle that is about to send shock waves across the United States. Could Jade lose her only child because of her faith? Only one man can help her in her darkest hour. And only one old woman knows the secret about that summer and the truth that can set them all free.